WASTED: PERFORMING AD

The Cultural Politics of Media and Popular Culture

Series editor:
C. Richard King
Washington State University, USA

Dedicated to a renewed engagement with culture, this series fosters critical, contextual analyses and cross-disciplinary examinations of popular culture as a site of cultural politics. It welcomes theoretically grounded and critically engaged accounts of the politics of contemporary popular culture and the popular dimensions of cultural politics. Without being aligned to a specific theoretical or methodological approach, *The Cultural Politics of Media and Popular Culture* publishes monographs and edited collections that promote dialogues on central subjects, such as representation, identity, power, consumption, citizenship, desire and difference.

Offering approachable and insightful analyses that complicate race, class, gender, sexuality, (dis)ability and nation across various sites of production and consumption, including film, television, music, advertising, sport, fashion, food, youth, subcultures and new media, *The Cultural Politics of Media and Popular Culture* welcomes work that explores the importance of text, context and subtext as these relate to the ways in which popular culture works alongside hegemony.

Also available in this series:

Wasted:
Performing Addiction in America

HEATH A. DIEHL
Bowling Green State University, USA

Routledge
Taylor & Francis Group

LONDON AND NEW YORK

First published 2015 by Ashgate Publishing

2 Park Square, Milton Park, Abingdon, Oxfordshire OX14 4RN
52 Vanderbilt Avenue, New York, NY 10017

Routledge is an imprint of the Taylor & Francis Group, an informa business

First issued in paperback 2020

British Library Cataloguing in Publication Data
A catalogue record for this book is available from the British Library.

The Library of Congress has cataloged the printed edition as follows:
Diehl, Heath A.
  Wasted : performing addiction in America / by Heath A. Diehl.
    pages cm. -- (The cultural politics of media and popular culture)
  Includes index.
  ISBN 978-1-4724-4237-6 (hardcover)
  1. Alcoholism--United States--History. 2. Drug addiction--United States--History. I. Title.
  HV5292.D54 2016
  362.29088'7910973--dc23

                                                                    2015030968

ISBN 978-1-4724-4237-6 (hbk)
ISBN 978-0-367-59752-8 (pbk)

Contents

For Gary and "the kids,"
"as long as we got each other/
we got the world spinning right in our hands"

Acknowledgments

First, foremost, always I need to acknowledge the unwavering support and the unconditional love that I experience every day from my partner, Gary Thurman. Thank you for giving me the time and space to write this book. Thank you for indulging me in conversations about addiction for the past four years—especially since most of the time you probably would have rather been doing almost anything else. And most of all thank you for loving me, and thank you for allowing me to love you.

To our "kids," Scooter, Licorice, Ani, Kit, Melba, Jules, and Allie: Words cannot begin to express how thankful I am for the privilege of being your human. I cannot imagine writing this book without having you on my lap and in my heart.

The mentorship of both undergraduate and graduate faculty with whom I have been privileged to work closely continues to shape and define the kinds of research questions that I pose, the types of critical lenses through which I respond to those questions, and the kinds of conclusions at which I ultimately arrive. I am particularly grateful to a small, but distinguished group of teachers who have nurtured my intellectual curiosity, have fostered my desire to ask difficult questions, and have tolerated my (sometimes obsessive) need to seek answers to those questions: Mary Boone, Rob Brown, Perry Bush, Gene Caskey, Diane Harris, Carl Holmberg, Simon Morgan-Russell, Mary Ellen Newport, Pat Rodabaugh, Jim Sargent, Sue Snyder, Mary Ann Sullivan, and Susan Weisenberger.

Special "Thank you"s to two faculty members who mentored me through my first major research project and who together introduced me to the pleasures of intellectual work:

Jeff Gundy: You once gave me the confidence that I needed to pursue a project that scared me more than anything I had ever to date pursued, to complete a project that challenged me in ways that I never had been challenged, and to see myself in ways that I had always wanted to but had never possessed the self-assurance to do.

Sharon Showman: Since I was 18 years old, you have been the yardstick against which I have measured my own accomplishments and "worth." You are my mentor. You are my friend. You are my role model. And you are one of the greatest gifts that the universe has ever given me. "Thank you" seems grossly insufficient, but it is all I have.

To three of the faculty who mentored me through graduate school and my dissertation:

Vicki Patraka: Working with you was one of the most difficult challenges of my professional life, but it also has been one of the most rewarding learning experiences that I ever could have imagined. Your influence is all over this book.

Ellen Berry: Thank you for teaching me to appreciate (and to indulge in) the near-infinite pleasures of theory, and thank you for always reminding me of the material consequences of doing so. Because of you, my work "matters."

Lisa Wolford: Thank you for encouraging me to follow my intellectual passions wherever they may lead. Your scholarship and your mentoring immeasurably has inspired my scholarship since graduate school and, without knowing you, *Wasted* would never have been possible. Rest in peace, Lisa.

Over the years I have been blessed with an especially generous, supportive, engaging, and thoughtful peer group. Some have provided me inspiration and motivation. Others have engaged meaningfully with me in some of the conversations that have shaped the contents of this book. Still others have been there "merely" to keep me sane and grounded. Whatever your contribution to *Wasted*—large or small, in the immediate present or in the distant past—I am grateful beyond measure for your friendship, your wisdom, and your being: Annie Adams, Angela Athy, Rachel Armstrong, Becky Becker, Nicole Buccalo, Jessica Chung, Maria Getz, Lisa Hanasono, Tiffany "Lady Teacher" Hyland, Kara Jennings, Kimberly Greenfield Karshner, Mary Krueger, Emily Lanik Parr, Ellen Larabee, Jeannie Ludlow, Carrie Mast, Paul Moore, Elisabeth Showalter Neal, Marissa Wagner Oehlhof, Mary Kate Riddell, Blaire Rideout, Leslie Robinson, Linda Rouse, Eric Severson, Diana Spiess, Christopher Stahl, John Thies, Sara Webb-Sunderhaus, Gus Weltsek, and Darius Omar Williams.

To one very special friend goes a very special "thank you." Amy Rybak: In the words of the incomparable Bea Arthur: "Your friendship is something I never expected at this point in my life ... and I couldn't have asked for a better surprise."

Within my immediate family, two aunts deserve special recognition.

Marsha Ward: You are owed more "thank you"s than I have space or time or words to pen. Suffice it to say: With you, I've truly had the time of my life.

Sharon "KK" Shaw: By taking me to see my first play, you sparked in me the life-long love affair with live performance that this book, and so much of my intellectual work, celebrates.

Finally, to my students (especially The Thesis Class): You constantly remind me of why I do what I do. You motivate me. You inspire me. You humble me. And I am thankful every day that I have been given the privilege of watching you grow as thinkers, as young professionals, and as human beings.

Preface:
On Being Wasted in America

> [O]ne cannot think without metaphors. But that does not mean there aren't some metaphors we might well abstain from or try to retire. And, of course, all thinking is interpretation. But that does not mean it isn't sometimes correct to be against interpretation.
>
> Susan Sontag, *AIDS and Its Metaphors,* p. 93

Wasted truly became "real" to me the night that Whitney Houston died. To that point, I periodically had entertained the idea of undertaking a writing project about contemporary cultural representations of addiction, although the ideas for that project were always only partially formed in my mind and those ideas did not yet have a coherent throughline to unify them. My long-standing interest in the subject of addiction was shaped primarily by three influences that were biographical, historical, and intellectual in nature. On the biographical front, I come from a family of addicts. Some of those ancestors are only as *real* to me as the family lore about their drunken exploits that was passed down to me throughout my childhood. One legend, for instance, suggests that one of my maternal great-grandfathers, an alcoholic who also was close friends with one of our city's funeral home owners, died after drinking pilfered embalming fluid for the "alcohol" content. Other family members I have watched impotently as the disease ravaged everything that was once meaningful to them, including, for some, their lives. And I myself have not been immune to the disease. For 12 years I was a cigarette smoker, and for most of that time, I actively resisted (both inwardly and outwardly) the label of *addict*, often going as far as re-producing the addict's go-to defenses like, "I can quit any time I want" and "Cigarettes—I can take them or leave them," when confronted by concerned friends and family members who pleaded with me to quit.

Historically, I am a child of the 1970s and my formative years were played out against the backdrop of the "Just Say 'No'" decade during which American politics were dominated by President Reagan's "call for a 'nationwide crusade against drugs'" (quoted in Grim 58), and substance abuse constituted the *de rigeur* subject for many a teen movie, Afterschool Special, and Public Service Announcement. Intellectually, I have, for over a decade, been struck by, on the one hand, the seeming resurgence of national interest in addiction (after a decade of virtual "radio silence" during the 1990s) and the concomitant barrage of cultural artifacts about the subject that have been and that are being produced in early twenty-first-century America. At the same time, despite the myriad of cultural artifacts about addiction currently flooding the cultural marketplace, as late as January 2012, I would have been hard-pressed to cobble together a coherent statement regarding what all of those artifacts collectively reveal about current American cultural attitudes toward addiction.

And then Whitney Houston died.

When the news of Whitney's death broke, my immediate reaction was textbook Elizabeth Kübler-Ross denial: "She can't be dead. She's only 48. And she swore to Oprah that she was not using anymore." That night, as I watched one news anchor after another confirm that initial devastating report, I experienced in no particular order, and with varying degrees of intensity, the next three stages of the Kübler-Ross model: anger (that is, "Why didn't someone help her steer clear of the drugs? Why didn't she help herself?"); bargaining (that is, "Please let this be another Internet hoax!"); and depression (that is, "Why? Why?!?"). Over the next few days, as I began to accept (that is, Kübler-Ross stage five) the reality of Whitney's death, I turned to social and mass media outlets, anxiously anticipating the announcement of the official cause of death, re-living (thanks to YouTube) some of Whitney's most memorable performances, and commiserating with other fans about the untimely death of the American icon whose music had served as the soundtrack for most of the major milestones of my life since age 12. Not surprisingly, Whitney's sudden death elicited an outpouring of grief, fond remembrances, and other reverential responses from fellow celebrities and from avid fans; but what did surprise me—perhaps "shock" and "disgust" are more apt terms—was the large number of people who expressed contempt or disdain for Whitney, or who turned her death into a punchline. Four days after Whitney's body was laid to rest in Fairview Cemetery in Westfield, New Jersey, *The National Enquirer* published a cover story, titled "Whitney: The Last Photo!," alongside photographs of Whitney's body laid out in her coffin. In September 2012, *TMZ* broke a story alleging that law enforcement officers who were on the scene at the Beverly Hilton Hotel made crude jokes about Whitney's nude corpse (see "Whitney Houston: Cop," "Whitney Houston: Corroboration," "Ray J"). And over the days and weeks following Whitney's death, all manner of discussions sprang up on the internet in which users seemed determined to outdo one another on creating the crudest joke, or making the cruelest remark about Whitney's death. A couple of representative jokes that surfaced on an Australia travel/entertainment site should suffice to illustrate the general attitude to which I refer here: "Whitney Houston to star in her new film. The Bodybag." and "What's black, lies on the floor, 'Will Always Love You' and has white stuff around it's [sic] nose? A border collie" ("Whitney Houston Jokes").

Equally curious (or, perhaps more accurately, disturbing) were the countless blogs, discussion boards, and "news" articles in which one author after another uncritically and unequivocally labeled Whitney's life a "waste." One representative example of such responses is a blog, titled "Retired in Delaware" and written by Ron, a 72-year-old man living in Milton, Delaware. On the night of Whitney's death, Ron posted a blog titled "Whitney Houston—A Wasted LIfe [sic]" that begins with the bold (and arguably offensive) statements: "Whitney Houston is dead at the age of 48. She had everything; [sic] beauty, talent, riches and fame. Like so many other talented performers before her, she blew all of her natural, God given [sic] talent and beauty on the selfish short term [sic] high of drugs." After cataloguing a string of other performers who also struggled with and succumbed to their addictions—including the predictable line-up of Dinah Washington, Janis Joplin, and Judy Garland—Ron concludes that Whitney's death will not change the behaviors of "any of the remaining celebrities who are sniffing coke" and closes the blog with the defeatist lament, "What a shame. What a waste."

Aside from Ron's rather problematic assumption regarding the cause of Whitney's death (that is, cocaine addiction), made over a month before the official coroner's report had been released, his claim that her struggles with addiction will overshadow the long and illustrious career that she enjoyed seems preposterous. Yet Ron's few blog followers echoed his sentiments in the comments that were posted over the coming hours. One follower, nicknamed Ur-spo, proclaims, "Addictions ruin people," while WillJ opens his otherwise perceptive comment with "The addiction won; Ms [sic] Houston's life and her gifts lost." Blogger Ron very actively engaged with his limited followers, insisting that Whitney "[threw away her God-given] gifts in a life of drug fueled [sic] haze" and that "she wasted her life because of her weakness for drugs."

As I perused pages and pages of articles, blogs, and discussion board posts that condemned Whitney for squandering her talents and wasting her life, I struggled to reconcile this image of the waste-of-life-junkie with the woman who earned the distinctions of being the most decorated and one of the best-selling solo female vocalists of all-time. Although admittedly I mourned Whitney's death, lamenting all of the music that she never would make and I never would hear, I simply could not concede to the claim that Whitney "wasted" her life and her incomparable vocal talents. For me, and for many, Whitney was The Voice—of a generation, of a lifetime, of all-time. In her prime, she racked up one number-one hit after another, accumulating Grammys, American Music Awards, and many other laudable distinctions through her long and unparalleled career in the entertainment industry. Her extraordinary life, including her many struggles with substance abuse and addiction, were writ large against the exploitative glare of the media spotlight and through every barb lobbed at her by ironic cultural bloggers, every unflattering paparazzi snapshot published by *TMZ* or *The National Enquirer,* and every probing inquiry made by "well-meaning journalists" like Diane Sawyer and Oprah Winfrey, Whitney weathered her celebrity and her struggles with addiction with grace, aplomb, and humility.

What, then, I wondered, could possibly prompt, let alone justify, the kind of vitriolic reactions that I repeatedly witnessed in response to Whitney's death? Were the reactions to Whitney's death fueled by an inability to reconcile the privilege associated with her talent/celebrity with the banality of her descent into addiction? Or were those reactions indicative of larger cultural attitudes toward addiction and addicts, celebrities or otherwise? In other words, was Whitney branded a "waste" because her critics truly believed that she had squandered her amazing vocal talents or did critics condemn Whitney for wasting her talents *because* she was an addict? And if an icon like Whitney could be reduced to a punchline or, worse, a "waste" because of her struggles with addiction, then how were garden variety addicts being represented within American cultural artifacts and treated within American culture at large? In other words, if Whitney was branded a "waste" because of her struggles with addiction, then what could her life and death tell us about what it means and how it feels to be addicted, or, in the language of this study, "wasted" in America?

Literature Review and Methodology

To be sure, scholars have long exhibited intellectual interest in the ways in which controlled and illicit substances both physiologically and psychologically impact the human body. However, to date, the bulk of extant scholarship on the subject of addiction hails from the natural and social sciences. Within the arts and humanities, significantly less attention has been devoted to the subject of addiction, and those scholars who have pursued this subject typically have self-identified as "historians" and their intellectual work has tended to concentrate on a select few concerns. In particular, historical research into this subject can be classified under two fairly broad areas of inquiry: one, studies that investigate the ways in which historical expressions of addiction have shaped and been shaped by "the American character" (for example, Courtright, 2002; Pegram, 1998; Tracy and Acker, eds, 2004); and two, studies that examine the socio-historical forces that have contributed to the rise and/or decline in popularity of a specific substance in a given historical moment (for example, Brandt, 2009; Courtright, 2001; Spillane, 2002). While this research provides an important backdrop for the kind of scholarship in which I engage in *Wasted,* my work in this current study diverges from a traditional historical approach in the emphasis that it places on the dynamic nature of history, culture, and lived experience, a difference that performance studies scholars often draw between the *artifact* and its *performance*.

Within the field of English studies, only a handful of books have been written and published on the subject of addiction, and all of these works take fairly conventional approaches to the subject matter. Some authors have taken a socio-biographical approach to the subject, considering the ways in which addiction impacted the writing processes and the literary output of canonical authors (for example, Boon, 2005; Djos, 2010). Other scholars within this field have considered the ways in which cultural attitudes toward addiction are mutually generative of specific historical/literary movements (for example, Banco, 2009; Gilmore, 1987).

Perhaps not surprisingly, many literary critics who have studied the subject of addiction have concentrated their attention on the nineteenth century—the moment during which "the addict" emerged as a stable, coherent identity construct in medico-legal discourse (for example, Reynolds and Rosenthal, eds, 1997; Warner, 1997; Zieger, 2008). Examining both canonical and lesser-known literary works by such representative nineteenth-century authors as Emerson, Dickinson, Poe, Hawthorne, Melville, and Stowe, these critics locate the experiences of addiction at the intersections of socio-cultural discourses regarding substance abuse and literary practices characteristic of the period. My work in the current study differs from these previously-published examples of literary criticism in three noteworthy ways: one, *Wasted* casts a much wider net in terms of the artifacts that are examined within its pages, deemphasizing canonical authors and texts; two, *Wasted* focuses on representations of addiction in as-yet-unexamined periods of American history (namely, late-twentieth and early twenty-first centuries); and three, *Wasted* marries two fields of study that to date have not been brought together—that is, addiction studies and performance studies.

At present, only three texts—Janet Farrell Brodie and Marc Redfield's *High Anxieties: Cultural Studies in Addiction* (2002), Anna Alexander and Mark S. Roberts's *high cu/ture: reflections on addiction and modernity* (2003), and James Reynolds and Zoe Zontou's *Addiction and Performance* (2014)—tackle the subject of addiction in a manner remotely similar to my approach in *Wasted*. Like these authors, I am deeply invested in understanding addiction through an interdisciplinary lens; also like these authors, I see addiction as a complex cultural production that exists at the intersections of a myriad of social institutions, power relations, historical forces, and discursive formations. However, *Wasted* differs markedly from these earlier studies (especially *High Anxieties* and *high cu/ture*) in terms of the scope of its inquiry and the target of its interdisciplinary approach. Both *High Anxieties* and *high cu/ture* begin with an interest in addiction as a "social construction" (Brodie and Redfield 10). The editors of *High Anxieties* identify their "principal object of inquiry" as "either the historical specificity of the discourse of addiction, or the power such discourses have had to position subjects, shape desires, and rechannel anxieties" (10), while the editors of *high cu/ture* indicate that the essays included within their anthology are principally concerned with how "addiction emerges directly alongside modernity, haunting the various discourses of digression, dissent, and the transcendence of the commonplace so often associated with the modern era" (Introduction 3). For the editors of both of these collections, then, addiction—a lived experience that is profoundly material and tangible—is relegated exclusively to the cerebral realms of language, ideology, and discourse. What is ignored by such an inquiry, and what I seek to recover in *Wasted*, is the sense of materiality (bodily, historically, and culturally) that anchors the lived experiences of addiction; in other words, in this book, I regard addiction not merely as a discursive "object," but simultaneously as a set of socio-cultural practices, historically-contingent events, and lived behaviors.

Of the three aforementioned texts, *Wasted* shares the most commonalities with *Addiction and Performance*. Both projects, for instance, take as a grounding assumption the idea that "the performative dimensions of drugs, drug use and addiction provide us with more than just an insight into an often hidden world; they are important and relevant ways of understanding much broader features of culture and society" (8). Like *Wasted*, too, Reynolds and Zontou's book places much greater emphasis on the materiality of the lived experiences of addiction than either *High Anxieties* or *high cu/ture*. *Addiction and Performance* differs from the current study, however, in terms of its more expansive topical scope and its methodological approach to those topics. In particular, Reynolds and Zontou cast addiction as an act of "symbolic politics" (4) and the authors examine that concept in relation to four broadly-defined topical areas: "the cultural representation of addiction, questions regarding the performance of self, methodologies of applied arts practice, and performances of addiction" (3).

By contrast, *Wasted* is much more focused in its subject matter and much more squarely rooted within the discipline of performance studies, rather than cultural studies. According to field pioneer Richard Schechner in his book *Performance Studies: An Introduction* (2013), "Performance studies starts where most limited domain disciplines end. A performance studies scholar examines texts, architecture, visual arts, or any other item or artifact of art or culture not in themselves, but as players in ongoing relationships, that is, 'as' performances" (2). To see cultural texts *as* performance is to regard them "as practices, events, and behaviors, not as 'objects' or 'things'"—in other words, to acknowledge that "[t]he artifact may be relatively stable, but the performance it creates or takes part in can change radically. The performance studies scholar examines the circumstances in which the painting was created and exhibited; she looks at how the gallery or building displaying the painting shapes its reception" (2).

To suggest that *Wasted* is grounded in the field of performance studies is to acknowledge, first of all, that *Wasted* is concerned chiefly with textual analysis. However, unlike traditional forms of textual analysis, this study defines "textuality" much more fluidly and loosely, and it resists the temptation to regard a text as an object to-be-read whose meaning is stable, unified, and monolithic. Instead, in *Wasted*, I approach the texts under study as dynamic entities, as *performances*, whose meanings shift (sometimes, as Schechner notes, quite radically) depending on the processes by which and conditions under which those texts have been created, the socio-historical context against which those performances are framed, and the audiences for which those performances are enacted/displayed. To ground this investigation in the field of performance studies also allows me to borrow quite freely on a wide variety of critical lenses through which to read these acts of performance. In doing so, I not only open the field of addiction studies up to a myriad of new critical questions and observations, but also encourage a more holistic understanding of addiction as at once a social problem (typically the domain of the social sciences), a physiological "experience" (typically the domain of the natural sciences), and a socio-historical phenomenon (typically the domain of the arts and humanities).

The Metaphor of Waste

Anchoring the argument of *Wasted* is a set of interrelated grounding assumptions regarding America's treatment of addiction in the current historical moment. Chief among these assumptions is the idea, adapted from cultural critic Susan Sontag in *AIDS and Its Metaphors* (1989), that we cannot think about the lived experiences of addiction without thinking metaphorically. In other words, to conceptualize the materiality of addiction in thought is to abstract those experiences in the form of metaphor. The disease model of addiction stands as a vivid illustration of how the lived experiences of addiction are abstracted, rendered metaphoric, through acts of interpretation. Dating to the 1784 publication of the pamphlet *Inquiry into the Effects of Ardent Spirits on the Human Mind and Body* by prominent American physician and Founding Father, Dr. Benjamin Rush, the disease model of addiction identifies genetic predisposition and/or environmental conditions as the primary contributing factors to the development of an addiction. The addiction itself is likened to a "chronic, progressive [illness]," "such as Type II diabetes and cardiovascular disease," and "is characterized by [an addict's] inability to reliably control his use of alcohol or drugs, and an uncontrollable craving or compulsion to drink alcohol or take drugs" (Clark). Although the disease model of addiction originated as a medical explanation for the nature of addictive behaviors, over time, that model has given rise to a set of cultural metaphors that stand in for and shape our shared understandings of addiction. These metaphors often are expressed as abstract equations (such as addiction = disease = weakness = moral corruption) that link addiction to moral corruption and sin by way of disease and "weakness."

The impulse to render the lived experiences of addiction abstract and metaphoric is reinforced by the fact that addiction constitutes "a felt-experience of pain" that "has no referential content" (Scarry 5). As Elaine Scarry explains in *The Body in Pain: The Making and Unmaking of the World* (1985), "[Pain] is not *of* or *for* anything. It is precisely because it takes no object that it, more than any other phenomenon, resists objectification in language" (5). Although Scarry's concern in this book rests squarely on the experiences of war and physical torture—subjects that Sontag, too, would later take up in *Regarding the Pain of Others* (2003)—her observations regarding the eponymous "body in pain" nonetheless speak quite convincingly to the lived experiences of addiction. Like physical pain, addiction occupies the "invisible geography" of the material body, and, as such, "has no voice" (3); yet because pain/addiction "comes unsharably into our midst as at once that which cannot be confirmed" (4), the experience demands a "language … capable of providing an external image of interior events" (8). Enter metaphor.

Metaphor typically is understood as a type of figurative language that "identi[es] one object with another and ascrib[es] to the first object one or more of the qualities of the second" (Holman and Harmon 287). For example, addicts sometimes are saddled with the label "zombies" not because they are literal manifestations of the recently deceased raised from the dead by some ancient form of voodoo, but because they are perceived to share certain characteristics with the classic movie monster: namely, they appear to exist in a "death-like state that strips them of cognition, will and other mental or spiritual traits most considered unique to humanity, esp. the soul" (Casciato). Yet, as Murray Knowles and Rosamund Moon suggest in *Introducing Metaphor* (2006), "metaphor is not just a kind of artistic embellishment, at the rarefied end of linguistic usage, divorced and isolated from everyday communication. It is instead a basic phenomenon that occurs throughout the whole range of language activity" (1). Like many studies before it, including George Lakoff and Mark Johnson's ground-breaking *Metaphors We Live By* (1980), *Wasted* operates under the assumption that metaphor constitutes not merely a linguistic flourish, but a way of seeing and engaging with the world. As Lakoff and Johnson explain, "Our ordinary conceptual system, in terms of which we both think and act, is fundamentally metaphorical in nature" (3). In other words, metaphor does not merely shape what we think, but it actively shapes how we think, determining "what we perceive, how we get around in the world, and how we relate to other people" (3). In this respect, metaphor simultaneously mediates and constructs social reality.

The central assertion in the current study is that our shared cultural understandings of addiction are shaped largely by a metaphor of waste. Within this metaphor, the addict is identified as "[s]omething wasted or destroyed," as "refuse matter" rendered as such by a causal agent (that is, the addiction) that charts a path of "[d]estruction or devastation" across the body of the addict, as well as within the personal and professional arenas of the addict's life. The addiction not only precipitates "[a] wasting of the body," but also fuels the addict's "[u]seless expenditure or ... squandering" "of money, goods, time, effort" ("waste, n."). Perhaps the most obvious and compelling manifestation of the metaphor of waste is the language that Americans have created to describe a type and quality of illicit substance (for example, crap = low-quality heroin; embalming fluid = PCP; garbage = inferior quality marijuana or heroin), to denote the places where drugs are consumed (for example, abandominiums = abandoned row houses where drugs are used), to identify addicts (for example, bed bugs; junkies; zombies), and, most pertinent to this study, to describe the experience of inebriation (for example, wasted) ("Street Names"). These examples of how contemporary discourses about addiction are circumscribed by the metaphor of waste might initially seem rather inconsequential in the face of such a devastating and far-reaching social problem. Yet as David Bleich reminds, "language is not separable from the behaviors of historically real human groups. Language is 'material' because it 'matters,' and because it *is* part of palpable social relations" (47). The language of addiction "matters" because that language gives both shape and meaning to social reality. To refer to an addict as a "junkie," for example, at once presupposes and actively creates a social identity for that person—an identity predicated on the assumption that that person is a non-entity, a waste, and his/her struggles with addiction insignificant.

While language perhaps constitutes the most immediately visible manifestation of the metaphor of waste, other, less obvious manifestations of the metaphor exact sometimes even greater consequences, and leave more indelible marks on the psyches, the material bodies, and the lived experiences of addicts. The metaphor of waste, for instance, shapes legislation around addiction, making it easier to justify public policy (for example, stricter laws and harsher penalties for drug-related offenses) that stigmatizes and further marginalizes addicts, that criminalizes a medical condition (for example, Levine and Reinarman; Loue; "Why Patient Advocacy"), and that works to publicly shame persons who are struggling with a legitimate psycho-physical dependence (for example, "Justice System Paradox"; Moore and Fraser). As one contributor to *USA Today* has written: "The USA has effectively criminalized addiction ... giv[ing] the land of the free the dubious distinction of having the highest incarceration rate in the world and, in the process, driv[ing] illicit drug use underground where it is harder to treat" ("Drug Addicts" 11a). The metaphor of waste also can stall the workings of

American jurisprudence, overwhelming the already resource-strapped court system with a seemingly ever-increasing caseload of drug-related offenses and necessitating the creation of a separate system of "drug courts" (for example, Turque and McKillop; Murphy, Jennifer).

A third manifestation of the metaphor of waste is the increased ease with which anti-drug advocates can block and/or re-channel the allocation of much-needed government funding, a move that can limit and, indeed, has significantly limited the range of treatment options available to addicts (for example, Miller). Not only can the metaphor of waste impact the number of treatment options available to addicts, but also it can impact the addict's willingness to seek, and ability to complete, a substance dependence treatment program, contributing at times to greater rates of recidivism (for example, Rengifo and Stemen; Krebs, et al.). Additionally, the metaphor of waste can limit individuals' housing options and job prospects (for example, van Olphen, et al.), and can inadvertently exacerbate other, related social problems such as poverty and homelessness (for example, Baumohl, "Editorial"), as well as domestic violence (for example, Macy, Renz, and Pellino). And the metaphor of waste does not just impact the addict; non-addicts, too, feel the consequences of the cuts in funding, the denial of treatment, and the criminalization of addiction that I discuss above. As clinical psychologist Dr. Richard Juman explains, "Untreated substance use disorders have ramifications way beyond those of most other diseases … the links between addiction and a host of other critical issues are direct and reciprocal …. Substance use disorders cause tragedy on a human level, of course. But the financial cost to society is also enormous."

Two additional grounding assumptions concern the key term at the center of this study: addiction. In simplest terms, "addiction" commonly is understood as "a chronic, relapsing brain disease that is characterized by compulsive drug seeking and use, despite harmful consequences" ("The Science"). This particular definition classifies "addiction" solely in terms of an individual's relationship with controlled and/or illicit substances—a fairly conventional view that has been mirrored in much of the extant scholarship on the subject of addiction. However, within the vernacular of twenty-first-century America, as well as within the field of psychology, which is principally responsible for diagnosing and treating Substance Use and Addictive Disorders, "addiction" is an increasingly elastic term whose definitional boundaries perpetually are challenged by everything from conventional behavioral disorders (for example, compulsive gambling, shopping, pornography consumption, and so on) to unusual "addictive substances" (for example, Ramen noodles, McDonald's hamburgers, Oreo cookies, and so on). In a similar manner, the recent revisions to the definition of "addiction" in the fifth edition of the *Diagnostic and Statistical Manual* (or *DSM V*)—the "Bible" of the psychology field used to "[categorize] mental illness and … determine insurance coverage and research agendas"

("Scientists Unveil")—has proven a bit too overinclusive of the kinds of conditions and behaviors that it classifies as "Substance Use Disorders" and "Addictive Disorders."

Once I committed to writing *Wasted*, I fairly quickly had to determine how I would be defining the term "addiction" throughout the study because that definition not only would shape the selection of texts to be investigated, but also, to some degree, would determine my approach to interpreting those texts. In some respects, *Wasted* approaches the subject of addiction in a fairly traditional manner, defining the term "addiction" in terms of an individual's dependence on controlled and/or illicit substances (that is, as a "brain disease"). At the same time, I make no distinction (as, say, a hard scientist would) between the different "families" (that is, nicotine, alcohol, opiates, cocaine and amphetamines, cannabis, caffeine, and hallucinogens) of drugs that I study because, regardless of an addict's drug of choice, there are important and noteworthy similarities in how addiction is framed within discourse and ideology, and how addiction is experienced and lived in the everyday. These similarities have rarely (if ever) been considered within existing scholarship, most of which either focuses exclusively on a specific drug or, within a given study, parcels out its consideration of specific drugs into individual chapters.

The Chapters

Wasted is divided into three parts that collectively seek to define the metaphor of waste (Part I), to trace its socio-historical origins (Part II), and to identify key effects of the metaphor on the everyday lived experiences of Americans (Part III). In the first part of the study, titled "Representing Wasted Metaphors," I describe the central, controlling metaphor that shapes and delimits the lived experiences of addiction in late-twentieth and early-twenty-first century America: the metaphor of waste. Chapter 1 opens the study on the premise that this metaphor is deeply imbricated in narratives of American nationalism, emerging directly from the compulsive acts of surveillance and policing that actively imagine and simultaneously create the body politic. Through a close reading of two texts about late comic-actor John Belushi—the Bob Woodward biography, titled *Wired: The Short Life and Fast Times of John Belushi* (1984), and the 1989 Larry Peerce film adaptation of Woodward's book—I examine the mutually generative relationship between narratives of American nationalism and the metaphor of waste. Specifically, I suggest that both of these texts, but especially the cinematic adaptation, encourage viewers to read Belushi's biography in allegorical terms, that is, as a "[displacement] of language" or "a way of saying one thing and meaning another" (Tambling 6). In this respect, the metaphor of waste is at once a metaphor of containment that actively "ferret[s] out" and isolates the addict-Belushi as a "socially deviant" Other whose identity and behaviors must be "feared," "vilified" (Alexander and Roberts 3), and ultimately displaced (all forms of ideological and emotional containment) in order to maintain the sanctity of the nation. At the same time, and in a strange narrative twist (especially for texts classified—at least loosely—as "biography"), both the print and the cinematic versions of *Wired* substitute for the tragic biography of John Belushi a narrative of fervent nationalism built squarely on the shoulders of patriot and Watergate journalist Bob Woodward (arguably the protagonist in both texts) and modeled closely on the classic American Dream mythos.

In the second part of the study, titled "Staging Wasted Histories," I identify four discontinuous origin stories for the metaphor of waste, tracing the evolution of that metaphor to several interrelated, but distinct, socio-cultural formations that both ideologically and materially give shape and meaning to the lived experiences of addiction. Chapter 2 locates the emergence of the metaphor of waste in the development of two parallel nineteenth-century cultural institutions: the circus sideshow, or "freak show," and the inebriate asylum. I examine contemporary reality television programs about addiction (focusing most particularly on A&E's *Intervention*), which typically highlight only the most extreme of situations around the lived experiences of addiction, inviting a gaze that simultaneously objectifies and exploits that which is strange within a given socio-historical framework, foreign to the (non-addict) self, and abject in its own right. I argue that this exploitation of the addict-as-freak resurrects the normalizing tradition and the normative practices of earlier efforts at addiction treatment, namely the inebriate asylums of the nineteenth century. This blending of the freak show and asylum traditions witnessed in a program like *Intervention* asserts cultural narratives about the lived experiences of addition that ultimately run counter to the stated objectives of a "self-help" reality program that "mak[es] expert claims about how to resolve various mental health problems" (Kosovski and Smith 852) and undermines the very treatment programs that the show's producers advocate. In doing so, the program places psychological barriers and socio-cultural obstacles in the path of individuals who struggle with substance abuse and addiction.

Chapter 3 returns to debates from the mid- to late 1980s regarding the political efficacy (especially for "marginal" groups, like addicts) of literary realism—a form that emerged in the Western literary tradition at the tail end of the nineteenth century. I focus on two texts originally published and eventually adapted for film during the "Just Say 'No'" era: Jay McInerney's *Bright Lights, Big City* (1984; film 1988) and Bret Easton Ellis's *Less Than Zero* (1985; film 1987). Specifically, I argue that the filmic adaptations of these two novels, both of which are realistic in form and conservative in polemics, identify literary realism as a site at which the metaphor of waste was born, marking either the addict (i.e., Julian in *Less Than Zero*) or the addiction (i.e., cocaine addiction in *Bright Lights, Big City*) as narrative refuse that must be expunged from the text to achieve resolution and closure.

The second part of the book concludes with a chapter that examines the role that Alcoholics Anonymous and other, similar 12-step programs have played in the dissemination of the metaphor of waste. Chapter 4 begins with the assumption that the founding of 12-step recovery programs marks a significant milestone in the metaphor's history—not as a site at which the metaphor originated, but as *the* site at which the metaphor gained its greatest foothold in America over the twentieth and into the twenty-first centuries. Anchoring this chapter's investigation into the 12-step recovery programs is *Drunks* (1997), an independent film that has been dubbed by its producers as "the first film to fully portray a meeting of Alcoholics Anonymous" ("DVD/Streaming"). I argue that *Drunks* marks an obvious departure from its predecessors in at least one significant respect: namely, the filmmaker's insistent desire to represent 12-step recovery as faithfully (read realistically) as possible. It is the staunch cinematographic verisimilitude of *Drunks* that at once identifies the film as an obvious and ideal site at which to consider not only how 12-step recovery is represented within the American cinema, but also how 12-step recovery has shaped—and, indeed, continues to shape—our shared perceptions of addiction in the everyday.

In the third part of the study, titled "Performing Wasted Lives," I explore some of the more insidious ways in which the metaphor of waste has come to bear upon the everyday lived experiences of addiction. In Chapter 5, I turn my attention to two contemporary anti-drug campaigns that make use of scare tactic appeals in an effort to curb drug use among specific populations: 1) Multnomah County's *Faces of Meth*; and 2) the Centers for Disease Control's *Tips from Former Smokers*. I argue that because such campaigns tend to target already disenfranchised groups as both their subject matter and their primary viewing audience, and because such campaigns typically perpetuate in an uncritical manner stereotypical images of both the disenfranchised groups and addicts generally, there is a strong likelihood that these campaigns could produce what social scientists refer to as a "boomerang effect"—that is, they "may be not only less effective than hoped, but actually have unintended negative effects" (Lang and Yegiyan 432). Focusing specifically on how addiction intersects with other "marginal" identity categories (like sexual orientation, biological sex, generationality, race, and class), I suggest that this boomerang effect potentially can intensify deeply-entrenched forms of institutionalized oppression, can inhibit an addict's willingness to seek and/or ability to complete treatment, and can exacerbate other related social problems facing such risk groups (including poverty, homelessness, increased incidence of depression and suicide, and/or increased rates of sexually-transmitted infections).

Fittingly *Wasted* ends where it began: with Whitney Houston. The final chapter of this study returns to some of the issues around American nationalism introduced in the first chapter of *Wasted*, most particularly the idea that addiction constitutes a locus of social control by which American citizenship is regulated and the "nation" itself is imagined, demarcated, and contained. Through a reading of the life, celebrity persona, and death of pop icon Whitney Houston, I suggest a set of consequences of the metaphor of waste that extend beyond the individual to the collective. I begin with the assumption that Houston's life should not be read as allegory, as I suggest readers do with John Belushi in Chapter 1; rather, Houston's life and, in particular, the aftermath of her death must be read as a cautionary tale regarding the extreme and systemic acts of exclusion (both ideological and material) faced by persons whose addiction is cross-cut by other marginal identities (for example, gender, sexuality, race, class, disability, and so on). In other words, although Whitney was the most decorated and one of the best-selling female solo recording artists of all-time, incidents surrounding her struggles with addiction and her death in February 2012 indicated that her musical and acting legacies would always be undercut by the addictions that marked her life as *tragic*, her as a *junkie*, and her talents as *wasted*.

The Point

Wasted proceeds under the hope that to be addicted in America is not of necessity to be useless, squandered, destroyed—in a word, wasted. Mine is arguably a lofty—perhaps borderline idealistic—hope given the current cultural mindset regarding addiction, which is both politically conservative and ideologically punitive. Yet I proceed because addiction and addicts *matter*. At their core, addicts are vulnerable human beings who deserve better than to be written off as refuse, garbage, waste. Addiction itself *matters* precisely because it is a collection of *lived* experiences that are made meaningful through the *material* body. In this respect, I acknowledge that, as a lived experience, addiction is not a metaphor, although it is profoundly metaphoric. And in the pages that follow, my chief concern is the metaphoric properties that shape and delimit the lived experiences of addiction—or, what Sontag in *Illness as Metaphor* (1978) terms "the punitive or sentimental fantasies concocted about that situation: not real geography, but stereotypes of national character" (3). As with physical illness, addiction is so deeply imbricated in metaphoric thinking that, to modify slightly one of Sontag's claims about illness, "it is hardly possible to take up one's residence in the kingdom of the [addicted] unprejudiced by the lurid metaphors with which it has been landscaped" (3–4).

And yet I proceed.

I proceed in reading against the current cultural mindset toward addiction—that is, against interpretation—in the hope that doing so will expose addiction as a significant social issue that is "messy—riddled with misconceptions" (Hoffman and Froemke 14), and that must be returned to the realm of the material (bodily, culturally, and historically). Thus, I begin with metaphor because that is the "kingdom" where addiction lives in twenty-first-century American culture. And, again in the words of Sontag, "[i]t is toward an elucidation of those metaphors, and a liberation from them, that I dedicate this inquiry" (4).

PART I
Representing Wasted Metaphors

Chapter 1
Writing Belushi/Performing America: Addiction, National Identity, and the Cultural Mythos of "Waste" in *Wired*[1]

Belushi: Woodward. I used to do that guy.

Angel: Now he's doing you.

Belushi: What do you mean?

Angel: He's gonna be your biographer.

Belushi: My biographer? Bob Woodward??? I'll go down in history.

Angel: Yeah. He gonna do for you what he did for Nixon.

Belushi: Nixon?

Angel: Gonna call the book *Wired*. Gonna trash your good name, hemo, from here to …

Belushi: I'm fucked.

—*Wired* (1989)

Larry Peerce's biopic about comic John Belushi, titled *Wired* (1989), includes a key scene in which Belushi's agent (under the pseudonym Arnie) attempts to persuade Pulitzer-Prize-winning journalist Bob Woodward to write the late comic's biography. Part of Arnie's pitch involves the form which Woodward's research should take: "It's not an article. It's not even a series of articles. It's a book. Belushi's a book. 'Cause it's not just Belushi's story. It's a story about America." There is one chief reason to doubt the historical veracity of this conversation—namely, because the "real" Belushi's agent, Bernie Brillstein, eschewed any association with Woodward's project under threat of legal action (hence Woodward's use of a pseudonym). Nonetheless, the fact that this line is reiterated twice within the script of *Wired*—once tellingly in the final, climactic scene that takes place at Belushi's deathbed—suggests that Arnie's somewhat lofty analogy between Belushi's life and the mythos of America performs an important function within the diegesis of the biopic.

---

1 A previous version of this chapter was presented at the Battleground States American Studies conference at Bowling Green State University in February 2013.

In *Whose Lives Are They Anyway?: The Biopic as Contemporary Film Genre* (2010), Dennis Bingham asserts that the biopic is centrally concerned with "dramatiz[ing] actuality and find[ing] in it the filmmaker's own version of truth" (10). Following Bingham's logic, I would suggest that this line asserts itself as "the filmmaker's own version of truth" in *Wired*—that is, the central thematic conceit that simultaneously unites the events of the film (as much as the events of *Wired* can be considered "united") and focuses the viewing experience. What, though, is the "version of truth" that Peerce asserts about Belushi in *Wired*? What link(s) does the film draw between Belushi and America? To what particular "story of America" does the film liken Belushi's biography? And how does (or, Does?) one "story" lend insight to the other? Of particular relevance to the current study: How does *Wired* address the problem of Belushi's addiction? How does the film frame that problem as a uniquely "American story"? And what, in the end, does *Wired* have to say about the experience (both material and ideological) of being wasted in America?

I would suggest that, in *Wired*, Belushi's biography functions as a national allegory regarding America's troubled relationship with addiction—that is, the film at once stands as a "[displacement] of language," or as "a way of saying one thing and meaning another" (Tambling 6). The diegesis of the film simultaneously concerns itself with two narrative threads: one, Woodward's research process that preceded the writing of the film's source text; and two, Belushi's own life-after-death journey through key moments in his biography. Within the diegesis of *Wired*, the filmmakers use this dual-narrative structure as a means of actively demarcating the contrasts between the subject of the biography (that is, Belushi) and the biographer (that is, Bob Woodward) and it is through these contrasts that the film articulates its "own version of truth" regarding the experience (again, both material and ideological) of being wasted in America.

As the son of Albanian immigrants who, in life, enjoyed a meteoric rise to superstardom unparalleled among any of his contemporaries, Belushi immediately fits the bill for an American Everyman defined principally by his ambition, his hard work, and his self-reliance. Yet within the diegesis of his own biography, Belushi is cast as an antagonist—as the chief adversary both to Woodward and to himself. To Woodward, Belushi represents an enigma to-be-unraveled through meticulous and probing research. To himself, Belushi represents his own worst demon: a willfully self-destructive force bent on moral and physical ruin. Woodward, by contrast, represents America and, more specifically, the classic American Dream mythos. Whereas *Wired* represents Belushi as addiction incarnate, Woodward is viewed as The American Patriot—the Pulitzer-Prize-winning journalist whose dogged pursuit of Truth and Justice previously allowed him to break Watergate wide open and, in *Wired*, enables him to understand why Belushi died and, of equal importance (at least in the film), what addiction "means" within the context of 1980s America. Both the print and the cinematic versions of *Wired*, then, layer onto the tragic biography of John Belushi a narrative of fervent nationalism built squarely on the shoulders of the "true" American Everyman, Bob Woodward (arguably the protagonist in both texts), and modeled closely on the classic American Dream mythos, first articulated by James Truslow Adams in *The Epic of America* (1931). Woodward's research allegorically mirrors the compulsive acts of surveillance and policing that actively imagine and simultaneously create the body politic and, as such, the film suggests that the metaphor of waste is deeply imbricated in the operations of American nationalism. In this respect, the metaphor of waste is at once a metaphor of containment that actively "ferret[s] out" and isolates the addict-Belushi as a "socially deviant" Other—one whose identity and behaviors must be "feared," "vilified" (Alexander and Roberts 3), and ultimately displaced (all forms of ideological and emotional containment) in order to maintain the sanctity of the nation.

Bob Woodward's *Wired*: A Brief Production and Reception History

Wired (the biography) began several months following Belushi's death, in the summer of 1982, when the late comedian's sister-in-law, Pamela Jacklin, approached *Washington Post* reporter, Bob Woodward, and "suggested [he] look into" the "many unanswered questions surrounding John's death" (Woodward 9). Jacklin was acting on the instructions of her sister, and Belushi's widow, Judy—as Judy told *Rolling Stone* reporter Lynn Hirschberg in September 1984, "[Woodward] was my idea" (37)—who saw Woodward as "someone you can trust" (37), thanks in large part to his ground-breaking reporting (with Carl Bernstein) on the Watergate scandal. For his widow, Belushi's death was shrouded in mystery; as Judy (Lucinda Jenney) explains to Woodward (J.T. Walsh) in the film adaptation of *Wired*, "There's so much confusion …. He didn't shoot up. I knew my husband and he hated needles. A doctor got out a needle, he would run from the room. How could he have died from a needle?" Not only did Woodward boast of award-winning skills in investigative journalism, but also his reputation as the "Watergate sleuth" (Colby) would—Judy and her sister, Pamela, felt—provide the "name" needed to gain entry to the insular worlds of Hollywood show business and Los Angeles law enforcement to procure the answers to the widow's lingering questions (Hirschberg 37).

Although Belushi "was not a natural subject for [Woodward's] reporting," which to that point (and since) had(/has) "concentrated on Washington stories (Woodward 9), the two shared a common history, both having grown up—albeit six years apart—in the same small, Midwestern town of Wheaton,

Illinois. In the introduction to *Wired*, Woodward explains that his curiosity about the unconventional project encouraged him to meet with Belushi's widow, Judy, on two separate occasions that summer—first, in July in New York City, then, three weeks later on Martha's Vineyard; these interviews would become the springboard from which *Wired* would be launched. At the tail end of the introduction to the book, Woodward identifies the key research questions that he sought to answer through the countless hours of interviews that he conducted with Belushi's family members, friends, and associates: "Belushi could have been, should have been, one of those comedians whose work was measured in decades, across generations. But it wasn't. Why? What happened? Who was responsible, if anyone? Could it have been different or better? .... Could success have been something other than a failure" (12)?

Even before *Wired* was published in early June 1984, the book was eliciting harsh criticism and sparking controversy in many corners of public life. At the heart of the controversy was Judy Belushi and her many questions about fidelity—that is, the accuracy with which Woodward represented "the short life and fast times of John Belushi" (the subtitle for the book that, in some respects, already points to the bias with which Woodward was charged). Ever since Judy read portions of an advance copy of the book, she has maintained that "[t]he man in *Wired* is not the man I knew" (quoted in Hirschberg 35). She has taken issue with the focus of the biography; as she revealed to *Rolling Stone* reporter Lynn Hirschberg in September 1984, Judy "had ... hoped for a sympathetic biography. Instead, she got 432 pages of cold facts, the majority of them drug related and ugly" (35). She has taken Woodward to task for his superficial portrayal of her late husband (for example, "I loved John because he was warm. He was a very likeable person. He had a terrific presence, and Woodward missed all that."). She has criticized the tone of the book as biased (for example, "I had expected the sadness in the book, but I thought it should be balanced by joy, the joy John had and the joy he brought others.") and has labeled Woodward's methods unethical and manipulative (for example, "He manipulated me. He essentially raped my memories. My mental image of John—which was very strong—was stolen and used as the main character in Bob Woodward's novel.").[2]

---

2 Judy Belushi's criticisms of the one-dimensionality of Woodward's portrayal of Belushi have been echoed on multiple occasions by disinterested book reviewers with no immediately discernible personal stake in Belushi's legacy. Stanley Booth of the *Times Literary Supplement*, for instance, contends that "*Wired* is an honorable but ill-advised attempt to apply a technique that has worked for Woodward before. He has pieced together hundreds of interviews to arrive at an acceptable version of facts, too many of which related to bad or unmade films and grubby drug transactions. In the end we are left with the gloom but without the comedy that characterized Belushi's

Judy Belushi, of course, was not alone in her criticism of *Wired*, though for the past three decades she has been the loudest and most vocal of Woodward's detractors, at least with respect to *Wired*. Three days after the book was published, Belushi's friend and Blues Brothers collaborator, Dan Aykroyd, called *Wired* "[e]xploitation, pulp trash" (quoted in Hirschberg 37) in an interview with the *Philadelphia Inquirer*. Like Judy Belushi, actress-director Penny Marshall admitted to feeling "manipulated" by Woodward, adding, "If he had said he was writing a book about John Belushi and drugs, no one would have talked to him. What would have been the point? John had bad habits. He died" (quoted in Hirschberg 42). *Saturday Night Live* writer Anne Beatts was more pointed in her criticism of Woodward, calling the journalist a "star fucker" and "an exploitative scum-monger" (42). Similar comments were echoed by actor and Belushi pal Jack Nicholson, who called Woodward "a ghoul and an exploiter of emotionally distraught widows" (37)—interestingly, a critique that finds its way, in slightly modified form, into the mouth of the Belushi character in Peerce's filmic adaptation. (As Belushi confronts Woodward on his deathbed: "[S]tay away from my old lady. That's what you're waiting for. You vulture. You fucking bloodsucker. That's what you want. 'I Watched Bluto Breathe His Last,' told by Bob 'Pulitzer' Woodward. And then I snaked his old lady.") Perhaps one of the least emotionally-charged reviews of *Wired* hailed from author Tanner Colby and was published 29 years after the initial publication of Woodward's biography. Colby is the co-author (with Judy Belushi) of *Belushi: A Biography* (2005)—a book whose genesis Judy Belushi explains as follows in her introduction to the book: "So why *now* am I diverting my energies to another 'John project'? .... [B]ecause I once mistakenly gave the key to John's story to the wrong person, and this was a chance to get it right" (Introduction).[3] In "Regrettable," Colby raises critical questions regarding Woodward's professional ethics and credibility, asserting,

---

short, fast life" (269). In a similar manner, Norman Snider of *Maclean's* concludes his review of *Wired* by suggesting that "Woodward's wearying account of Belushi's short and desperate life will have to suffice until a more talented biographer comes along. The reader gets the distinct impression that the story would have fared better in the hands of a writer like Hunter S. Thompson ... who has a good sense of life lived out on the edge. With the stolid Woodward in charge, the reader feels none of the exhilaration of all those wild nights—just the sodden exhaustion of the morning after" (54).

3 In September 2013, news broke that the Belushi Pisano/Colby biography was being adapted for screen with a projected "spring 2014 shoot in New York." In all of the subsequent press releases about the project, the persons involved in writing, producing, and making this film implicitly but very self-consciously craft an image of this film as the anti-*Wired*. Although the project is, as of this writing in May 2015, still in pre-production, it will be interesting to see how (or even whether) the resulting film treats the late comic's addictions (Kit).

"The simple truth of *Wired* is that Bob Woodward, deploying all of the talent and resources for which he is famous, produced something that is a failure of journalism. And when you imagine Woodward using the same approach to cover secret meetings about drone strikes … you have to stop and shudder."

In response to much of the criticism that *Wired* has received, Woodward has hidden behind a very carefully crafted façade of objectivity. In the initial pages of *Wired*, Woodward marks the origin of the factual information contained within the biography, noting: "All the information in this book comes firsthand from witnesses or records" (10). As the controversies regarding accuracy and fidelity heated up—at one point, Judy Belushi charged, "People claim [the book is] all facts. It's not all facts. It's a bunch of people's opinions and memories put forth as facts" (quoted in Hirchberg 35)—Woodward stuck very closely to his objectivity defense. As he revealed to Hirschberg, "I think the facts loom so large in this book that they outweigh any analytical comments I might have made. The facts told a tremendous amount. And that's part of what this controversy is about: seeing and accepting those facts" (38). For Woodward, the facts surrounding Belushi's untimely death were so self-explanatory that the biographer could forego any form of editorial commentary in *Wired*, a technique for which Woodward has often been taken to task in his journalism.[4] And Woodward holds that it is precisely the unsettling nature of these self-explanatory facts that prompted Judy Belushi's criticisms. As he told Hirschberg, "John Belushi died of drugs. And it's awful and it's sad and *it was preventable*. All but the ending was written. Judy said it many times. But she didn't see the ending or know when the ending would come. And when it did come, she wasn't there. *I* showed Judy the ending. And that's what this is all about. *I showed Judy the ending*. It's that simple and that complicated" (41).

Woodward in Adaptation: Larry Pearce's *Wired*

Promoted almost from the very beginning of its production history as "the film Hollywood didn't want made," Peerce's *Wired* boasts of an origin story as convoluted and controversial as that of its source text.[5] According to most

---

    4   For example, a writer for *Kirkus Review* writes that in *Wired*, "Woodward offers—without shape, depth, or viewpoint—the dankly depressing, morbidly detailed life of John Belushi," concluding that "Woodward seems to have no idea what's involved in turning bare facts (or reconstructed dialogue) into a satisfying biography. So the result here, though scrupulously documented, is a dreary, empty chronicle, with enough real substance, perhaps, for a New York magazine article" (Rev. of *Wired*).

    5   Nina J. Easton and Jack Mathews of *The Los Angeles Times* provide a brief,

accounts, Woodward began trying to sell the film rights to *Wired* as early as 1984, the same year that the biography originally was published. Although threats of blacklisting and, in at least one instance, physical violence by Belushi's friends, relatives, and associates kept many prominent Hollywood producers from investing in the project, Woodward eventually sold the rights to his book in 1985 and, over the next four years, the project was inundated with unparalleled casting, production, publicity, and distribution problems that, at every turn, nearly ended the project before its cinematic release. *Wired* was screened at the Cannes Film Festival in May 1989 and opened to a wide release in August of that year.

The diegesis of *Wired* simultaneously follows two narrative threads. The first—which is both somewhat factual and somewhat realistic—accompanies Woodward along the research trail that eventually led him to write *Wired*. Like the storyline of *All the President's Men* (1976), this narrative thread is a reconstruction of an extra-diegetic series of events that features Woodward (J.T. Walsh) as a fictional character—perhaps *the* central fictional character—in a film purportedly *about* someone (that is, Belushi in the case of *Wired*) or something (that is, Watergate in the case of *All The President's Men*) else. In fact, Vincent Canby of *The New York Times* makes a similar observation, although he concedes that "'Wired' can't easily be turned into the mystery story that 'All the President's Men' resembled." The events of the narrative unfold chronologically, from the moment that Woodward first reads about Belushi's death in an AP report to his final visit to the site at which Belushi died: cabin #3 at Hollywood's Chateau Marmont. Throughout the film, Woodward (the character) interacts with a wide variety of fictional characters who represent Belushi's (the man's) family members, friends, and acquaintances—though, unlike in a conventional biopic, many such figures appear under pseudonyms after the real people on whom those fictional characters were based threatened legal action if their likenesses appeared in the film. The arc of this narrative thread is unified (as much as the narrative of *Wired* can be considered *unified*) by a simplified version of the research questions that open Woodward's book. As Woodward asks a dying Belushi (Michael Chiklis) in one of the final scenes of the film, "Why the drugs, John? Hmmm? Why the needle? That's what *I* need to understand."

The second, wholly fictionalized narrative thread places the late comedian at center stage, although the focus is not so much on Belushi's life as it is on a fantastical life-after-death scenario in which he, like Woodward, ponders the choices that he made that led to his death at the age of 33. This narrative picks up in the immediate aftermath of Belushi's death as his corpse is wheeled on a gurney into the Los Angeles County Morgue. After being unceremoniously ensconced in the autopsy room by a morgue attendant (Finis Henderson III),

---

but comprehensive, overview of *Wired*'s complicated production history in their co-authored article "Another Chapter in the Strange Odyssey of 'Wired.'"

Belushi emerges—sweat-soaked, frightened, and disoriented—from within the bodybag, unsure of where he is, how he arrived there, and what his purpose is in being there. He panics. He scurries around the autopsy room. Eventually he runs screaming from the morgue and manages to hail a taxicab, asking the driver to take him back to the Chateau Marmont. The driver, as it fortuitously turns out, is a former-addict-turned-guardian-angel tellingly (if not creatively) named Angel (Ray Sharkey). When the pair reaches the hotel, they watch as (in a strange temporal twist—the first of many in this film) Belushi's corpse is rolled out and loaded into the morgue van; it is at this point that Belushi finally realizes (or accepts) that he is dead. Over the course of the film, Angel leads Belushi through a series of flashbacks, flash-forwards, and even an occasional flash-sideways—all drawn (albeit sometimes quite loosely) from the real Belushi's biography. Spectators look on, for instance, as Belushi recreates one hilarious *Saturday Night Live* sketch after another, mugs for the camera as Bluto in the cafeteria scene of *Animal House* (1978), muses about life and death with pal Dan Aykroyd (Gary Groomes), sinks deeper into his cocaine addiction on the set of *The Blues Brothers* (1980), and is warned repeatedly to quit using drugs by physicians, friends, and family members. Throughout all of these remembrances of things past, Belushi struggles (ultimately in vain) to discover, in his words, "What the hell happened in [the Chateau Marmont]?" In other words, the Belushi narrative, fantastical as it may initially appear, attempts to identify the factors that contributed to the comic's devolution into addiction and eventual death from drug-related causes—a similar objective to Woodward's in the parallel narrative of *Wired*.

The plot of *Wired* seemingly inevitably moves toward a head-on collision of these two narrative threads, a climactic clash in which Woodward and Belushi, against the logic of temporality, spatiality, and historical accuracy, meet in-person at the deathbed of Belushi in the final moments of the late comic's life. This surreal meeting takes place in cabin #3 of the Chateau Marmont and depicts Woodward engaging Belushi in a wholly fabricated deathbed conversation that begins with Woodward insistently asking, "Why the drugs, John? Hmmm? Why the needle? That's what *I* need to understand …. Judy said that you were afraid of needles. That you hated them. If you hated them so much what were you doing sticking them in your arm? Huh, John? C'mon now. Answer me now." To label this scene as "heavy-handed" seems rather an understatement given the hyperbolic emotional valence that circumscribes its action. Over the nearly 15 minutes of back-and-forth dialogue between a stoic Woodward and a gasping Belushi, the Belushi figure alternates almost schizophrenically from one emotion to another, covering the entire emotional gamut from self-loathing (for example, "I'm out of control when I take heroin.") to self-aggrandizement (for example, "Society fucked me over like Lenny Bruce!"). Meanwhile, Woodward adopts a variety of roles vis-à-vis the dying Belushi, from objective interlocutor (for example, "Judy said that you were afraid of needles. That you hated them. If you hated them so much, what were you doing sticking them in your arm? Huh, John? C'mon now. Answer me now.") to armchair psychologist (for example, "Why didn't you ever want to go home? What was so painful that you couldn't even close your eyes at night without drugs?"). Belushi lobs one criticism after another at Woodward, calling him a "cold bastard" and a "fucking bloodsucker" and echoing—in sentiment, if not in verbatim word choice—the many criticisms that had, by that point in time, been leveled against the source text for the film, most vehemently by Judy Belushi herself.

The climax of this scene (and, indeed, the film) centers on a series of questions that Belushi puts to Woodward in the final moments of the film: "So, what'd you find out that I didn't already know? Huh, Mr. Straight-A-Honor-Society? We expected you to come up with something. What'd you find out?" This speech marks an interesting moment in the film—a moment at which Belushi (the character) meta-fictively aligns himself with the extra-diegetic audience of both *Wired* and its source text (suggested by the use of the first person plural point-of-view) and demands that Woodward perform the job of biographer and draw some sort of conclusion from his research. (Again, by the time of the production and release of the film, this was a demand that many critics were making of Woodward for the source text.) In typical Woodward fashion, the Woodward character disavows this responsibility: "There's no mystery here. You did it to yourself, John. Had help. But you did it to yourself." At one hour forty-five minutes into the film, *Wired* has returned viewers decidedly back to its initial five minutes when the morgue attendant rolling Belushi's corpse into the Los Angeles County Morgue unceremoniously condemns Belushi, who "had it all," for being "Stupid" and overdosing. Even more interesting, and, I would argue, disturbing, is the dying Belushi's final line: "I can't breathe. Breathe for me, Woodward"—a directive that signals Belushi's concession of narrative voice and authority in his own biography to Woodward. (I analyze this scene in much greater detail later in the chapter.) The stripping away of the addict's voice and autonomy, so common not only in cultural artifacts that represent the lived experience of addiction, but also in the philosophies of predominant treatment models, marks one cornerstone tenet of the metaphor of waste that I will discuss both in this chapter and throughout the second and third parts of this book.

Larry Pearce's *Wired*: A Brief Production and Reception History

With Belushi as its subject, and Woodward as its source author, *Wired* should have been met with a wealth of acclaim and financial success when it opened in theaters on 25 August 1989. Yet the film universally was panned by critics and movie-goers alike, the $13 million motion picture pulling in only a little over $1 million in box office sales. (Apparently time has done little to soften the critical reaction to the film. As of January 2014, the film boasted a 0% on Rotten Tomatoes's Tomatometer, with an average audience rating of 2.4/5.) And *Wired* fared even worse in the popular media, producing a mound of scathing, if quote-worthy, reviews. Mike McGranaghan of Aisle Seat labeled *Wired* "[o]ne of the all-time worst. An offense," while James Sanford of the *Kalamazoo Gazette* punctuated his review with, "The word that comes to mind is 'ghastly'" (quoted in *Wired* [1989]). Roger Hurlburt, a contributor to the *Sun Sentinel,* was alone in his criticism of the subject matter of the film, calling *Wired* "a lot of hoopla about a man who just doesn't seem to be all that beloved anymore."

Most critics of *Wired* highlighted what one *Rolling Stone* writer termed the "surreal, stupefyingly silly script"—a script penned by American novelist and screenwriter Eric Mac Rauch, whose writing credits to that point included *New York, New York* (1977), *A Stranger is Watching* (1982), and *The Adventures of Buckaroo Banzai Across the 8th Dimension* (1984) (Rev. of *Wired,* dir. Larry Peerce). *Time* magazine's Richard Zoglin generously called the film "an ambitious, if muddled, attempt at surrealistic psychodrama." But others were not so diplomatic. Jack Mathews of *The Los Angeles Times* described the plot of the film as "a surreal mélange of events," while *The Humanist*'s Harry M. Geduld labeled *Wired* "an incoherent mishmash that answers none of the questions the film provokes." There also were the to-be-expected charges against what some perceived to be an exploitative and offensive treatment of the biography of America's Guest. Rob Gonsalves of eFilmCritic.com called the film "[a] profoundly trivial and tasteless affair" (quoted in *Wired* [1989]) and Desson Howe, a colleague of Woodward's at *The Washington Post,* wrote, "Certainly Belushi deserves as much scrutiny as the next public figure who died after heavy drug use, but this autopsy seems unnecessary."

Three especially quotable reviews of the film serve to summarize the kinds of problems that the film suffered, as well as the level of confusion that it inspired even among seasoned film critics. Michael Wilmington of *The Los Angeles Times* called *Wired* "a multileveled hipster exposé: a whacked-out docudrama, 'Citizen Kane' squeezed through 'Saturday Night Live' and basted with National Lampoon blood and bile." By contrast, a *Rolling Stone* reviewer offered two equally strange analogies, suggesting on one hand that *Wired* was "even more of a gloss than the candy-assed view of Jerry Lee Lewis in *Great Balls of Fire*" and, on the other, that "*Wired* packs all the investigative wallop of a Care Bears flick" (Rev. of *Wired*). Roger Ebert perhaps offers the clearest and most definitive response to the film, writing, "*Wired* ... is such an ungainly and hapless movie, so stupidly written, so awkwardly directed and acted, that it never gets off the ground."

Truth, Accuracy, and the Biopic

Woodward himself has long attributed much of the film's failure to the fact that "[a] large portion of Hollywood didn't want this movie made because there's too much truth in it" (Zoglin). Woodward's explanation of why *Wired* flopped both financially and critically might initially spark confusion; after all, he is talking about a biography (a genre that most people associate with factuality, Truth) that features guardian angels, a risen-from-the-dead celebrity, and strange temporal and spatial manipulations that are neither directly nor indirectly attributed to Belushi's drug use. In other words, if Woodward defines "truth" as historical accuracy, or narrative verisimilitude, or even adherence to the laws of physics, then his claim stands on very shaky ground, given that within the context of what is supposed to be a biopic, viewers witness not just historical reconstruction, or even the application of creative license, but outright fabrication. However, if the word "truth" is defined not in terms of how accurately the film "*corresponds* to reality," but in terms of how "through an act of interpretation or construction" the film *ideologically produces* reality, then Woodward might be onto something. The idea here is that "truth" (or, perhaps more precisely, "meaning") does not "objectively" exist within a cultural artifact like *Wired*, but rather the meaning of that artifact derives from "a meeting between what's out there and what we bring to it" (Ford 128). In short, textual meaning is actively constructed and negotiated in the meeting of author, text, and reader; in this respect, the act of reading/interpreting (what Wolfgang Iser terms "the unfolding of the text") becomes "a living event" (Iser 290).

At its core, the biopic is a genre that asserts itself as a meeting among author (filmmaker), text (biography subject), and reader/viewer/critic. The biopic "narrates, exhibits, and celebrates the life of a subject in order to demonstrate, investigate, or question his or her importance in the world: to illuminate the fine points of a personality; and for both artist and spectator to discover what it would be like to be this person, or to be a certain type of person" (Bingham 10). From *Sweet Dreams* (1985) to *Cinderella Man* (2005) and *Milk* (2008), biopics may focus their attention on a range of figures from many different arenas of public life, but they collectively share at minimum three characteristics that work to differentiate them from other genres of film. First, biopics assert a concentrated focus on the biography of a public figure of *significance*, although what constitutes *significance* will differ based on historical moment, culture, and even sometimes producer. Second, biopics offer a chronological recounting of key events from the significant figure's life—or, as George F. Custen explains in *Bio/Pics: How Hollywood Constructed Public History* (1992), the biopic "sets up the moment of a life when we can witness the birth of a particular talent—seldom the character's literal birth" (51).

The third common characteristic of the biopic is that the film articulates an overarching thematic that identifies the enduring significance of the figure's life, career, and/or key accomplishment. In "Does the Biopic Constitute a Genre?," the author alludes to this common feature when s/he suggests that "[w]hat the 'biopic' does indicate for audiences ... is that they are witnessing factual information about the real lives of individuals, and there is also a moderate expectation that viewers are likely to discover a previously hidden truth about the subject in question." In some instances, this "previously hidden truth" emerges from a concentrated investigation into the biography of a significant public figure. In most instances, however, the "previously hidden truth" is imposed onto the biography by the filmmakers in an act of creative interpretation. As Bingham notes, "[S]ince historical fiction stems from the desire to see biographical and historical figures living before us, there are instances where the filmmakers see the need to 'complete' history to fill in what didn't happen with what a viewer might wish to see happen" (8). Later in his book, Bingham goes on to note that the "previously hidden truth" put forth by a biopic is "the filmmaker's own version of truth" (10). Bingham's point here resonates quite profoundly with the process by which the *real* becomes the *representational*. Narratives—whether literary or filmic, fictional or non-fictional—demand a kind of thematic (and temporal) coherence uncharacteristic of life outside of books or the cinema. Specifically, such narratives insist upon closure (that is, the iteration of a "previously hidden truth" that "completes" history) that can only ever be achieved through the assertion of a unifying theme that guides the selection of key events presented within the diegesis (thereby simultaneously providing a clear and logical organizational plan for the narrative); this unifying theme, while manufactured, nonetheless provides the audience with a clear "take away" message about why the figure is *significant* and worthy of a much-coveted place within "the pantheon of cultural mythology" (Bingham 10).

In the introduction to this chapter, I assert that the "previously hidden truth" about Belushi that is advanced in *Wired* rests firmly on the link that Arnie draws between the late comic and the mythos of America. I go on to suggest that the film invites viewers to read Belushi's biography as an allegory—that is, as I note above, as "a way of saying one thing and meaning another" (Tambling 6). More specifically, I argue that the film stands as a national allegory regarding America's troubled relationship with addiction. This reading of the film draws heavily on the work of historian Hayden White who, in his seminal text *Tropics of Discourse: Essays in Cultural Criticism* (1986), conceives of historiography not as an objective textual rendering of historical fact (that is, Authoritative History), but as an active (re)construction of "the objects which it pretends only to describe realistically and to analyze objectively" (that is, multiple and invested histories)

(2). The practice of historiography, according to White, involves an imaginative blending of factual information and literary tropes. As White explains:

> The reader, in the process of following the historian's account of those events, gradually comes to realize that the story he is reading is of one kind rather than another: romance, tragedy, comedy, satire, epic, or what have you. And when he has perceived the class or type to which the story that he is reading belongs, he experiences the effect of having the events of the story explained to him .... They are rendered comprehensible by being subsumed under the categories of the plot structure in which they are encoded as a story of a particular kind. (86)

In this passage, White asserts that the historian renders historical events both understandable and meaningful by framing them within familiar tropes—that is, genres, character types, and/or narratives that are part of both the historian's and the reader's "cultural endowment" (86). Such tropes play an explanatory role in the reading process, enabling the historian to corral the often discontinuous events of history into a cohesive (and usually causal) narrative while simultaneously signaling to readers why a particular event/personage is regarded as "historically significant."

In a similar way, the biopic (itself a subgenre of "History," broadly conceived) announces itself as a representational form that both "describes realistically and analyzes objectively" (White 2) an historical subject. (Note here the striking similarity between White's assertion regarding the descriptive and analytical nature of the historical record and Bingham's suggestion that biopics "dramatize actuality and find in it the filmmaker's own version of truth.") Indeed, any biopic that has ever been produced can be meaningfully interpreted from within the framework of White's "tropics of discourse." For example, *Coal Miner's Daughter* (1980) casts the life of Loretta Lynn as a fairy tale—a rags-to-riches story, not unlike "Cinderella," that follows the country-western singer from her humble beginnings in Butcher Hollow, Kentucky, to the apex of her career performing at the Grand Ole Opry. *Mommie Dearest* (1981) is a tabloid-like tell-all about the scandalous private life of actress Joan Crawford. *Ghandi* (1982) is an epic, as is *The Passion of the Christ* (2004). And *The Whistleblower* (2011) is a "feminist" informant story in the tradition of *Silkwood* (1983) and *Erin Brockovich* (2000). Like many biopics that focus on a public figure who suffered an untimely and traumatic death [for example, *Selena* (1997) or *Boys Don't Cry* (1999)], *Wired* is framed principally as a tragedy. However, unlike some similar biopics, *Wired* casts Belushi's biography as a tragedy *of national proportion*, a not-unsurprising choice on the part of the filmmakers given that Belushi's struggles with addiction (the primary focus of the film) were historically played out against the backdrop of the "Just Say 'No'" decade.

Wired as Tragedy

At its most basic, tragedy traces the degradation of a character of some significance due to circumstances that are identified at once as both preordained and avoidable. To establish Belushi as a figure of significance, *Wired* waxes nostalgic regarding the comic's involvement in *Saturday Night Live* (1975–1979), re-casting that period of the comic's life as the apex of his brief but prolific career and using his unprecedented success on the late-night program as a means of underscoring the "tragic" nature of his death. In this respect, Belushi's stint as one of *Saturday Night Live*'s original cast members becomes within the diegesis of *Wired* what Custen identifies as a central feature of the biopic: namely, "set[ting] up the moment of a life when [viewers] can witness the birth of a particular talent—seldom the character's literal birth" (51). The prominent role that *Saturday Night Live* plays within the narrative of *Wired* is hinted at in the very first scene of the film and then echoed in the final one. The film begins with an extended re-creation of Belushi's classic bee routine, the opening credits being played out against the soundtrack of Belushi belting out "I'm a king bee, baby, and I want you to be my queen." *Wired* closes with another extended re-creation of an iconic Belushi routine—this time, the Joe Cocker imitation that Belushi originated during his time as a cast member of The Second City comedy troupe (1971–1972) and refined during his tenure on *Saturday Night Live*. These two performances occupy prominent places within *Wired*, together bookending the viewing experience and providing the spectator tangible (and familiar) touchstones by which "to demonstrate, investigate, [and] question [Belushi's] importance in the world" (Bingham 10), another key feature of the biopic. That these characters are instantly recognizable as iconic Belushi creations underscores my claim here that, in *Wired*, *Saturday Night Live* serves as the primary sieve through which Belushi's *significance* as a tragic figure is filtered and as the key piece of evidence for why Belushi has entered "the pantheon of cultural mythology" (10). Through its repeated references to Belushi's iconic performances on *Saturday Night Live*, *Wired* over and again identifies Belushi as a figure of significance whose comedic talents marked him as "better than ordinary people" (Holman and Harmon 479) and thus worthy as a subject of both biography and tragedy. Even more telling is the fact that the filmmakers opted to foreground one of the characters that the real Belushi loathed (but Belushi fans loved); in *Belushi: A Biography*, a number of Belushi's associates from the *Saturday Night Live* days vividly recall Belushi's disdain for the bee sketches. Rosie Schuster, a writer for *Saturday Night Live*, for instance, recalls, "The bees were on every show for a while, and John just felt it was so beneath him," while Al Franken, another *Saturday Night Live* writer, states simply, "He hated being a bee" (Chapter 5).

Of course, not only does *Saturday Night Live* feature prominently in the opening and closing of *Wired*, but also references to its significance recur throughout the film as a reminder to viewers of "the class or type to which the story that [they are] reading belongs" and, by association, how to read the film, how to understand Belushi's enduring cultural legacy. Within the film, there are at least three additional extended *Saturday Night Live* performances that are re-created for viewers—a lengthy Blues Brothers routine, a skit in which Belushi plays Bob Woodward to Dan Aykroyd's Conehead Nixon, and a skit featuring the Samurai at the World Series—none of which advance the plot in any meaningful way. Furthermore, during his deathbed tirade against Woodward's journalistic methods, Belushi slips in one of the catchphrases for which he was known on *Saturday Night Live* (that is, "But nooooooo!"). What such re-creations/allusions do is invite the viewer into the world of the film, allowing him/her to "[see] an actual person who did something interesting in life, known mostly in public, transformed into a character. Private behaviors and actions and public events as they might have been in the person's time are formed together and interpreted dramatically" (Bingham 10). Once the viewer's interest is piqued by these scenes that reference classic Belushi performances (that is, "public events as they might have been in the person's time"), s/he is reminded on two separate occasions—once near the opening of the film and once at its close—that Belushi's enduring significance is deeply imbricated in his work on *Saturday Night Live*. Near the opening of the film, Judy Belushi reveals to Woodward that Belushi was "proudest" of his work on the sketch show, while, near the end of the film, Cathy Smith (Patti D'arbanville) in voice over reveals that "[t]he only laugh or good time John had that last week was watching a re-run of *Saturday Night Live*." In *Wired*, *Saturday Night Live* represents the height of Belushi's creativity and celebrity, and the cornerstone of his cultural legacy—that is, one key reason that his biography is being written/adapted for film in the first place. The film suggests that viewers should care about the late comic because of his innovative comic stylings, his musical talents, and his acting abilities—all of which were nurtured, at least according to the revisionist history asserted in *Wired*, during his tenure as a member of the Not Ready for Primetime Players.

Tragedy not only demands a figure of significance, but also presupposes "an unhappy catastrophe" in which the tragic figure is "brought from happiness to misery" (Holman and Harmon 479). This catastrophe (a term that is synonymous here with "conclusion" or "*dénouement*," rather than with "calamity" or "disaster") can be precipitated by a number of causal factors—external forces, internal "flaws," biographical circumstances, and so on—and, in *Wired*, the filmmakers trot out all of the usual suspects for a cameo appearance. Not surprisingly, *Wired* draws a fairly explicit causal link between Belushi's death and Cathy Smith's administration of a speedball in the hours immediately preceding that event; however, the film tellingly omits any mention of Cathy's conviction for involuntary manslaughter and subsequent 15-month stint in prison.[6] This omission does not necessarily exonerate Smith of any wrong-doing in Belushi's death, but at least within the diegesis of *Wired*, it does significantly shift the balance of blame to other targets—chief among them, Belushi himself. In addition to Cathy Smith, the filmmakers indict a variety of other people and institutions in the death of Belushi. From the opening scenes of the film, when the iconic Hollywood sign can be glimpsed through the morgue window, the institution of Hollywood haunts the biography of the dead comic, offering up one rather compelling (if expected) alternative cause for Belushi's addictive and ultimately fatal behaviors. An early lesson with an acting coach from 1972, for instance, implies that the nature of great comedy (arguably the cornerstone of Belushi's legacy) is excess: "John, there's a light in you. When you burn it out, *burn it out!* Cut the demons loose, John. Cut 'em loose. That's where your characters come from …. Comedy's an assault." Belushi's agent, Arnie, draws an even more explicit causal link between celebrity and addiction, regarding "drinking and fucking and drugs" as Hollywood's commonplace, as simply "what stars do when they're not working."

Of course, Hollywood not only fosters, but also enables Belushi's addictions in *Wired*. At one point, for instance, Woodward interrogates an apathetic movie studio executive about Belushi's $2,500/week per diem, most of which Belushi would use to purchase illicit substances; later in the film, a music producer justifies giving Belushi amphetamines by noting, "It was

---

6 One could argue, of course, that Smith's prison sentence, which spanned from December 1986 through March 1988, post-dates both the publication of the source text (that is, 1984) and the diegetic time of the film (roughly 1972 through several months following Belushi's death in February 1982) and therefore its omission within the film is not particularly surprising. However, it is not uncommon for filmmakers of biopics to employ a pre-end-credits montage in which they briefly explain what happens to the "characters" after the diegetic "end" of the film [for example, *Sid and Nancy* (1986), *The Doors* (1991), or *Big Eyes* (2014)]. By the time *Wired* was in production, Smith already would have completed her prison sentence and, given the strange temporal twists and turns that the film makes, this type of fast forward would not have been either unexpected or particularly jarring by the film's close. Moreover, the source text itself does offer a similar type of closure, although again its publication pre-dates Smith's prison sentence by more than two years. In that text, Woodward checks in with all of the major, and many of the minor, players in Belushi's biography in the year or so following his death. That the film omits any mention of Smith's fate subtly directs attention back to Belushi himself (or, more specifically, his willful self-destructiveness) as the causal agent in his own addiction and untimely death; in short, Smith may have administered the speedball that killed Belushi, but, the film makes perfectly clear, she did so on Belushi's orders.

a $40,000 recording session. John had to be on and it was the only way to ensure he'd stay awake." Fans, too, are implicated in Belushi's demise. In one especially strange (even for *Wired*) scene, an adoring fan offers Belushi a vial of cocaine while the two are standing together at the urinals of a trendy nightclub. Belushi refuses the cocaine, but once the fan exits the club bathroom, the hand soap and towel dispensers inexplicably begin to serve up a never-ending supply of cocaine. While each of these causal agents is offered up as a potential contributing factor in the untimely demise of Belushi, ultimately none is explored as thoughtfully as need be in order to convince viewers that it is the reason Belushi died. In this respect, these alternative causes become interesting anecdotes that add color and dimension to the comic's biography (or, in the words of Bingham, that help to "dramatize actuality"), but they do not constitute the "previously hidden truth" that "completes" Belushi's biography.

Blaming and Shaming

To discern the "previously hidden truth" that *Wired* advances about Belushi, we need to look first at that final, climactic scene in which Woodward and Belushi square off. As I note above, this scene builds to the moment when the dying Belushi asks Woodward, "So, what'd you find out that I didn't already know?" Woodward's deceptively simple response points directly and authoritatively to the "previously hidden truth" about Belushi's tragic downfall—a "previously hidden truth" that, I would argue, is in plain sight from the very opening credits of the film. Woodward replies, "There's no mystery here. You did it to yourself, John. Had help. But you did it to yourself."[7] In essence, this film reiterates the party line of many a 12-step program: namely, that addiction is a self-destructive choice that individuals make. (I take up the topic of 12-step programs and their embeddedness in the metaphor of waste in Chapter 4 of the current study.)

---

7   This "climactic" conclusion is foreshadowed much earlier in the film when Woodward, after reading the Coroner's report on Belushi's autopsy, lightly ponders, "Accidental? What is this: a *Saturday Night Live* routine?" Both within the diegesis of *Wired* and outside of it, Woodward often functions as the voice of authority, an omniscient, God-like presence whose meticulous research lends credibility to his "incisive" observations about his subjects. The frightening part of this attitude, as has been noted by many of the real Belushi's former friends and family members, is that if an observation comes from Woodward's mouth (or pen), then "people will believe [it]. After all, *Bob Woodward* wrote it. He's God. He's Watergate" (Tim Kazurinsky quoted in Hirschberg 41). In other words, this "blame the addict" mentality reflects antiquated notions of the nature of addiction, and yet, in the mouth of even a fictional Bob Woodward, it takes on more than a ring of Truth.

Within this tragic narrative, Belushi is cast as addiction incarnate, a willfully self-destructive force bent on moral and physical ruin. What results is a very familiar narrative that simultaneously blames and shames the addict-Belushi for his tragic death.

This narrative of blame and shame is introduced in the opening credits of the film when the title, *Wired*, flashes across the screen. According to Belushi's sister-in-law, Pamela Jacklin, the title *Wired* was one of the most significant bones of contention between Judy Belushi and Bob Woodward. From Judy's perspective, the title "focused [too much] on the negative—the drugs" and, in so doing, "missed the man" (Hirschberg 38). Interestingly, in the cinematic adaptation of *Wired*, the filmmakers implicitly acknowledge Judy Belushi's criticism of Woodward's book when her filmic counterpart tells Woodward "I want people to see [John] as he was. The drugs *and more*" (emphasis added). To his credit, Pamela Jacklin recalls, Woodward did attempt to alleviate Judy's anxieties regarding the title, explaining "his triple-entendre theory that 'wired' meant (a) vibrant and alive, (b) successful and plugged into the system and (c) drugs" (quoted in Hirschberg 38). Yet Woodward's explanation of the title smacks of disingenuousness, especially coming from a Pulitzer-Prize-winning journalist whose long and illustrious career is built squarely on the foundation of precise diction. After all, as the *Oxford English Dictionary* confirms, only one of the meanings that Woodward cites for the term "wired" (that is, letter *c*) has ever been in use in the English language. Furthermore, the first international use of the term "wired" to denote the experience of being "[i]ntoxicated or 'high' on drugs, esp. so as to become hyper or overstimulated" occurred in Australia in 1977, just seven years prior to the publication of Woodward's *Wired: The Short Life and Fast Times of John Belushi*. In America, the first noted usage of the term was, perhaps quite coincidentally, in the Style section of *The Washington Post* on 13 December 1978 ("wired, adj."). In short, the title of Belushi's biography and its adaptation unequivocally identifies Belushi as first and foremost an addict. At times, this narrative focus stands in direct opposition to the focus on Belushi's comedic virtuosity on *Saturday Night Live*, while at other times the manic performances that are re-created in *Wired* only work to reinforce the focus on Belushi's tragic devolution into drug abuse and addiction.

Throughout the film, Belushi repeatedly is blamed and shamed for his addictive behaviors. Indeed, against the logic of prevailing neurobiological theories regarding the nature of addiction, the comic himself repeatedly is regarded by other characters as, in the words of one of the fictional Los Angeles detectives investigating the case, "just another fat junkie that went belly up"—a fairly stark contrast to the rose-colored nostalgia through which some of Belushi's *Saturday Night Live* sketches are refracted. In the second scene of the film, for instance, a morgue attendant wheels a gurney carrying the recently-deceased Belushi toward the autopsy room. After the attendant passes a large picture window through which the iconic Hollywood sign can be glimpsed in miniature in the distant background, he voices his disgust for Belushi, calling the comic "Stupid" for having every opportunity and wasting them. Moments later, after the dead-Belushi escapes from the morgue, his taxi driver/guardian Angel recognizes the comic, saying, "I remember you played a coke addict. Yeah. Yeah. You was a funny guy. But you died in the end. You were fucked up." Interesting here is the blurring of fact and fiction that occurs in Angel's line—the taxi driver simultaneously recognizing dead-Belushi as a celebrity, and mis-recognizing his off-screen substance addictions both as a fictional narrative (that is, Belushi "*played* a coke addict," emphasis added) and as the source of his fame. This blurring of fact and fiction lends authority and credence to the "previously hidden truth" advanced in the film, which has both diegetic implications for Belushi and extra-diegetic implications for addicts—a point I discuss in greater detail at the close of this chapter.

There are, of course, many other instances in the film when Belushi is identified as the root source of his tragic demise. When Angel and dead-Belushi arrive at the Chateau Marmont, they watch—in one of the film's confusing moments of temporal blurring—as Belushi's corpse is wheeled out by the Coroner. Belushi's reaction is to ask in a panicky voice, "What the hell happened in there?" to which Angel replies, "You are officially dead .... 'cause you are stupid." Near the mid-point of the film, as Belushi devolves into increasingly erratic and self-destructive behaviors, he visits a physician who advises him to stop using drugs and twice explicitly warns Belushi, "You're killing yourself."[8] Like Belushi's physician, Judy Belushi indicts the late comic for having "a life pattern of binges," an indictment that is reinforced by Belushi on several occasions, such as when he pleads, "I want some coke .... I need it. I can't do the scene without it" or when he demands "Shoot me up" immediately preceding Cathy Smith's injecting him with that final, fatal speedball hours before his death. In each of these instances, *Wired* targets Belushi's own ("stupid") actions as responsible for his death. Despite the warnings against such actions by medical professionals and concerned family/friends, he repeatedly "chooses" to use drugs—the notion of choice being powerfully reinforced by the very language Belushi uses (for example, "Shoot me up" is a directive issued from superior to subordinate). Also telling is the

---

8 Interestingly, this scene is surrealistically replayed on the night before Belushi's death. At a club, as he ingests increasingly greater quantities of cocaine and other drugs, Belushi witnesses this scene with his doctor playing out on one of the club's television screens. In the role of the doctor is an exaggerated, Groucho-Marx-type figure. I would suggest that narratively the scene functions as a kind of strange foreshadowing of Belushi's imminent death as well as a reminder (albeit a grotesque, drug-induced one) of the film's condemnation of Belushi as solely responsible for his demise.

fact that *Wired* never once entertains the notion that addiction is anything other than a series of morally-questionable choices. There is no consideration of the disease model of addiction, no sense that an addict might be driven by anything—most particularly, a neurobiological condition precipitated by repeated, heavy substance abuse—other than a broken moral compass.

One of the most explicit instances in which the biopic shames and blames its subject occurs during the autopsy scenes. An autopsy enacts a literal and a figurative violation of the human body—literally, a breach of its natural boundaries by foreign objects (for example, a scalpel), and figuratively, a laying bare of the body's most intimate secrets to the probing gaze of others. These scenes are shot largely in extreme close-up with the camera either pointed upwards at the Coroner's face (from Belushi's perspective on the autopsy table) or downwards at Belushi's countenance (from the Coroner's perspective). The focus is on the facial expressions of those involved in the action rather than on the action itself. For instance, the Coroner, his mouth covered by a mask, disinterestedly narrates the process by which Belushi's innards are dissected, measured, and catalogued, while Belushi screams and wildly contorts his face with every cut and slice that happens off-camera. In much the style of classical Greek tragedy, the film (thankfully) isolates the more graphic aspects of the autopsy off-camera, yet, in doing so, the film powerfully emphasizes the systemic acts of surveillance that persistently violate the individual's civil rights and rights to privacy—especially if that individual is a celebrity who dies as a result of addiction. Through its concentrated (and extreme close-up) focus on the individual's reaction, the choice of shot in the autopsy scene gives spectators a front row seat in the viewing theater of Belushi's postmortem, calling attention not only to the act of looking, but also to the near-obsessive curiosity, the desire to know, that often consumes Americans when a celebrity succumbs to addiction. (This topic will be examined much more fully with respect to the death of Whitney Houston in Chapter 6 of this study.) But the autopsy also provides ample fodder for the judgment that the film makes against Belushi. As Belushi's corpse is dissected and the ravages of addiction catalogued, the body repeatedly supplies ample physical evidence of the comic's willful self-destruction and his poor moral judgment—from the four to five needle marks intended to point to the "reason" Belushi died, to the distended bladder and the enlarged heart (big "even for someone his size") intended to document addiction's path of destruction through Belushi's body. At the same time, the autopsy gives lie—both diegetically and extra-diegetically—to the comic's protestations that he wasn't an addict by documenting the impact of drugs on his body and linking that impact causally to his eventual (and inevitable) death.

22

Conclusion

Of Belushi's addiction, *Wired* unapologetically advances a fairly straightforward and ideologically unequivocal narrative—one that originated in the nineteenth century and one that identifies the addict as morally corrupt and willfully self-destructive. (I examine the origins of this narrative in much greater detail in the next two chapters.) But Belushi's story is also, as Arnie reminds Woodward early in the film, "a story about America"—more specifically, I would argue, a narrative that locates the metaphor of waste in the processes by which the American nation is imagined and performed. My understanding of "the nation" derives from Benedict Anderson's classic study *Imagined Communities: Reflections on the Origin and Spread of Nationalism* (1983), in which the author defines "the nation" as "an imagined political community—and imagined as both inherently limited and sovereign" (6). As Anderson explains:

> It is *imagined* because the members of even the smallest nation will never know most of their fellow-members, meet them, or even hear of them, yet in the minds of each lives the image of their communion …. The nation is imagined as *limited* because even the largest of them encompassing perhaps a billion living human beings, has finite, if elastic boundaries, beyond which lie other nations …. It is imagined as *sovereign* because the concept was born in an age in which Enlightenment and Revolution were destroying the legitimacy of the divinely-ordained, hierarchical dynastic realm …. Finally, it is imagined as a *community*, because, regardless of the actual inequality and exploitation that may prevail in each, the nation is always conceived as a deep, horizontal comradeship. (6–7)

"America" as a "nation" is limited by the geographical boundaries of land mass and the storehouses that bankroll physical and/or financial conquest; such boundaries can be challenged and re-drawn over time, as historically the boundaries of America have been re-drawn through the operations of imperialism, but those boundaries are, at any given historical moment, conditionally finite and limited. It is precisely this sense of limit that enables the emergence of unique national identities within and among a global community and allows individuals to differentiate Self from Other. It is also this sense of limit that enables the citizens of a nation to imagine *and* enact a seemingly coherent and stable internal identity—what Anderson terms a "comradeship"—that supersedes and, in many instances, covers over "the actual inequality and exploitation that may prevail" among individual Americans.

In *Wired*, there is no place for the addict in the story of America, except as an antagonist bent on disrupting the order and dismantling the unity of the imagined community from within its limited, albeit violable, boundaries. Just as the dead-Belushi repeatedly threatens to unravel the narrative coherence of *Wired* by violating the laws of physics as well as the generic expectations of biography, the addict unsettles the "deep, horizontal comradeship" that Americans imagine they share by violating some of the cornerstone tenets of the classic American Dream mythos. As in the case of Belushi, the addict may very well be a self-made man, but his ambitions and his successes are always and already undercut by the self-destructive impulses that contribute to his stagnation, rather than his progress. (And, of course, these self-destructive impulses are causally linked to the addict's addictions.) Degradation and death, then, rather than material prosperity and personal fulfillment, are identified as the inevitable outcomes of the addict's journey/biography. It is precisely due to the challenges that the addict poses to the American Dream mythos that his very presence within the nation-state initiates (nay, demands) a re-mapping of citizenship along the axis of sobriety and enables the emergence of a coherent and stable (at least temporarily) collective identity through the simultaneous identification and ostracization of that which is antithetical, Other, and abject to it (that is, the inebriate, the drunkard, the junkie, the addict). Sobriety thus aligns with, indeed is put forth as synonymous to, America itself.

If *Wired* represents Belushi as antithetical to the nation, the film casts Woodward as the symbol around which the imagined community unites. This contrast between Belushi and Woodward is hinted at early in the film (and explored a bit more fully in the source text) when Woodward off-handedly reveals to a *Washington Post* colleague that he and Belushi hail from the same small, Midwestern town of Wheaton, Illinois. Throughout the film, the filmmakers increasingly draw sharper contrasts between the two men, perhaps most pointedly during a scene in which Woodward asks his *Washington Post* editor for advice about whether to take on the Belushi project. His editor advises against the project, explaining to Woodward that "you're the *straightest* guy I know. Even if you did that story, you wouldn't understand what they're saying" (emphasis added). In this context, the term "straight" denotes rationality, restraint, sobriety—all adjectives that place Woodward in direct opposition to the uncontrollable, excessive, and "wired" force that was Belushi. Moreover, that the editor suggests that a decorated and seasoned journalist like Woodward "wouldn't understand" Belushi's life underscores how radically different the two men's biographies actually were. Like Belushi, Woodward is a self-made man, although his biography is characterized by progress, virtuosity, and success. Such differences are explicitly referenced by the dying Belushi, who disdainfully refers to the journalist as "Bob 'Pulitzer' Woodward" and "Mr. Straight 'A'

Honor Society," both monikers that should be read as an ironic commentary on the ways in which Belushi's addiction facilitated a perversion of the American Dream mythos and ultimately precipitated his own devolution.

Woodward, though, is not merely cast as Belushi's foil—the sober, straight-man to the wired funnyman; rather, Woodward stands in this film as the mouthpiece of America itself. In some respects, this characterization of Woodward-as-America does not require a great logical leap of faith given the celebrity persona that Woodward has enjoyed since he and Carl Bernstein first reported on Watergate in 1973.[9] Watergate forever cemented the intimately-bound relationship between Bob Woodward and the American nation, identifying the former as a dogged champion, even a symbol, of the very ideals (for example, Truth, Justice, Transparency, and so on) at the heart of the latter. Thus through Woodward, viewers understand not only why Belushi died (that is, "There's no mystery here. You did it to yourself, John."), but also what addiction should "mean" to an imagined community of contemporary American citizens. The addict squanders the nation's resources. The addict undermines the foundational principles of the nation. The addict threatens the order and unity of the nation with chaos and confusion. In short, the addict is always and only a waste that must be identified, contained, and expunged in order to maintain the sanctity of the nation and its citizens. This is the story of *Wired*. And *Wired* is the story of America.

---

9   To understand the point that I make here regarding the post-Watergate personification of Bob Woodward as America, one need only cursorily examine some of the ways in which Watergate typically is framed within the historical imaginary. In the opening paragraph to the Introduction of *Watergate: The Corruption of American Politics and the Fall of Richard Nixon* (1994), Fred Emery frames the Watergate affair as a narrative of fervent nationalism, suggesting that "Watergate is a compelling story of botched government." Emery goes on to write: "If it was a self-destruct tragedy for Richard Nixon, for the American people it was a drawn-out ordeal that tested the robustness of democratic processes. Despite some alarms, institutions held steady, law was upheld, and a chastened republic survived" (ix). Similarly, in *Watergate in American Memory: How We Remember, Forget, and Reconstruct the Past* (1992), Michael Schudson views Watergate "as a piece of political theater" that "stresses the value of the American Constitutional order and the need to protect it from arbitrary executive power" (xiv). As one of the journalists responsible for exposing the highest political office in the American government to unprecedented forms of public scrutiny and accountability, Bob Woodward not surprisingly has come to embody the fearless, uncompromising protector of "American Constitutional order" and the Nation—The American Patriot who safeguards the very ideals of nationalism that social historians like Emery and Schudson have long used to frame narratives of national success and tragedy.

PART II
Staging Wasted Histories

Chapter 2

Welcome (Again) to the Circus: Resurrecting the Freak Show and the Inebriate Asylum in A&E's *Intervention*[1]

The assumption of identity always entails the acquisition of desired attributes and the refusal of the intolerable abject. Freaks embody this cast off refuse.

Rachel Adams, *Sideshow U.S.A.: Freaks and the American Cultural Imagination*, p. 7

In February 2011, during a Q&A session at Oxford University, actor David Hasselhoff offered the following boldfaced observation about contemporary popular culture: "Reality television has ruined television. It is exploitation of youth" (quoted in Rainey). Hasselhoff represents an unlikely source for such frank (and on-target) criticism of what has become television's most profitable and popular genre. Widely known in the United States for leading roles in the kitsch classics *Knight Rider* (1982–1986) and *Baywatch* (1989–1999), Hasselhoff has, over the past decade-plus, largely fallen outside of the American limelight. In fact, of late, Hasselhoff's reputation and popularity—at least outside of Germany where the Hoff's short-lived singing career in the late 1980s still garners him an arguably large fan base—has been built almost exclusively on his participation as an "expert" judge on such reality programs as *America's Got Talent* (2006–2009) and *Britain's Got Talent* (2011–present) and as a contestant on *Celebrity Apprentice Australia* (2012). Although Hasselhoff has frequently used the platform of reality television as a means of self-promotion, his indictment of the genre nonetheless rings quite true. Reality television has, indeed, become increasingly more exploitative since its debut on American television in 2000. Writer Stephen Galloway, who regularly contributes to *The Hollywood Reporter*, documents this change as follows: "Since launching in the U.S. with *Survivor* in 2000, unscripted television has moved beyond the competitions and dating foibles that defined its youth. Increasingly, the popular shows (especially cable) document weaknesses of the human condition."

---

1 A previous version of this chapter was presented at the Ray Browne Conference on Popular Culture at Bowling Green State University in February 2013.

Within the past half-decade especially, reality television programs about the lived experiences of addiction have blossomed both in number and in popularity. Joe Lynch of *The Fix*, for example, notes that "[t]elevision shows about addiction and recovery are so commonplace today that it's almost impossible to remember a time when cable wasn't populated with real-life stories about people abusing drugs, overeating, swallowing Kleenex, and hoarding." Such programs range from the clinical (for example, *Addicted*) to the quackish (for example, *Celebrity Rehab with Dr. Drew*), from the serious (for example, *Intervention*) to the outlandish (for example, *My Strange Addiction*), and from the tragic (for example, *Hoarders*) to the inspirational (for example, *The Biggest Loser*), and encompass experiences as diverse as self-mutilation, over-eating, extreme couponing, hoarding, gambling, and garden variety substance abuse.

One of the most illustrative examples of this trend in reality television programming is The Learning Channel's (TLC's) *My Strange Addiction* (2010–present). Premiering in December 2010, this program focuses on some of the most bizarre compulsive behaviors ever grouped (however erroneously) under the rubric of "addiction." While *My Strange Addiction* has featured persons who suffer from marginally traditional addictions (for example, 44-year-old Theresa who huffs gasoline), the program typically features eccentric, bizarre, and strange behaviors that do not meet the *DSM*'s criteria for "Substance Use Disorders" or "Addictive Disorders"—like the woman who compulsively licks cats, or the man who is romantically involved with his automobile, Chase, or the woman who has spent $250,000 on 22 breast enhancement surgeries. *TV Guide* correspondent Rich Juzwiak acknowledges that while "[m]any of these [behaviors] … stretch the definition of the word 'addiction' beyond normal parameters," *My Strange Addiction* "is maybe the most entertaining freak show on television now," "more of a platform for reasonably coherent people to share their weirdness" than an exploration of the actual lived experiences of addiction ("There's Nothing Strange").

Juzwiak is not alone in his invocation of the freak show as a kind of catch-all for the myriad types of "weirdness" that are the stock-in-trade of contemporary reality television programming. Indeed, the phrase has entered the vernacular both in America and in Britain as a short-hand way to classify virtually any non-normative behavior, practice, or identity. As of this writing in May 2015, *Urban Dictionary* lists 13 definitions of the term, with only one making either direct or veiled reference to the nineteenth-century tradition of exhibiting human oddities for entertainment and profit. The other 12 definitions offer riffs on a single theme that perhaps is best summarized in the third definition listed: "A people-watching term used to describe any situation where you encounter unusual people, or people doing unusual things. *Burning Man is a total freakshow.*" While "freak show" is used to describe a wide range of deviations from the perceived "status quo," the phrase gets an inordinate amount of mileage in discussions about reality television programming.

In this chapter, I suggest that those cultural commentators and entertainment journalists who have somewhat carelessly lobbed the generic moniker "freak show" at all manner of reality television programs are not as far from the mark in their assessment as it initially might appear. However, unlike the aforementioned writers, I seek to historicize the "freakishness" witnessed in contemporary reality television programming by locating the "origins" of such representations in two parallel nineteenth-century traditions: the freak show and the inebriate asylum. Throughout this chapter, I focus almost exclusively on examples drawn from A&E's *Intervention* (2005–2013) because, as the flagship reality addiction program, it laid the groundwork—both production- and reception-wise, both narratively and ideologically—for subsequent offerings within the genre. As such, *Intervention* provides a compelling case study from which to extrapolate observations regarding the operations of the genre generally.

What *Intervention* reveals is that reality programs about addiction constitute a genre deeply imbricated in and actively productive of the metaphor of waste. Like the nineteenth-century freak show, such programs typically highlight only the most extreme of situations around the lived experiences of addiction, producing what cultural critic Rosemarie Garland Thomson terms "the exceptional body" (1). Within such programs, the "exceptional" and freakish body of the addict invites a gaze that simultaneously objectifies and exploits that which is strange within a given socio-historical framework, foreign to the non-addict self, and abject in its own right. I argue that the exploitation of the addict-as-freak resurrects the normalizing traditions and the normative practices of earlier efforts at addiction treatment, namely the nineteenth-century inebriate asylums. The legacy of the inebriate asylum produces the exceptional body of the addict as that which "compel[s] explanation, inspire[s] representation, and incite[s] regulation" (Thomson 1)—in short, a body that must be controlled, confined, and condemned. But that body, like the body of the nineteenth-century freak show performer, also embodies "the intolerable abject" (Adams 7)—that is, the narrative and ideological refuse of a culture that unconditionally champions sobriety. Trapped in a no-win binary within which s/he is either moralized against or marginalized, the addict featured in episodes of *Intervention* and like reality programs is divested of her/his subjectivity and rendered an object-to-be-exploited and -condemned within a formulaic cautionary tale.

The Structure of an *Intervention* Episode

Although certain aspects of *Intervention* varied over the program's original fourteen-season run, generally all episodes have conformed to a common format, one that borrows quite heavily on the realist tradition discussed in Chapter 3. Each episode of the program has a run time of approximately 43 minutes (sans commercials) and focuses on one or, less commonly, two individuals suffering from a substance dependence, although rare episodes have examined behavioral addictions like gambling, shopping, exercising, and video game playing.

The opening minute of each episode confronts viewers with a quick-cut montage of some of the most dramatic moments from the upcoming episode, underscored by the frenetic theme music used since the airing of *Intervention*'s inaugural episode. And the more sensational the moment, the more likely it will appear in the opening montage. Following a brief title sequence, also underscored by the same frenetic music used in the opening montage, the episode proper begins with a segment, usually running about seven minutes in length, devoted to establishing the "problem" that will be explored and "solved" during the episode. The primary purpose of this segment is to provide exposition and the primary voice in this segment typically belongs to the addict him-/herself. In fact, the mini-climax of this segment is an extreme close-up shot of the addict in first-person confessional announcing, "My name is ____ and I'm addicted to ____." (On rare occasions, someone other than the addict will perform this role.) Borrowing openly on the discourse and practices of Alcoholics Anonymous and other like 12-step programs, this announcement serves as the centerpiece of the opening segment, its *raison d'être*, although the revelation gains its impact from a series rhetorical strategies that repeatedly underscore the severity of the individual's addiction.

One commonly employed strategy is a fade-to-white and a direct presentation of backstory to viewers by way of simple black text; less frequently, this information is textually layered over the live action at the bottom of the screen. These fades-to-white can be used as a means of providing viewers information about the severity of the addiction: for example, "Coley has been on a drug binge for the past year. He snorts up to 20 lines of meth a day" ("Coley") or "Last year, Kristine was drinking up to a gallon of vodka a day" ("Kristine"). They also are used merely to advance the narrative and to introduce a plot point that otherwise would be awkward for the "characters" to speak to one another: for example, "When Aaron was 8, his mother and two brothers moved to Nebraska. Aaron stayed in California with his father." ("Aaron and Andrea") or "Marci's brother Chris has a life-threatening heart condition. A month ago, Marci's family abandoned plans to have an intervention on Marci due to Chris' declining health." ("Marci"). The fades-to-white often reveal surprising information about the addict: for example, "Trent was once a chef at four-star restaurants. He has been homeless for six months" ("Trent"). And they also can be used to point up the damaging consequences of addiction: for example, "Chronic heroin use can cause collapsed veins, heart infection, liver disease and kidney disease. —National Institute on Drug Abuse" ("Tom") or "Smoking crack can cause seizures, paranoid psychosis, heart attack and death. —Drug Enforcement Administration" ("Richard"). Regardless of the specific content, these fades-to-white serve both functional and ideological ends.

Also employed within this opening sequence are a series of then/now juxtapositionings that establish how significantly the individual has changed as a result of his/her addiction. Most commonly achieved through quick cuts between live action scenes from the addict's current life and still photographs of the addict in younger, usually happier times, this series of juxtapositionings works to reinforce the by-now familiar equation between addiction and personal devolution. It does so by "normalizing" the addict's life prior to the onset of addiction, thereby heightening the contrast between then and now, between sobriety and addiction, and increasing the narrative tension that both "characters" and viewers feel as the addict later devolves further into his/her addiction and (often unknowingly) moves closer to that "rock bottom" moment of intervention.

The middle segment of *Intervention*, which constitutes the bulk of the program (approximately 27 minutes), is dedicated to building a veiled causal argument for how and why the addiction developed, peddled not as loose interpretation but as hard fact. Typically, the episodes of *Intervention* assert a pseudo-Freudian narrative that implicates childhood trauma at the hands of biological parents, stepfamilies, siblings, grandparents, and/or other "relatives" as the chief determinant for later addictions.[2] In "Everybody Hurts: Addiction, Drama, and the Family in the Reality Television Show *Intervention*," Jason R. Kosovski and Douglas C. Smith acknowledge that

[w]e are perfectly willing to believe … that addicts are often part of particular risk groups which can include those from broken homes and traumatized children and young adults. What *Intervention* does, however, is to depict their presence

---

2 I am not suggesting that childhood trauma and addiction share no relationship; indeed, much research suggests that the former is a key antecedent of the latter (for example, Dube, et al.; Gordon). However, none of the credible extant research goes as far as *Intervention* producers do in identifying childhood trauma as a chief causal determinant of later experiences. I would suggest that the advancement of this narrative trope—one that is both titillating and taboo—by the producers of *Intervention* is merely one example of the operations of exploitation in reality television programming about addiction.

within these risk groups not as possible influences on addiction but rather as the sole and universal causes of such behaviors. In only rare exceptions do addicts featured on *Intervention* not belong to one or both of these groups. (854)

The concept of "risk groups" historically has been especially appealing with respect to complex social problems (for example, poverty, crime, illiteracy) that simultaneously defy easy causal explanation and demand a swift, conclusive, and very public remedy. With respect to addiction, *Intervention* isolates the unwieldy social problem within recognizable risk groups whose members are predisposed to the condition, suggesting that one who is not a part of the aforementioned "risk groups" is safe from developing an addiction. One of the most common "benefits" of risk groups is that they pacify (usually only temporarily) a concerned, but largely ignorant, public by suggesting a measure of institutional control and knowledge that the powers-that-be do not actually possess. Although the producers of *Intervention* rarely draw explicit causal links between the addiction and childhood trauma, the editing of the episodes makes quite clear what conclusion viewers are supposed to draw. Through careful and pointed sequencing of confessionals, live action, and still photography, the producers weave a coherent, chronological narrative that ultimately manufactures the necessary connecting causal links between the addict's past and present.

In addition to a primary narrative arc that identifies childhood trauma as "the sole and universal cause" of an addiction, the middle portion of an *Intervention* episode also typically presents a series of character and thematic tropes that reinforce cultural stereotypes about the addict and the lived experiences of addiction. Often the addict is infantilized, depicted as a self-consumed child with little to no regard for the physical health and emotional well-being of others. Usually the self-involved addict is identified as the cause of a string of damaged/broken relationships with children (many of whom have been seized by Child Protective Services), spouses (who usually are estranged or divorced), and relatives. Always the addict is shown participating (even relishing) in self-destructive behaviors that contribute to his/her diminishing self-respect. Often these self-destructive behaviors are criminal in nature, with theft, domestic violence, and prostitution topping the list of common criminal offenses.

Approximately 30 minutes into the 43-minute episode, the focus shifts from the addict and his/her self-destructive behaviors to the pre-intervention and intervention proper. This segment varies very little from one episode to the next, except for the specific interventionist tapped to facilitate the meeting and for the severity of the drama involved. Prior to the intervention proper, the interventionist meets with relatives and friends of the addict and strongly advises them to be firm in their demands that the addict accept treatment or else suffer the consequences. If there are co-dependent family members/friends, then the interventionist will advise those people to receive treatment as well. This pre-intervention segment usually runs between three and five minutes in length. The intervention segment typically opens with a suspense-building montage that juxtaposes live action sequences featuring the addict preparing for his/her final interview for the fake documentary and live action sequences of the assembled family and friends anxiously awaiting the addict's arrival. The addict's arrival at the site of the intervention is met with one of three reactions: confusion (that is, "What is this? Grandma, why are you here?"), confirmation (that is, "I knew this was *Intervention*!"), or anger (that is, "An intervention?!? You have to be {bleeping} kidding me!"). The interventionist calmly invites the addict to sit down and listen to what the assembled family members and friends have to say—a strategy that typically works to at least momentarily calm the addict and advance the narrative of the episode. Next, the family members and friends who are present read prepared letters to the addict that: 1) express their love, concern, and support for the addict; 2) document the ways in which the addict wronged him-/herself and the letter writer; and 3) stipulate the consequences that the addict will incur if he/she does not enter into a rehabilitation program immediately. Although the consequences vary slightly in terms of specificity, they typically involve some form of forced estrangement from the assembled loved ones. Emotions are heightened throughout the intervention segment. A lot of tears are shed—often by the most unlikely of persons. Usually the addict becomes defensive, at least momentarily. The interventionist, depending on the "character" selected to facilitate the meeting, will attempt a variety of strategies to cajole the addict into accepting the gift of treatment—including threatening the addict with consequences (a strategy for which one interventionist, Donna Chavous, earned some notoriety).[3] The addict's response to these tactics varies, but ultimately the program offers the addict only two options: accept the treatment (which is always and only 90-day, in-patient rehabilitation patterned on the twelve steps) and be welcomed back into the fold of family, friends, and society, or refuse the treatment and

---

3 The controversy to which I refer centered on a season 12 episode featuring Courtney, a 20-year-old heroin addict. During the intervention segment of this episode, Chavous invoked the power of Florida's Marchman Act to threaten Courtney with imprisonment if she refused to enter treatment. Reactions to Chavous's heavy-handed approach were largely condemnatory, with posts on the A&E website referring to Chavous as a "power hungry bully" and warning A&E producers to "get rid of her before she gets someone killed" (quoted in Ferrero). For more on this controversy, see: Raymond G. Ferrero III's *A&E "Intervention" Condones Addict Abuse By Donna Chavous of Intervention911 and Silences Audience Outrage.*

be ostracized. Commercial breaks are cleverly placed to heighten the suspense of the intervention.

Each episode of *Intervention* concludes with a brief segment (typically between two and three minutes in length) that resolves the narrative in one of two ways: either the addict successfully completes treatment or the addict relapses.[4] For those who successfully complete treatment, the emotional valence of the final segment is upbeat and hopeful. The music throughout the segment is cheerful, buoyant, lilting—a dramatic contrast to the frenetic theme music that underscores the action of the majority of the episode. The addict has undergone a marked transformation not only in appearance, but also in attitude and in self-perception.[5] This new outlook is accompanied by a series of self-revelations that the addict apparently has made during his/her time in rehabilitation. Families are reunited. Social roles are reaffirmed. Sobriety is championed. For those who do not successfully complete treatment, the concluding segment still underscores these themes, but does so by exploiting the addict-as-scapegoat trope. In doing so, reality television returns viewers to a very familiar narrative (born of literary realism, which I discuss in Chapter 3) in which the addict must be moralized against and/or marginalized; however, reality television introduces another component to this narrative—that is, the exploitation of the addict as an abnormality, an abjection, a "freak."

Controversy Around *Intervention*

Over its original 14-season run, *Intervention* sparked its share of commentary and controversy. One of the most frequently-voiced criticisms of reality addiction programs like *Intervention*—as is true of reality television programs generally—is that they thrive on the exploitation of their subjects. One especially vocal critic of the program is Matthew Gilbert of the *Boston Globe*, who has

---

4 Some might suggest that death operates as a third possible narrative outcome, since 12 of the addicts featured over the original run of *Intervention* have subsequently died, and at least one of those deaths (that is, Bret Cansler, season 7) was reported on the original airing of the episode. However, I would argue that death works merely to punctuate the "sin" of relapse, standing as a possible—albeit perhaps extreme—consequence of "falling off the wagon."

5 In "The Family on Reality Television: Who's Shaming Whom?," Galit Ferguson suggests that "transformation" operates as a common thematic motif in reality television programs. The author writes that "[o]ne of the most blatant discourses of these family-help programs is that of transformation." Ferguson goes on to explain, "Family-help shows perform other functions as well as disciplining and teaching: they can helpfully be regarded as sites where tensions of ideological and psychic reformation are played out" (88).

labeled *Intervention* "one of the rankest" examples of a genre that he terms "faux reality philanthropy." At its core, Gilbert argues, *Intervention* "is about watching broken addicts destroy themselves," "mak[ing] prime-time sport of vulnerable, desperate people and their spiral to the bottom." Gilbert suggests that *Intervention* is "an exercise in fraud," and likens its producers' tactics to the old "bait-and-switch" and "a media ambush." Of particular concern for Gilbert is the emphasis that *Intervention*'s producers place on "the details of [the addicts'] habits"—an emphasis that Gilbert terms "almost fetishistic." Gilbert's criticisms of *Intervention* are neither surprising nor especially original. Indeed, many critics have analyzed the ways in which the seemingly inherent voyeuristic qualities of the reality genre breed exploitation. I would, however, argue that the form that exploitation takes on in reality programs about addiction is quite different than the form it takes on in other reality programs. To understand how exploitation manifests itself in a program like *Intervention*, we first need to look at the four primary means by which the producers of *Intervention* "put damaged lives on display to attract our pitying eyes" (Gilbert).

Exploiting "Normalcy"

First, producers of the program typically chose to feature only those individuals who initially would appear least likely to develop an addiction. Dan Partland, Executive Producer of *Intervention*, has said, "We have a very long list of different elements we try to find in a story. The most important one is, will the story in some way challenge the stereotype of what addiction is?" (quoted Lynch). That the producers of *Intervention* sought to "challenge the stereotype of what addiction is" was quite clear from the inaugural episode, which aired in March 2005. When the episode originally aired, it featured two addicts: Alyson, a former White House intern turned morphine and crack addict, who steals painkillers from her terminally ill father, and Tommy, a former stockbroker who sacrificed the spoils of his successful career to bankroll his cocaine addiction. However, in subsequent airings (including the version that, as of this writing in May 2015, was available on the A&E website), the episode was re-cut to focus exclusively on Alyson; this alteration was made, according to a disclaimer that airs just before the opening montage, "[d]ue to overwhelming viewer response." That Alyson, and not Tommy, captured the interest of A&E viewers is not particularly surprising.

From the initial moments of this episode, Alyson is cast as a prototypical American Everywoman—an exemplar of the American Dream mythos whose addictions to morphine, heroin, and crack have halted her upward mobility and have, according to the causal logic of the episode, sent her into a downward spiral, both health- and morality-wise. Early in the episode, Alyson's sister,

Kara, reveals in first-person confessional, "[Alyson] could have been something wonderful in life. But she just threw it away." Kara's observation is underscored by her mother, who, also in first-person confessional, notes, "[Alyson's] wasting every day of her life with drugs." Interestingly, both Kara and her mother perpetuate the metaphor of waste in the rhetoric that they employ to describe their sister/daughter. Both women cast Alyson as someone who willfully and actively squanders all of the opportunities that racial and socioeconomic privilege have afforded her for the fleeting pleasures that accompany drug use. (And even those pleasures are challenged when Alyson early in the episode wails, "I don't feel good …. I don't like this feeling.") Several years prior to her appearance on *Intervention*, Alyson was awarded a full-tuition scholarship at a "prestigious university," but dropped out after only attending for one semester due to her addiction. Alyson also was among an elite group of young adults selected as White House interns. These are the spoils of her privilege that Alyson has wasted. At the same time, Alyson cannot shake that privilege; indeed, it is precisely the specter of "former White House intern" that looms large over the episode, exacerbating the pathos of Alyson's current addictions. In this respect, *Intervention* transforms both the stereotype of the "skid row bum" and the "normality" against which it is perpetually contrasted into commodities that are trafficked among the A&E viewership.

And Alyson is only the first in a lengthy series of prototypical Americans who have succumbed to addiction and whose downward spiral is documented in graphic detail on *Intervention*. Season two, for example, featured 18-year-old Corrine, a former honor roll student and star athlete, who turned to heroin and methamphetamine after being sexually abused by a babysitter at age 14; that season also featured Antwahn, a former NBA star who was homeless and bankrupt as a result of a crack addiction. The cast of season 3 included heroin addicts Trent, a former four-star chef whose clientele once included U.S. Presidents and Hollywood actors, and Ricky, whose image as the All-American "Golden Boy" had been overshadowed by his addiction. Forty-nine-year-old meth addict Dawn, whose story was part of the season four line-up, once worked as a successful model. Alcoholic Derek from season five was once a championship bodybuilder. And season nine's Adam formerly was one of America's top skiers until Post-Traumatic Stress Disorder for tours as a Marine in Iraq and Afghanistan led him to alcoholism. Across its original 14-season run, *Intervention* chronicled the devolution of countless All-American boys, girls-next-door, athletes (both amateur and professional), mothers and fathers, grandmothers and grandfathers, sons, daughters, garden variety housewives, rugged family men, and even a former beauty queen. While these addicts differed in terms of age, race/ethnicity, socioeconomic status, profession, and a number of other factors, there is an uncanny sense of sameness among the 200-plus addicts who were featured on the program between 2005 and 2013—a sameness that stems from similarly "normal" backstories shared by the featured addicts. Among these featured addicts, their former sobriety connotes a certain type of "normalcy" that contrasts sharply with their current suffering and it is precisely in the contrast between then and now, between who the addict *was* and who the addict *is* that exploitation occurs. In this respect, normalcy is not merely commoditized, but it is fetishized—the object of irrational reverence and obsessive devotion to which nearly every episode of *Intervention* pays homage. Viewers tune in to the program to bear witness to the dramatic transformation of the normal into the abject (the central thematic conceit on which all episodes of *Intervention* turn), and the more "normal" the addict's former life (where "normal" does not necessarily equate to "common"), the more dramatic the transformation and the more pathos engendered by the addict's current suffering. In short, in episodes of *Intervention*, sobriety/normalcy becomes the locus of exploitation, and contrast becomes the rhetorical means by which exploitation occurs.

Exploiting Severity

Second, episodes of the program tend to highlight only the most extreme forms of addiction. Indeed, garden variety alcoholism rarely (if ever) warrants the "gift" of in-patient treatment and the Warholian "15 minutes of fame" engendered by a reality television cameo. The exploitation of extreme personal suffering is a fairly common occurrence in reality television programming, and, in fact, in one of the most illustrative examples of such exploitation, ABC's *Extreme Makeover: Home Edition* (2003–2012) earned a great deal of criticism for targeting vulnerable individuals. In 2006, The Smoking Gun exposed "ABC's 'Extreme' Exploitation" by making public a memo in which a Producer/Family Casting Director strongly urges those responsible for casting decisions to look specifically for persons who had been "victimized" either by rare medical conditions or at the hands of other human beings.

So many episodes of *Intervention* quantify an addiction in terms of the amount of a particular substance that is ingested per day in order to emphasize the extent and severity of said addiction. A select group of representative examples include: Betsy, of season two, who consumes up to five bottles of Chardonnay per day; Vinnie, of season eight, who smokes crack cocaine up to eight times per day; and Britney, of season 13, who shoots up suboxone and bath salts nearly 30 times per day. At work in these and like episodes of *Intervention* is a type of emotional manipulation through which producers simultaneously incite the viewer's compassion for the suffering of other human beings and exploit the viewer's scopophilic desire to bear witness to the addict's self-destruction. Executive Producer Partland, for instance, notes that the program "put[s] the audience in the uncomfortable position of perversely hoping for failure, because those are the most dramatic moments" (quoted in Kaufman). Stated differently, the emotions that such episodes provoke are similar to the emotions provoked by the axiomatic train-wreck—the desire to look away, but the inability to do so. The extremity of the addiction marks the addict as pitiful and as worthy of the viewer's compassionate gaze. But it also provokes the perverse desire to see even greater depravity, to be invited even deeper into the intimacies of the individual's struggles with addiction. Viewers may even find themselves, as Partland suggests above, rooting for the addict to refuse treatment, to relapse, or even to die because such events would make for a more exciting "narrative." In this respect, the "fly on the wall" verisimilitude of reality television in its original iteration is sacrificed over and again for (melo)dramatic moments and manufactured or, at the very least, heightened crises that exploit both the addict and the addiction. Furthermore, what is lost in all of this manufactured drama is the addict's very real struggles with addiction. Viewers are not simply desensitized to the pain and the suffering that are intimately a part of addiction, but they also are encouraged to view addiction as merely another narrative trope—as the makings of dramatic television programs without any "real world" implications. And this, of course, is its own form of waste—a jettisoning of the materiality of addiction and its concomitant suffering for ratings, profit, and viewer pleasure.

Exploiting Causality

A third common form of exploitation regularly witnessed on episodes of *Intervention* is a type of fear-mongering and fallacious causality that identifies addiction as the sole cause of a variety of other self-destructive behaviors. In fact, most episodes of *Intervention* draw their ideological impact and their persuasive force from the perpetuation of a slippery slope fallacy that links addiction to a wide variety of extreme behaviors that are identified as direct and inevitable consequences of an individual's addiction. The key problem with slippery slope causality is that worse case scenarios are erroneously proffered as inevitable rules to a given situation, rather than as rare exceptions. Also ignored are other factors that might have contributed to the emergence of a particular behavior, as well as other potential relationships that might exist between the two variables that initially were identified as related by simple cause and effect. While fallacious, this logic often can be quite persuasive precisely because it preys on and exploits some of the most basic fears that human beings harbor.

The producers of *Intervention* regularly present a causal narrative arc within which the addiction incites a series of increasingly self-destructive behaviors that inevitably lead the addict to his/her "rock bottom." One of the most common causal equations asserted in episodes of *Intervention* is drawn between addiction and prostitution. Indeed, this narrative arc recurs no fewer than a dozen times over the series run (for example, Rachel, season 1; Kristen, season 5; Miriam, season 9). Of course, prostitution is not the only devastating consequence of addiction targeted by the producers of *Intervention*. Stripping is identified as an inevitable outcome of addiction in no fewer than three *Intervention* episodes, including those featuring: Cristy (season 2), Jessie (season 2), and Sarah (season 8). Homelessness is identified as an inevitable outcome of addiction in no fewer than a dozen *Intervention* episodes (for example, Troy, season 2; Hubert, season 3; Eddie, season 11). And felonious assault and/or theft is identified as an inevitable outcome of addiction in no fewer than 14 *Intervention* episodes (for example, Chuckie, season 2; Donald, season 7; Shantel, season 11). And these examples reflect only the most frequently rehearsed causal narratives asserted in *Intervention* episodes. Some "consequences" are featured in only a single episode of *Intervention*, and yet still powerfully reinforce the fallacious causal links between addiction and criminality, between addiction and self-destruction. Season one, for instance, featured 29-year-old Jerrie who forged physician signatures to support her addiction to Vicodin, while season eight featured Robby, a former member of a Grammy-nominated R&B group who drank his way into bankruptcy.

If exploitation entails the transformation of "intimacy into a commodity," then here exploitation is commodified simultaneously as criminality, as propriety, and as scopophilia. All of the aforementioned examples beg the question, "How far will they go?," where "they" refers both to the addicts and to the producers. With regard to the addicts, viewers take scopophilic pleasure at being invited (albeit at a safe remove) into the unpredictable, dangerous, and often illegal worlds that the program's subjects inhabit. Heightening this pleasure-in-looking is the presentation of the subject's dangerous/illegal activities as an "open secret"—that is, as something that, thanks to it having been aired on A&E, is now widely known among the American public but that the addict does not want to publicly admit. Ultimately what makes viewers tune in to *Intervention* is the taboo prospect of witnessing criminal activity first-hand—something that A&E delivers in great quantity. With regard to the producers, viewers marvel at how they repeatedly "[push] the boundaries of television voyeurism in search of another hit" (Peters)—how they look on disinterestedly[6] as these subjects increasingly spiral out of control. In

---

6 For an extended examination of "the sticky [moral and legal] situations that reality-show producers can find themselves in as they document unpredictable and unstable subjects and situations," see Jeremy W. Peters' "When Reality TV Gets Too Real."

this respect, what is being sold is propriety itself, or more aptly, the breach of propriety that is enacted through the performance and documentation of addiction-as-intimacy.

Exploiting Causality, Redux

Fourth, episodes of the program tend to assert sensational causal narratives that explain why the individual developed an addiction. Most often these causal narratives center on some childhood trauma that the addict suffered at the hands of a family member or close friend. The abuse can be psychological, physical, and/or sexual in nature, but always the trauma is targeted as the root and source of later addictive behaviors.[7] The 14 original seasons of *Intervention* are rife with episodes that feature this narrative arc and, indeed, virtually any episode of the program could be used as an illustration of my point. I briefly will discuss the first episode of the fourteenth season, featuring heroin addict Jessica, in part because it very clearly foregrounds the "childhood trauma" narrative arc, and in part because its currency reveals the stranglehold that this narrative had over *Intervention* throughout its original run.

From early in the Jessica episode, Jessica's belonging to the particular risk groups that Kosovski and Smith mention above (that is, "those from broken homes and traumatized children and young adults") is highlighted as the addict's primary character arc. Only minutes into the episode, viewers learn that Jessica's biological parents were either absent, as was the case with her biological father, or negligent, as was the case with her biological mother. Through the signature fade-to-white/fade-to-text transitions, the producers inform viewers that Jessica's biological father abandoned the family "shortly after Jessica was born," and that her mother remarried a man named Gary when Jessica was eight years-old. Through first-person confessionals, viewers learn that Jessica "wanted attention. She wanted to feel wanted." Jessica admits that when her mother married Gary, she "felt like [she] lost [her] mom." She also reveals, "I really don't think [Gary] ever cared about me," an observation that is confirmed not only by her mother (who says that Gary and Jessica never bonded) but also by Gary (who, in first-person confessional, admits in a dry monotone that

---

7 Of course, I am not suggesting that there is no correlation between the two variables. As neuroscience journalist Maia Szalavitz notes, "[c]hildhood trauma has long been known to raise a child's odds of developing depression and addiction." And much research supports the correlation that Szalavitz identifies. However, I do take issue with the relationship that A&E producers repeatedly seem to draw between the two variables, which seems both deterministic and inevitable, and which also runs counter to much of the currently available research on the topic.

"[a] lot of the things I had interest in, [Jessica] really didn't have any interest in. It's just hard to have that really tight bond that you can develop when you have something in common.").

Later in the episode, the causal links between traumatic childhood experiences, poor parenting, and addiction are made even clearer. Following a segment that documents the devolution and death (by overdose) of Jessica's biological father—ironically, only two months after he introduces Jessica to heroin—viewers are informed that "[a]fter her father's death, Jessica started injecting heroin up to six times a day." Immediately following the presentation of this fact, the program cuts to a clip from a first-person confessional with Jessica's estranged husband, Marty, who reiterates the causal equation between Jessica's father's death and her severe drug abuse by noting, "Everything just spiraled out of control. Hopelessly out of control. There was no saving it." Marty's comment is punctuated in the next shot by a zoom in on a slack-jawed, passed out Jessica. Although the producers never explicitly draw a causal link between Jessica's addiction and her childhood trauma (that is, her parents' divorce, her father's addiction and death, and so on), the editing of the episode makes quite clear what conclusion viewers are supposed to draw. Through careful and pointed sequencing of confessionals, live action, and still photography, the producers skillfully manufacture the connecting causal links between Jessica's past and present.

There are two interrelated aspects of this narrative arc that I find especially exploitative. First, as above, the program dwells on these possible trigger experiences, offering up one graphic recollection after another for over 30 minutes, to the point that the backstory seems gratuitous, performed over and again exclusively to titillate and shock the viewing audience. Indeed, in so many episodes of *Intervention*, the producers almost seem to badger the addicts by repeatedly cajoling them to discuss/re-live the myriad abuses that they have suffered. And the point of such repetition seems to lie in the response—the guttural sobs, the angry lashing out, and, of course, the manic ingesting of copious amounts of controlled/illicit substances to dull the pain. In other words, everything about childhood trauma makes for "good television" and the producers of *Intervention* capitalize on the drama, the unpredictability, and the graphic nature of these experiences not only by probing their depths, but also by devoting a disproportionate amount of time to that probing, which is the second exploitative aspect of this narrative arc. Within any given episode of *Intervention*, the eponymous intervention is given at most about 12 minutes of attention—and that time span includes the pre- and post-intervention sequences. In some ways, this distribution of time makes sense given that, from one episode to the next, the intervention varies quite negligibly, except with regard to the addict's initial response and the eventual outcome of the intervention. The routineness of the intervention proper makes for bad television programming in general, but makes for especially poor fodder for reality television where shock, titillation, and boundary pushing are staples of the genre and certainly the most common and effective means to ensure viewers, ratings, and program longevity. Thus, in a narrative structure in which the climax (that is, the intervention) is almost anti-climactic, the producers need to shift the focus away from the formulaic and emphasize the unpredictable—a strategy that smacks of exploitation, especially when the unpredictable element is an addict whose past and current traumas are being mined for their most gasp-worthy moments and whose struggles with sobriety are being exacerbated for entertainment and profit.

Description of the Freak Show

The kinds of exploitation witnessed on *Intervention* find an historical precedent in the nineteenth-century freak show—a performance tradition that is roughly coterminous with the emergence of "the addict" as a distinct and recognizable identity construct. Although the freak show dates at least to the seventeenth century in England, "it was not until the nineteenth century that freak shows and novelty acts caught the imagination of a larger viewing public willing to pay for the opportunity to witness human medical oddities" (Grande). It was also during this time period that the freak show took on the form that is most recognizable in the contemporary historical moment. The Victorian era is widely regarded as "the heyday of the freak show" precisely because "[i]t was an age of scientific and medical advancements and, consequently, the public was naturally curious about unexplained oddities" (Grande). The freak show of nineteenth-century popularity most often is understood to be a mobile and nomadic performance "troupe" that traveled from one town to the next as part of an elaborate "amusement industry circuit" (Bogdan 74), somewhat akin to the medicine or Wild West shows of the same period; however, in actuality, the freak show enjoyed a much richer and more diverse performance history, one that implicates some of the most prominent institutions of the nineteenth-century amusement industry. Human curiosities, for instance, "were the major attraction" of P.T. Barnum's American Museum, located in New York City, from the mid-nineteenth-century onwards, and they also constituted "the main attraction of most dime museums of the period 1870–1900" (Bogdan 37). Freak shows were important parts of other amusement institutions as well, including circuses, World's Fairs, amusement parks (like the quintessentially American amusement park, Coney Island), and carnivals.[8]

---

8   A more elaborate discussion of the freak show's performance history can be found in: Robert Bogdan's *Freak Show* (esp. chapters 2 and 3); Frederick Drimmer's

Regardless of whether the freak show occupied a singular, fixed location, or traveled from city to city, whether it was a stand-alone entity or part of a pre-existing entertainment institution, all such attractions shared some important commonalities, chief among them the mission of exploiting "human oddities" for entertainment and profit. These oddities could be "real" or perceived, congenital or manufactured, but they had to tap simultaneously into what Lillian Craton, in *The Victorian Freak Show: The Significance of Disability and Physical Differences in 19th-Century Fiction* (2009), describes as the public "fascination with physical difference and the exploitative nature of much bodily spectacle" (2) if they had any hope of attracting the curiosity and the financial backing of the public. Some of the most widely-recognizable "human oddities" exhibited during the Victorian period include: conjoined twins Daisy and Violet Hilton, who continue to fascinate viewing audiences as evidenced by the recent release of the documentary *Bound by Flesh* (2012); "fat lady" Ella Milbauer, who was billed under the tagline "586 Pounds of Feminine Charm"; Myrtle Corbin, the four-legged woman; General Tom Thumb, whose height topped out at just over three feet; Isaac W. Sprague, the "human skeleton"; Annie Jones, the bearded lady; and Joseph Merrick, the elephant man. Some of the "human oddities" that were exhibited as part of the nineteenth-century freak show merely represented rare medical conditions that, at the time, were undiscovered, such as Julia Pastrana, dubbed "the Baboon Lady," whom, scientists later determined, suffered from congenital generalized hypertrichosis terminalis (CGHT) with gingival hypertrophy, a genetic disorder that "is characterized by excessive growth of dark hairs all over the body, distorted facial features, and enlarged gums" (*Genes of 'Bearded Lady' Revealed*). Some were outright frauds—such as Pasqual Piñon, "the two-headed Mexican," whose second head was rumored to be either "a tumor that was outfitted with facial features" or simply a "false head" (Bogdan 85). And some were part of the wider mapping of "ethnographic exhibition of human beings that has taken place in the West over the past five centuries" (Fusco 143), such as Ota Benga, a Congolese pygmy who was featured in an exotic human exhibit at the Bronx Zoo around the turn of the twentieth-century.

Over its lengthy history, one which spanned from the early nineteenth century to the mid-twentieth century,[9] the freak show employed an estimated

---

Very Special People; Leslie Fiedler's *Freaks*; and C.J.S. Thompson's *The History and Lore of Freaks*. For a thoughtful bibliography of resources related to carnival and sideshow history, see: *Carnival and Sideshow Bibliography*.

9 This is not to suggest that the freak show merely died out at a particular point in history, though it is to recognize that, by the mid-twentieth century, the form was in a state of marked decline, especially with respect to popularity among American audiences. Some old school freak shows continued to travel and exhibit for many years after this

35,000 individuals (Verner) and took a number of forms—sometimes simultaneously—and therefore it is difficult (albeit not impossible) to generalize about how human oddities were exhibited. However, what all of these freak shows had in common was an elaborately-conceived architecture of information that served to frame the exhibits as oddities, as freaks. Through mass-produced leaflets, professionally painted banners, and thoughtfully-detailed programs, those who bankrolled the freak shows aggressively packaged, exploited, and sold "the freak" as commodity to a curious mass audience. Such promotional materials supplied a backstory for the exhibit, one that often was only marginally grounded in fact. Professional grifters, known in the patois of the sideshow as "showmen," "systematically and pervasively misrepresented their exhibits to the public" (Bogdan 85), manufacturing sometimes entire histories to explain the origin of a specific attraction's freakishness. Indeed, as historian Laura Grande notes, "The larger-than-life personalities of Victorian-era showmen became an art form in and of itself, as they created narrative histories for each of their freaks in order to create drama and heighten the excitement of the audience."

To understand the ways in which the nineteenth-century freak show laid the groundwork for some of the forms of exploitation witnessed in contemporary reality addiction programs, we might examine one representative example of the architecture of information that participated in the construction of the "freak role": a flyer for an exhibit known as "WHAT IS IT." From the onset of this advertisement, the creators establish a standard of normalcy that the exhibited oddity not only fails to meet, but consistently challenges, attacks, and undermines. To ask "WHAT IS IT" is to stress how this "FREAK of NATURE" so actively resists standard identity categories as to invite curiosity, shock, and perhaps even disgust. The freakishness of the exhibited oddity is underscored textually through the use of the indeterminate pronoun "it," through the frequency with which the "WHAT IS IT" question is posed, and through the use of all capital letters in the presentation of that question. In the description of this exhibit, too, the advertisers simultaneously convey the implied "norm" as well as the many ways in which this exhibit deviates from that norm. For instance, this "most extraordinary Being" is compared and contrasted to an "ORDINARY SIZED MAN"—described as having "Features, Hands, and the upper portion of its Body" that "to all appearances [are] Human," but having "hind Legs, and Haunches, [that] are decidedly Animal!" Neither quite human,

---

decline began. This is the part of sideshow history that is fictitiously imagined in FX's series *American Horror Story: Freak Show* (2014–2015). Furthermore, new iterations of the freak show (such as the Jim Rose Circus Sideshow, Circus Amok, The Happy Side Show, Tokyo Shock Boys, and the Kamikaze Freak Show) have subsequently been born. However, the freak show would never be the same once its "golden age" had passed.

nor fully animal, this "Being" exists somewhere in the murky space between those two categories—an abjection that "disturbs identity, system, order" and that fails to "respect borders, positions, rules" (Kristeva 4). Such rhetoric would have been employed not only in leaflets such as the one I reference here, but also in posters adorning the performance site, in the cat calls of the sideshow showmen, and in the dramaturgy of the performance itself. Here, then, the "ORDINARY SIZED MAN" functions as the standard of normalcy against which the exhibited oddity repeatedly is contrasted, a contrast that manufactures the aura of "freakishness" that frames the performance, that inspires curiosity and horror in the public, and that ultimately fills the coffers of the exhibitors. In a similar manner, in contemporary reality addiction programs, the sober person functions as the implied standard of normalcy against which the addict repeatedly is contrasted and it is precisely in the act of contrast that the addict is framed as a freak whose life is exhibited for the profit of television executives and for the perverse entertainment of television viewers.

This advertisement also manufactures a series of sensational causal narratives around the exhibited oddity to explain, or provide an etiology for, his freakishness. In reality, "WHAT IS IT" was an African-American man named William Henry Johnson who was born "about 1840 in the eastern United States" and who, if alive today, "would be diagnosed as mentally retarded, with microcephaly" (Bogdan 134). (Bogdan provides a thoughtful overview of Johnson's backstory and involvement in the sideshow industry in Chapter 5 of his book.) By contrast, the advertisement mentions that "WHAT IS IT" was recently "caught" (not discovered, not encountered) "in the WILDS of CALIFORNIA"—an origin story that instantly identifies the exhibited oddity as an uncivilized beast (perhaps, as the opening hook suggests, "the long sought for LINK between Man and the OURANG-OUTANG"). Identifying California as the point of origin for "WHAT IS IT" underlines the bestial and savage qualities that are attributed to the exhibited oddity given that, in the nineteenth century, much of the western United States still was unexplored and therefore regarded as untamed. Moreover, "WHAT IS IT" is described as even less civilized than the "Tribe of Indians" with whom he spent the past 10 months. Within the American cultural imaginary, Native Americans (presumably the "Indians" to which this advertisement makes reference) historically have represented the original savages and therefore, to contrast "WHAT IS IT" with "Indians," marking the former as more uncivilized than the latter, only further reinforces the abject qualities of the exhibited oddity. The causal narratives that are advanced in episodes of contemporary reality addiction programs and that link addiction to, for instance, childhood trauma operate in a similar manner; such narratives underscore the "freakishness" of the addict by simultaneously claiming that the addict is abject and therefore resistant to explanation and providing the very explanation that they claim cannot be offered.

Finally, the hyperbolic allusions to the savagery of "WHAT IS IT" are echoed in the extreme representations of addiction and addiction-related behaviors on contemporary reality programs. Like the "Indian," to which he is contrasted (at least in terms of degree of savageness), "WHAT IS IT" is identified as "THE WILD MAN OF THE PRAIRIES" who cannot "speak, Read, or Write." Johnson's abilities to communicate (that is, speak and write) or understand others (that is, read) might have been compromised by his neurodevelopmental disorder, but Bogdan notes that "[h]e was verbal and apparently an active participant in the construction of his freak role" (134). However, it is significant that the advertisement focuses specifically on deficiencies in speaking, reading, and writing since such skills are assumed to be the chief defining characteristic that differentiates human beings from beasts and other creatures (like, of course, the savage "Indian"). The comparison to a "Monkey" and the aside about "WHAT IS IT"'s diet further supports the (missing?) link between this "FREAK of NATURE" and the savage, the uncivilized. And, of course, during an historical moment when westward expansion was advanced and justified on a platform of staunch and exclusionary nationalism, this kind of rhetoric would have been especially compelling for an American audience.

An Abbreviated History of Inebriate Asylums

If the freak show is the site at which nineteenth-century Americans learned to commodify and exploit the (addict-)Other, then the inebriate asylum was the site at which they learned to contain, sanitize, and dispose of the threats that that Other portended. Inebriate asylums gained popularity (if, indeed, such institutions could ever lay claim to having been "popular") in the two centuries that led up to the ratification of the Eighteenth Amendment to the United States Constitution (1919) when addiction, at least in American culture, was cast as moral degradation, personal corruption, and sin. Across this time period, pro-Temperance posters announced in no uncertain terms that addiction was the result of moral failure and the concomitant poor choices that stem from such moral failure. One particularly illustrative example is a poster from the British Temperance movement, which shared some important commonalities with its American counterpart and therefore invites the comparison that I draw here. In the bottom left quarter of the poster is an etching depicting a rather ordinary-looking man seated on a cot in a jail cell; he gazes forlornly at a series of placards that are affixed to the cinder-block wall and that list a variety of "sins," including: Murder; Sabbath Breaking; Disobedience to Parents; and Drunkenness. The remainder of the poster is devoted to block-style text that reads, "DRINKING LEADS TO NEGLECT OF DUTY, MORAL DEGRADATION AND CRIME."

This poster establishes quite vividly some of the most salient features of nineteenth-century pro-Temperance rhetoric. The argument put forth in this poster rests squarely on a series of problematic causal linkages that encourage readers to avoid alcoholic beverages lest they succumb to "neglect of duty" (read "Disobedience to Parents"), "moral degradation" (read "Sabbath Breaking"), and "crime" (read "Murder"). Part of the potential impact of this argument, then, relies on the extremity of its claims—specifically, that drunkenness leads not simply to criminal behavior like forgery, theft, or even battery, but to the most morally abhorrent and legally severe of all crimes: murder. For a God-fearing nineteenth-century American audience, these ideas would have been very subtly, but very persuasively underscored by the Biblical allusion to the fall of Babylon. Like the disembodied hand whose writings on the Babylonian palace walls foretold the murder of the king and the fall of his kingdom, the "writing" on the cinder-block walls of the jail cell in this poster alludes to the "imminent doom or misfortune" that results from profane and ungodly behaviors: namely, drunkenness. The nineteenth-century addict, then, invites not only legal sanctions, but also spiritual condemnation for his moral depravity.

During the eighteenth and nineteenth centuries when this view of addiction initially gained prominence, the public treatment movement was dominated by an initiative, spearheaded by Dr. Benjamin Rush, to "[treat] inebriates in specialized institutions modeled on insane asylums." The idea of an inebriate asylum dates to 1810 when Dr. Rush "first proposed a 'sober house' for drunkards" (Baumohl 1187). Inebriate asylums constituted one response to the "dramatic rise in alcohol consumption in the United States between 1780 and 1830 and the subsequent increased consumption of opium and morphine" (Weiner and White 15). In "'What shall we do with the inebriate?': Asylum Treatment and the Disease Concept of Alcoholism in the Late Nineteenth Century," Edward M. Brown suggests that "[m]any factors combined to make the times right for the creation of inebriate asylums." Brown explains, "Frustration over the shortcomings of prohibitory legislation and the recidivism of those jailed for drunkenness as well as the influx of Irish and German immigrants gave the temperance question a certain urgency."

Dr. Rush "advocated not only personal abstinence from hard liquor, but also a return to strict communal sanctions against drunkards." Dr. Rush further argued that "[d]runkards ... were the antithesis of virtuous citizens" precisely because they were "incapable of managing their own affairs, could become mentally enfeebled, and certainly could not be responsible enough to vote" (Lender and Martin 38). This view gained much wider support among medical practitioners and the general public around 1835 when Samuel Woodward, "the patriarch of institutionalized psychiatry in North America, and a renowned temperance orator, published ... the first widely read (and widely copied) tract in support of inebriate asylums" (Baumohl 1187).[10]

Although "[a]sylum enthusiasts dominated the [nineteenth-century] public treatment movement" (Baumohl 1187), very few inebriate asylums were actually built and opened and most such institutions had been either closed or converted for other uses by the time of Prohibition in 1920. The first American inebriate asylum was founded in Binghamton, New York, in 1864,[11] and, according to one estimate, "by 1902 over 100 [such] institutions ... were operating" throughout the United States (Brown, "English Interest" 549). However, it should be pointed out that Brown's estimate here ambiguously references "institutions," not specifying whether this estimate includes only inebriate asylums or other types of institutions that dealt with the treatment of inebriates (for example, sober houses, inebriate homes, private cure hospitals). Of the 100-plus inebriate asylums operating in America throughout the nineteenth and into the twentieth century, conversions were fairly common, with some (such as those in Minnesota and California) occurring even before any inebriates were admitted for treatment. In fact, the asylum at Binghamton had, by 1879, been "converted to an insane asylum" (Baumohl 1189). Furthermore, some inebriate asylums (like those in Texas and Washington, D.C.) "were chartered but never opened" (1189).

Modeled both ideologically and architecturally on insane asylums, inebriate asylums were large, public institutions that offered confinement (either voluntary or involuntary) as "a medical solution to the vast problem of drunkenness." Such institutions typically were "isolated in rural areas," staffed by trained physicians, and "organized into elaborate systems of wards to segregate patients by social and diagnostic criteria and voluntary or involuntary status" (Baumohl 1189). Most such institutions also were equipped to handle several hundred patients at any given time. Within the asylums, addicts faced a fairly standard (at least for the nineteenth century), but "highly structured" treatment regimen that included "bed rest, a healthy diet, and therapeutic baths (hydrotherapy), followed by the discipline of useful labor" (Baumohl and Jaffe).[12]

---

10 See Samuel B. Woodward.

11 For an extended history of the founding of this inebriate asylum, see: J. Edward Turner's *The History of the First Inebriate Asylum in the World By Its Founder*, and John William Crowley and William White's *Drunkard's Refuge: The Lessons of the New York State Inebriate Asylum*.

12 For more extensive descriptions of the treatment regimens commonly employed in inebriate asylums, see: "Our Inebriates, Classified and Clarified"; J.W. Palmer's "Our Inebriates Harbored and Helped"; and James Parton's "Inebriate Asylums, and a Visit to One."

Architecture and Ideology in the Inebriate Asylums

Those who advocated the effectiveness of asylum-based treatment "considered the architecture of their hospitals, especially the planning, to be one of the most powerful tools for the treatment of the insane"; in fact, as Carla Yanni explains in *The Architecture of Madness: Insane Asylums in the United States* (2007), "[f]or most of the nineteenth century, doctors believed that between 70 and 90 percent of insanity cases were curable, but only if patients were treated in specially designed buildings" (1). As I note above, inebriate asylums were modeled on insane asylums, often sharing with their predecessors general building plans, specific architectural features, and underlying ideological justifications; as a result, the parallels that I draw between these institutions throughout the following discussion are, I think, more than justified.

The American asylum tradition was dominated by a building type known as the Kirkbride Plan. Named for Dr. Thomas Story Kirkbride, "an influential advocate of an asylum system based on the tenets of Moral Treatment," the Kirkbride Plan "promoted a set of detailed principles that influenced the construction and operation of many [Victorian-era] American asylums" ("History").[13] The Kirkbride asylum was organized around a central administration building that was flanked on either side by two linear wings of "tiered wards." In *On the Construction, Organization and General Arrangements of Hospitals for the Insane* (1854), Kirkbride suggests that "the best and the most economical form will be found to be a centre building with wings on each side, so arranged as to give ample accommodations for the resident officers and their families, and for the classification and comfort of the patients" (12). The central building of the asylum was designed to house the administrative offices as well as the infrastructure of the institution (that is, the kitchens, the laundry, and so on), but it also served as the bridge between outside and inside, between sanity and madness. Of the wings that branched off of this central administration building, Kirkbride writes,

---

13　Here, I focus the discussion exclusively on the contributions made to asylum architecture by Kirkbride because his ideas were the most widely influential in America at the height of the asylum tradition. As Yanni notes, "[f]or most of the nineteenth century, from about 1840 to about 1880, [Kirkbride] was the single most important nineteenth-century psychiatrist when it came to matters of architecture." Yanni goes on to acknowledge that "[t]his is not to suggest that his authority was absolute, but his ideas were the standard against which alternatives had to be tested" (38). For a more thorough examination of what Yanni describes as the "social and cultural history of a building type" (that is, the asylum) (12), see: Christopher Payne's *Asylum*; and Leslie Topp, James E. Moran, and Jonathan Andrews' *Madness, Architecture and the Built Environment.*

The wings should be so arranged as to have eight distinct classes of each sex; each class should occupy a separate ward, and each ward should have in it a parlor, a dining room with a dumb waiter connected with it, and a speaking-tube leading to the kitchen or some other central part of the basement story, a corridor, single lodging rooms for patients, an associated dormitory for not less than four beds, communicating with an attendant's chamber, one or two rooms of sufficient size for a patient with a special attendant, a clothes room, a bath room, a wash and sink room, and a water closet. (13)

Kirkbride also stipulated that each wing should be outfitted with "one infirmary for patients who are too ill to remain in their own chambers, two work rooms, a museum and reading room, a school room, a series of drying closets, at least one on each story, and various other fixtures" (13).

The Kirkbride Plan promoted the asylum as a site at which the architectural confinement of "sick" individuals (where "sick" denotes either insanity or inebriety) symbolically served to create a more orderly, understandable, and safe "outside" world. Indeed, the notion of "confinement" has been central to the institution of the asylum since its founding in the late seventeenth century. In his classic study of the relationship between *Madness and Civilization* (1965), Michel Foucault identifies the Age of Enlightenment—the period that gave birth both to the concept of "madness" and to the institution of the insane asylum—as an age of "confinement" (65). Foucault writes, "Confinement hid away unreason and betrayed the shame it aroused; but it explicitly drew attention to madness, pointed to it. If, in the case of unreason, the chief intention was to avoid scandal, in the case of madness that intention was to organize it" (70). In both the design of the asylum, and in the execution of its various treatment programs, the institution systematically segregated the insane/inebriate from the larger social milieu and simultaneously identified the affliction from which the individual suffered; both actions were intended to mitigate the moral and physical threats that the insane/inebriate potentially posed to others through the geographical, institutional, and conceptual organization of insanity/inebriety. In what follows, I will discuss three specific forms of confinement and classification that contemporary reality addiction programs borrow from the asylum tradition, discussing specifically how the forms of confinement and classification work to manufacture and perpetuate the metaphor of waste.

A Return to the Asylum in Reality Television

With respect to inebriate asylums, confinement of the addict began with the geographic placement of the institutions, which typically were built outside the city limits, isolated in the country and "embosomed in rural seclusion"

(Turner 230). Kirkbride notes, for instance, that "[i]t is now well established that [insane] hospitals should always be located in the country, not within less than two miles of a town of considerable size" "in a healthful, pleasant and fertile district of country" to afford its residents "views … [of] life in its active forms" (7). The rural seclusion of these institutions served both symbolic and pragmatic ends. The geographic distance manufactured between inebriates and their nineteenth-century sober brethren reinforced the notion of the addict as a corrupting, immoral force by drawing distinct geographic boundaries between the inside and the outside, between the normal and the abnormal, between sobriety and addiction. The segregation of the inebriate to the margins of the nineteenth-century American city, then, provided non-addicts a false sense of security by suggesting that the immorality of the inebriate, as well as the physical and spiritual damage that that immorality might cause, was safely contained by and controlled in the asylum. Like the television screen that safely distances a twenty-first-century viewing audience from the volatile, dangerous, and corrupt addicts featured on programs like *Intervention*, the placement of the asylum at the outskirts of the planned city both literally and symbolically segregates the inebriate from the larger social milieu, enclosing him/her within the clearly-demarcated and rigidly-policed boundaries of the institution. (Such acts of confinement also perpetuate the widely-held belief that addicts "look different" than non-addicts, which often prolongs the time it takes for an addict to receive and accept treatment, especially those who are "high-functioning.") For the nineteenth-century inebriate, geographic isolationism served more pragmatic ends. The secluded rural location removed the inebriate from the pressures and demands of his everyday life, thereby also presumably eliminating the environmental triggers for his addiction. Moreover, the serenity of the pastoral setting was believed to provide the relaxation and rejuvenation necessary to successfully remedy inebriety. In some ways, isolationism continues to be a part of some addiction treatment programs, most particularly in-patient treatment where the buildings typically are isolated in idyllic (and often pastoral) environs like the beach or the woods and the addicts are removed from their everyday lives for extended periods of time (usually between 30 and 90 days). This same kind of treatment is the "gift" offered to addicts at the climax of *Intervention* episodes.

 Once inside the institution, the inebriate was subjected to additional forms of segregation and additional layers of confinement. Indeed, even before the inebriate was literally confined to the institution, representatives of the asylum worked systematically to identify the particular affliction or malady from which the individual suffered—a type of psychological triage—based on highly structured diagnostic criteria which, since 1952, have been documented in the *Diagnostic and Statistical Manual of Mental Disorders* (or, *DSM*). In the insane asylum, this process involved the identification of the specific mental disorder from which the patient suffered; in the inebriate asylum, this process typically involved an assessment of the severity and type of addiction, as well as a decision about the most appropriate course of action. This process of categorization—a process typically mirrored in the distribution of space within the asylum—sought to make sense of that which often defied logic and order (that is, madness, addiction, and so on), but it also identified the treatment of insanity and inebriety as principally bureaucratic in nature. (The emphasis that such treatment institutions placed on bureaucracy was echoed in design: specifically, the concentration of the administration infrastructure at the visual and architectural center of the building.)

Like the asylum, reality television programming about addiction seeks to codify and contain the addict, rendering him/her understandable within a familiar and limiting narrative trajectory patterned on literary realism and borrowed verbatim from 12-step programs. One of the most obvious ways by which reality addiction programs like *Intervention* mirror the bureaucracy of nineteenth-century inebriate asylums is through the obligatory naming of the addiction and an explicit act of confession. As I note above, each episode of *Intervention* begins with a diagnosis, usually conveyed in the form of a first-person confessional by the addict. In *The History of Sexuality, Volume 1: An Introduction* (1978), Foucault notes that "[s]ince the Middle Ages at least, Western societies have established the confession as one of the main rituals we rely on for the production of truth" (58). The confession not only provides an etiology for the addict's actions, rendering often unpredictable behaviors understandable, but also explicitly draws attention to the addiction as an identity category that defines the speaking individual. In other words, by identifying his/her affliction, the addict marks him-/herself as different from an implied norm—a norm that, again as I note above, is repeatedly referenced in both implicit and explicit ways throughout each episode of the program. Here, the confession simultaneously segregates and confines the individual into the recognizable identity construct of the morally degenerate addict (or, the skid row addict).

Once committed to the asylum, the inebriate was assigned to a specific ward based on the initial (bureaucratic) diagnosis of his condition, proposed treatment program, and commitment status (that is, voluntary or involuntary). Obviously, the use of wards to segregate the patients served as a form of confinement, though according to the Kirkbride Plan, even this design feature also was intended to serve a pragmatic end: "this arrangement would make patients' asylum experience more comfortable and productive by isolating them from other patients with illnesses antagonistic to their own" ("History"). The ward system further worked to distance, or segregate, the addict from the outside world by using the central administration building, as well as the series of locked doors leading into and out of each ward, as a literal means of containment to separate the outside from the inside. On the wards, the behavior of inebriates was highly structured around a series of mandatory daily activities, including physical labor. Interestingly, this feature of early asylum treatment has carried over to contemporary in-patient treatment programs; Anne M. Fletcher discusses common treatment regimens in contemporary in-patient programs in her book *Inside Rehab: The Surprising Truth About Addiction Treatment—And How to Get Help That Works* (2013). The common space of each ward typically featured a wall of windows that looked out onto the bucolic natural setting of the institution, identifying the inebriate as a voyeur whose successful treatment was at least partially dependent on his/her willingness to examine "life in its active forms." But the inebriates were not just voyeurs; they also and simultaneously were objects-to-be-looked-at by the physicians and staff of the asylums. Like specimens in a cage, their every move was documented and analyzed and this, of course, is perhaps the most significant way in which contemporary reality addiction programs borrow on the asylum tradition. As I discuss above, the addicts featured on episodes of *Intervention* are exploited as "freaks" to be scrutinized (albeit at a safe remove) by the television viewing audience. Their self-destructive behaviors become fodder for water cooler discussions with colleagues. We celebrate their successes. We decry their failures. But most of all we watch. And in our watching, we reveal the cultural work that inebriate asylums in the nineteenth century, and reality addiction programs in the twentieth and beyond, do for the metaphor of waste.

Conclusion

In the end, every episode of *Intervention*, regardless of the specific outcome of its storyline, leaves viewers with the same basic message—a message not unsimilar to the theme conveyed through the pro-Temperance poster I discussed earlier in this chapter. Addiction "leads to neglect of duty, moral degradation and crime." It is a cautionary tale that *Intervention* weaves—one that repeatedly reminds viewers of the thin line between sobriety and inebriety, between the self and the Other, between sanity and abjection. This cautionary tale always and only reminds addicts (even, and perhaps especially, those who have successfully completed treatment) that they are little more than morally bankrupt sinners—disposable, expendable, corrupt. In a word: waste. From the freak show and the inebriate asylums, then, contemporary Americans have inherited an image of the addict as what Rachel Adams has, in reference to freak show performers, termed "the intolerable abject" (7). The very category of "the addict"—that is, of a self that is both knowable and recognizable through the invocation of the phrase "the addict"—presupposes, indeed demands, the existence of an "intolerable abject," which we initially might understand simply as the absolute inverse of sobriety and, more generally, normality. But the "intolerable abject" is not merely an opposite of an identity category; it also and simultaneously is the absolute negation, even annihilation, of identity itself. Through the "almost fetisthistic" emphasis on "the horrors of addiction," programs like *Intervention* reinforce the values of sobriety, moderation, and personal accountability, thereby simultaneously confining and exploiting the excesses, the unpredictability, and the madness of addiction within the institution of the asylum and, later, the genre of reality addiction programming. The lived experiences of addiction, then, always and already presuppose the identification, containment, and annihilation of "the addict." In short, the metaphor of waste—as the controlling narrative "logic" of the intolerable abject—is an *a priori* condition of the identity of "the addict."

The types of confinement witnessed in the asylum (and on reality addiction programs like *Intervention*) not only isolate the addict and identify him/her as the "intolerable abject," but also enable the non-addict to confront the Otherness of addiction safely. In *Sideshow U.S.A.: Freaks and the American Cultural Imagination* (2001), Adams suggests that nineteenth-century freak shows performed similar functions. Adams writes, "Although they have often been treated as an ephemeral form of amusement, freak shows performed important cultural work by allowing ordinary people to confront, and master, the most extreme and terrifying forms of Otherness they could imagine, from exotic dark-skinned people to victims of war and disease, to ambiguously sexed bodies" (2). In *Freakery*, Garland Thomson also contends that the cultural construction of the Other in the form of the freak show enabled the emergence of a particular form of "normality" that was trafficked among nineteenth-century audiences: "The exaggerated, sensationalized discourse that is the freak show's essence ranged over the seemingly singular bodies that we would now call either 'physically disabled' or 'exotic ethnics,' framing them and heightening their differences from viewers, who were rendered comfortably common and safely standard by the exchange" (5). Both Adams and Garland Thomson regard the performance of "freakishness" as an active "exchange" among the framed performance event, its performers, and their spectators. Both critics suggest that viewers were affirmed in their ordinariness, their normality, through the exhibition, display, and witnessing of the freak show. Through the heightened contrasts that were drawn between the exhibited freaks and their "safely standard" spectators, the freak show worked to reinforce the nineteenth-century status quo in its myriad forms. But it also served as a vehicle by which those nineteenth-century spectators could "confront" and, given the many layers of confinement embedded within the freak show, "master" the fears that they harbored. Such fears often were moral in nature, but also could take more general forms (for example, fear of change or fear of the unknown). Regardless of the specific fears that were manifested and managed, the nineteenth-century freak show used the body of the "human oddity" as a means through which all manner of meaning and truth were produced, codified, and circulated. Arguably one of the most enduring truths to emerge out of this tradition was what I have termed the metaphor of waste.

As with the freak show, *Intervention* and like reality addiction programs traffick in the body of the "addict," using that body as a means through which to produce, codify, and circulate "truths" about the lived experiences of both addiction and, by extension, sobriety. In other words, in the safety of our own homes, and within the clearly-demarcated boundaries of the television screen, we confront the intolerable abject in all of its excesses, unpredictability, and unreason and, in that confrontation, we learn much about the ways in which addiction is understood and lived in this historical moment. We also learn a great deal about how we (the sober) are supposed to relate to addicts, to the issue of addiction, and to ourselves. We learn that the addict is undisciplined and self-destructive and, as such, must be brought into submission (by coercion, by consent, or by force). We repeatedly are exposed to an addict who is both "diminished in ... health" and "morally marred or defiled" ("wasted, adj."). The addict's self-destructiveness not only is employed as justification for the paternalistic attitude that the sober are encouraged to adopt toward him/her, but also as the go-to defense for the many ways in which Americans lay waste to addicts. Furthermore, the addict's squandering of his/her health, talent, wealth, and potential—akin in our context to the squandering of the American Dream—is regarded as a rejection of citizenship. Addiction, then, effectively exiles the addict to a spiritual, moral, and even often legal wasteland. Because this metaphor is reiterated *ad infinitum* in programs like *Intervention,* what is wasted in virtually every episode of reality addiction programs is the opportunity to challenge pre-existing and limiting models of addiction that always and already cast the addict as a sad, lonely example of moral corruption that must be contained and excised from the fabric of contemporary American culture. Through the containment and discarding of the addict as waste, such programs also tell their viewers much about what it means to be sober. Sobriety confers value (moral, cultural) on an individual. Sobriety begets reason and order. To be sober is to be a "normal," upstanding American. In short, sobriety simultaneously produces and affirms citizenship, whereas addiction always and only signifies waste.

Chapter 3

Re-Visiting Literary Realism: Adaptation, Ideology, and the Metaphor of Waste in Jay McInerney's *Bright Lights, Big City* and Bret Easton Ellis' *Less Than Zero*

[I]t is still only by distancing ourselves from the familiar modes of representation that we can expect to identify the areas on which ideology is silent.

Catherine Belsey, *Critical Practice*, p. 137

In *Inventing the Addict: Drugs, Race, and Sexuality in Nineteenth-Century British and American Literature* (2008), Susan Zieger locates the "birth" of the modern *addict* in the century between 1820 and 1920. Zieger suggests that due to a myriad of changes in the Western socio-political landscape of the nineteenth century—including "bourgeois self-making, commercial imperialism, metropolitan consumerism, reform movements, a widening public sphere, and modernizing medicine" (8–9)—"addiction and the addict became newly visible" (18). In this study, Zieger (following the methodological lead of Michel Foucault) historicizes the emergence of "the addict" as a recognizable identity construct—one that draws on and adapts earlier tropes of addiction (for example, drunkards, opium-eating scholars, vicious slave masters, dissipated New Women, and queer doctors)—arguing that this figure arises out of a complex interplay of social and political forces that most vividly came to the fore in nineteenth-century British and American cultures. For Zieger, the popular and medical literature of this period become the sites at which these larger socio-political constructions of "addiction" and "the addict" are made legible, a kind of *tabula rasa* onto which those constructions freely are inscribed. Absent from Zieger's discussion, however, is a consideration of the ways in which the literature itself (and, in particular, literary form) actively participates in the construction of the modern addict and the lived experiences of addiction.

Literary realism emerged at a historical juncture roughly coincident with the period examined in Zieger's book and it found its roots in a variety of sometimes discordant voices and contexts across the European continent—from Emile Zola's gritty realist novels that explored "the consequences upon his characters of their birth and background" (Styan 6) to the ruthlessly candid "problem plays" of Henrik Ibsen in which "the characters circle and evade the taboo subjects" (28) and Konstantin Stanislavsky's actor training method that "work[ed] towards a greater psychological realism of character" (79). Literary genres have long been viewed not merely as products of their times, but as active "agents" in the construction of the socio-historical and poltico-cultural landscapes from which they emerge. In this respect, literary realism constitutes a site at which nineteenth-century constructions of "addiction" and the "addict" not only might be discursively inscribed, but also might be ideologically produced.

This chapter returns to debates from the mid- to late 1980s regarding the political efficacy of literary realism. I focus on two works of transgressive fiction originally published and eventually adapted for film during the "Just Say 'No'" era: Jay McInerney's *Bright Lights, Big City* (1984; film 1988) and Bret Easton Ellis's *Less Than Zero* (1985; film 1987). Specifically, I argue that the filmic adaptations of these two novels, both of which are realistic in form and conservative in polemics, identify literary realism as a site at which the metaphor of waste was born, marking either the addict (i.e., Julian in *Less Than Zero*) or the addiction (i.e., cocaine addiction in *Bright Lights, Big City*) as narrative refuse that must be expunged from the text to achieve resolution and closure.

The Realism Debates

In *The Feminist Possibilities of Dramatic Realism* (1996), Patricia R. Schroeder defines "a realist play" as

> one that reflects a specific social milieu in a particular era; that develops according to cause-and-effect sequences of actions; that ends with the resolution of some problem; that includes characters who react to the environment and act in complex and clearly motivated ways; and that attempts to convince the audience by all available theatrical means that the onstage action is, in fact, real (not fictitious) and occurring before them as they watch. (17)

Although Schroeder specifically concerns herself with stage realism, her observations regarding the generic characteristics of the form hold consistent across other modes of realistic representation. At its core, realism chiefly is concerned with the principle of verisimilitude, or the likeness of diegetic action to extra-diegetic reality. The fictional environment created within the text is detailed and specific to a temporal and spatio-geographic locale. Characters interact with and are influenced by their environment and the storyline in which the characters are involved proceeds causally to a logical resolution.

Literary realism has long constituted a site of ideological contention—a disputed representational terrain that, within contemporary literary and critical theory, has repeatedly pitted politically conservative critics against politically progressive critics in a territorial battle over what it means to represent in a "realistic" manner, who has access to the form (and who is silenced within it), what experiences can be "realistically" represented (and what experiences remain invisible), and how the representational apparatus might (or might not) be "valuable" to various artists, standpoints, and/or polemics. At the center of these long-standing debates is the assumption that, as Catherine Belsey articulated in her seminal study *Critical Practice* (1980), "literature represents the myths and imaginary versions of real social relationships which constitute ideology, but also that classic realist fiction, the dominant literary form of the nineteenth century and arguably the twentieth, 'interpellates' the reader, addresses itself to him or her directly" (56–7). In other words, realism has played such a central role in shaping the concerns of certain branches of literary theory for the past three-plus decades in part because realism *is*, and long has been, the "dominant literary form" in American (and, arguably, Western) cultural productions. The sheer volume of cultural artifacts that can be classified as "realistic," not to mention its overwhelming visibility in publication and exhibition venues, the significant shaping influence that realism has exerted over non-realistic forms, and its pervasive presence in both mainstream and avant-garde canons, all underscore the deep need for a comprehensive understanding of the form. Moreover, the emphasis that realism places on verisimilitude suggests to critics that the form shares an intimate relationship with the "social reality" that is purports to represent, thereby casting the form as profoundly constitutive of both diegetic and extra-diegetic ideology.

On one side of the conversation are those critics who acknowledge, as William W. Demastes does in the Preface to *Realism and the American Dramatic Tradition* (1996), that realism is not "a structurally unambitious, homogenous, tunnel-visioned form, its every product churning out the same fundamental message and denying creation of a more open, pluralistic theatre" (ix). Rather, such critics regard realism as "chameleon-like," as "changing colors at almost every turn and blending into a context appropriate for [the artist's] goals" (x). One of the most vocal proponents of a "chameleon-like," "flexible" realism is Schroeder. In "Locked Behind the Proscenium: Feminist Strategies in *Getting Out* and *My Sister in This House*," Schroeder acknowledges that while "the proscenium stage offers playwrights built-in opportunities for dramatising the traditional systems of enclosure that restrict women" (164), "a flexible realism can depict the values encoded and disseminated by a patriarchal culture, assess the consequences of oppression by powerful cultural agents, and simultaneously support the alternative values—such as autonomy and female community—that feminism espouses" (160–61). Like Schroeder, Sheila Stowell, in *A Stage of Their Own: Feminist Playwrights of the Suffrage Era* (1992), rejects the notion of a monolithic Realism that portrays "an arbitrary but self-serving orthodoxy as both neutral and inevitable"; instead, Stowell argues for her own kind of "flexible realism," asserting that "[w]hile genres or styles ... may not be politically neutral, they are surely capable of presenting a range of ideological positions ... dramatic forms are not in themselves narrowly partisan. They may be inhabited from within a variety of ideologies" (100–101). All three of these critics regard representational form as a dynamic ideological entity capable of responding to ever-changing socio-cultural conditions in ways that are specific to a temporal and cultural milieu, as well as to an artist's goals and standpoint. In this respect, realism does not *a priori* follow a limited and "narrowly partisan" ideological course on its path toward resolution. Rather, realism is inhabitable by, and can reflect the interests of, a variety of ideological standpoints.

On the other side of the conversation are the politically *progressive* critics—referred to as such because typically they are aligned with progressive social justice movements. Following the lead of Belsey, such critics acknowledge, as Les Brookes does in his book *Gay Male Fiction Since Stonewall: Ideology, Conflict, and Aesthetics* (2009), that realism "cannot break entirely free of the ideology that envelops and engenders it" (42). One of the earliest feminist critics of classic realism was theater scholar Sue-Ellen Case who, in *Feminism and Theatre* (1988), characterizes realism as "a 'prisonhouse of art' for women," explaining that "[r]ealism, in its focus on the domestic sphere and the family unit, reifies the male as sexual subject and the female as sexual 'Other.'" Case goes on to provide examples of the multiple ways in which the realist form locates the female subject in the position of sexual "Other": from "their confinement to the domestic setting," to "their dependence upon the husband," and "their often defeatist, determinist view of the opportunities for change" (124).

Like Case, theatre and performance scholar Jill Dolan has written about the ways in which "realism continue[s] to construct [womens'] conditions of objecthood" (160), although her indictment of realism focuses specifically on the representation of lesbian subjectivity within the form. In *Presence & Desire: Essays on Gender, Sexuality, Performance* (1993), Dolan asserts,

> bourgeois realism reinstates the unitary, transcendent lesbian caught in a binary opposition with heterosexuality. Realism is not recuperable for lesbian theorists, because its ideology is so determined to validate dominant culture

that the lesbian position can only be moralized against or marginalized. The lesbian subject most readable in realism is either dead or aping heterosexual behavior. (162–3)

At the center of Dolan's (and others') critique of realism is the assumption that realism engenders/fosters a relationship of complicity between the "invisible [male] spectator" and "the patriarchal biases" of the form—that is, as Schroeder explains in *The Feminist Possibilities of Dramatic Realism*, "that the spectacle is designed precisely for a male viewer to identify with and for his eyes voyeuristically to devour" (28). For materialist feminist critics like Dolan, this complicitous relationship is inherent to the realist form—the product of an age-old marriage among gender, genre, and ideology—and is predicated on a simultaneously passive but receptive voyeurism. From the vantage point of dominant ideology (which is, within this theoretical framework, always and only maniacally heteronormative in nature), the lesbian subject is cast as a complication—arguably *the central* narrative complication—that precipitates tensions between characters and that moves the plot inevitably toward both climax and *dénouement*. As a narrative complication in a form that is "determined to validate dominant culture," the lesbian Other must be sacrificed (or, in Dolan's terms, "moralized against or marginalized") in order for the drama to achieve both narrative and ideological closure. For the invisible but ever-present dominant culture spectator (who may or may not self-identify as biologically male), the death, ostracism, or conversion of the lesbian Other that signals the *dénouement* of the drama reads as "right," "just," "natural" precisely because the invisible, but pervasive, ideological operations of both realism and dominant culture are simultaneously coercive and maniacally heteronormative.

With respect to the realism debates, I tend to take a "moderate" stance. Like Stowell in "Rehabilitating Realism," I would suggest that when engaging with a realistic text (what Belsey terms a "familiar mode of representation"), the reader needs simultaneously to consider formal, "historical, contextual and phenomenological" concerns, not simply (and unequivocally) dismissing realism as not recuperable for a particular type of critic or in service of a particular political agenda.[1] In doing so, the reader can "identify the areas on which ideology is silent" (Belsey 137) and can begin to untangle the ideological

---

1 To be fair, Dolan does temper the conclusions that she draws in the chapter about realism in the introduction to *Presence & Desire*. Writing in the wake of the publication of Stowell's "Rehabilitating Realism," Dolan notes that "even though the basic outline of [realism's] conservative ideological implications has been thoroughly established," "Stowell does make several important points that suggest rejecting realism out of hand is presumptuous." Ultimately Dolan concludes that "returning to realism frequently to check its status and its meanings seems inevitable" (27).

shackles that bind writers, readers, and characters. In the two sections that follow, I examine the filmic adaptations of *Bright Lights, Big City* and *Less Than Zero* respectively, paying particular attention to how form and historical context together shape the ideologically conservative representations of addiction. The filmic adaptations identify realism as one site at which the metaphor of waste was born, marking the addiction or the addict as narrative refuse that must be expunged from the text to achieve resolution and closure.

Bright Lights, Big City in the Realist Tradition

That the film adaptation of *Bright Lights, Big City* borrows heavily on the ideological prescriptions of both literary realism and the metaphor of waste is most overtly conveyed through the radical transformation that the protagonist (named "Jamie" in the film version) undergoes over the film. That Jamie (Michael J. Fox) will undergo this transformation and emerge, at the close of the film, a reformed man is intimated at in the initial moments of the film. Although the opening scene of the film is lifted almost verbatim from the opening pages of the source text (including the employment of voice over narration in second-person point-of-view), there are a couple of seemingly slight alterations that impact the plot and its ideological valence quite profoundly. As in the novel, the film opens at a trendy, "vaguely tribal" (2) nightclub where Jamie is being engaged in conversation by a bald woman (Marika Blossfeldt). However, in the novel, the bald woman (merely another patron) "is saying this [nightclub] used to be a good place to come before the assholes discovered it" (2), while, in the film, the bald woman (re-cast as a bartender) subjects Jamie to some armchair psychology and, in so doing, establishes quite clearly the thematic and ideological arcs for the film. As Jamie stares blankly into his drink, nearly oblivious to the sensory overload surrounding him, the bald bartender inquires, "Why so sad?" The question startles Jamie, who grunts for clarification as his glassy-eyed gaze trails slowly upward from drink to bartender (into whose point of view spectators have momentarily been cast). Again the bartender inquires, "Why so sad?" and she then follows up with, "Trouble with some woman?" Jamie's response, though vague, nonetheless acknowledges the accuracy of the bartender's guesswork: "Something like that." *Bright Lights, Big City* was produced and released during an historical moment when *Cheers* (1982–1993) was at the height of its popularity and the "bartender," at least within American culture, was regarded not merely as a service provider, but as an amateur therapist.[2] Within this context, the

---

2 This image of the bartender as an untrained, but highly perceptive, psychologist is comically referenced in a fourth season episode of *The Golden Girls*, titled "Stan

initial scene of the film, in which a bartender serves as interlocutor for the protagonist, takes on a heightened thematic and ideological importance in framing the narrative action. Specifically, this scene casts the film as a kind of "character study" that takes quite literally the question that its protagonist poses near the close of his initial internal monologue: "How did you get here?" This question stands as the inciting incident for the narrative action that unfolds over the film, as well as the central thematic conceit, suggesting that, in adaptation, *Bright Lights, Big City* chiefly is concerned with tracing an etiology of Jamie's addiction—that is, how and why did it develop? That the director places spectators within the point of view of the bartender when Jamie responds to the question suggests that this concern (i.e., Why *is* Jamie so sad?) not only is of utmost importance to her, but also should be to those who are voyeuristically consuming this film.

That an introspective examination of Jamie's character is of central concern to the film adaptation of *Bright Lights, Big City* is visually underscored by the presence of a wall-length mirror in this opening scene, as well as by the protagonist's engagement with that set property across the film. The looking glass boasts of a rich history in Western art/culture, typically signifying a character's willingness (and capability) to undergo self-examination. When Jamie, in voice over, "speaks" his initial line of dialogue—that is, "You are not the kind of guy who would be at a place like this at this time of the morning"—viewers witness Jamie, captured in medium shot, gazing meaningfully at his reflection in the mirror across the bar. The visual, then, reinforces the reflective quality of the verbal. In looking at himself and in recognizing the disparity between who he "really" is and who he has "become," Jamie foregrounds a series of etiological and causal questions that serve as the underlying narrative preoccupations of the film: If Jamie is "not the kind of guy who would be at a place like this," then who is he? What kinds of factors contributed to the changes in Jamie? And how might Jamie find his way back to himself?

A second appearance by the symbol of the mirror not only confirms how it is thematically employed within this opening scene, but also conveys how theme

---

Takes a Wife." As the title suggests, this episode centers on the decision by Dorothy's (Bea Arthur) ex-husband, Stanley (Herb Edelman), to re-marry. In the climactic scene, Stanley's betrothed, Katherine (Elinor Donahue), who suffers from momentary misgivings regarding her impending nuptials, steals away to the hotel bar for a cocktail:

Bartender: What can I get you, lady?

Katherine: How about a shot of self-confidence?

Bartender: Let me guess. You didn't come in here to drink. You've got a problem and you need someone to talk to. Am I right?

Katherine: That's right.

Bartender: Then take a quarter and call a shrink. This ain't *Cheers*.

functions ideologically within the adaptation of *Bright Lights, Big City*. Late in the film, at a party thrown by a mutual acquaintance, Jamie finally comes face-to-face with his estranged wife Amanda (Phoebe Cates), who greets Jamie by asking simply, "How's it going?" The flippancy of this greeting, when contrasted with the gravity of their months-long estrangement, causes Jamie to erupt in a fit of hysterical laughter which is punctuated by a cocaine-induced nosebleed. Jamie's friend, Tad (Kiefer Sutherland), escorts him to the bathroom, where Jamie gazes into the mirror over the sink and says to himself: "How's it going? I need some help. Whatever that is. Can't straighten everything out in one night." Here, introspection is made manifest as a self-talk monologue in which Jamie assesses his situation and prescribes a course of action (however vaguely defined) based on that assessment. In this respect, the moment stands as the ephiphanic climax of the film. Narratively this scene represents the plot point on which all of the preceding action converges and from which the narrative arc turns. With respect to characterization, this scene represents at once a moment of self-realization—during which Jamie directly acknowledges the addictions that have ravaged his life, his career, and his personal relationships—and a moment of self-actualization—during which Jamie commits to change (read sobriety).

Of course, this scene does not stand alone in revealing the epiphanies both large and small that assist Jamie on the journey back to himself. Indeed, such epiphanies are sprinkled throughout the film—some merely isolated and highlighted from the source text, while others are specifically added to the adaptation to more clearly delineate the ways in which the source text was sanitized (both content-wise and ideologically) in order to pacify conservative Hollywood and Right-Wing America.[3] One of the more telling moments occurs in the scene when Jamie is fired from his job at *Gotham* magazine by the school-marm-ish Clara (Frances Sternhagen). In both the source text and the adaptation, Clara begins the conversation by saying, "I would like to know what happened," to which Jamie, again in both texts, responds, "I screwed up," referring to his botched attempt at fact-checking an article about the French elections. In both the source text and the adaptation, Clara concludes the scene by saying, "I'm sorry." However, in the source text, the narrator disavows much (if not all) of his responsibility for the erroneous story that will most certainly compromise the reputation of the newsmagazine (104) through his internal monologue: "You might add that the writer of the piece in question really screwed up, that you improved the thing immeasurably, and that the change of scheduling was ill-advised. But you don't" (103). Moreover, Clara's "apology" is terse and unaccompanied by any description that would indicate how the dialogue is delivered or intended to be received. By contrast, in the film, Jamie's

---

3 For a thorough account of the politics and "poetics" of adapting *Bright Lights, Big City* from page to screen, see Caryn James, "'Bright Lights, Big City'—Big Trouble."

"I screwed up" stands alone, sans internal monologue or commentary of any sort, whereas Clara's apology is punctuated by tears.

Although these two scenes bear strong resemblances to each other, the slight differences in characterization that can be glimpsed in Clara and the protagonist clearly point to the conservative ideological turn that *Bright Lights, Big City* takes in its realistic adaptation. Jamie's stark admission of culpability in the loss of his job, as well as his inability to manufacture a sarcastic defense that implicates the article author and/or Clara (as he does throughout this scene in the source text) marks the admission as an epiphany. What Jamie realizes here, but fails to act on until much later in the film, is that his addiction to cocaine is compromising his ability to succeed in the professional arena. He cannot write fiction—his preferred profession which is emphasized in the film by the use of the typewriter sound effects between different "chapters" of the film. (This point is emphasized the one time that Jamie actually sits down at his typewriter to write and is interrupted by Tad, who is looking for a wingman for a night of drugs, alcohol, and sex.) Jamie cannot even verify facts in articles written by "real" authors. And all of these "screw ups," spectators are to assume, derive from Jamie's dependence on "Bolivian Marching Powder." At the same time, the changes witnessed in Clara's character help to reinforce the idea that Jamie is principally responsible for his own poor choices. In the novel, Clara's terseness allows the reader to more easily hold her at least partially responsible for the protagonist's downfall; after all, by this point in the novel, the protagonist has, for most readers, probably attained a strong degree of likeability despite, or maybe because of, his many character flaws while Clara, as the nemesis of McInerney's protagonist, often comes off as unduly strict. But in the film, the tears that accompany Clara's unwarranted apology, in combination with the admission that she has "given [Jamie] the benefit of the doubt before," identifies Clara, not Jamie, as sympathetic. Clara is the savior figure who could not help the self-destructive addict because he was unwilling to help himself (read stop using). Thus, the addict must be moralized against and marginalized (i.e., fired) within his workplace environment—a narrative expectation both of realism and of the metaphor of waste.[4]

---

4 Another similar example occurs later in the film when Jamie visits Megan's (Swoozie Kurtz) apartment for dinner. In the source text, this scene is truncated quite dramatically, with the bulk of the implied exchange between the protagonist and Megan reduced to the explanation, "You eventually give Megan the gist of [what happened with Amanda]" (140). Moreover, in the source text, the protagonist passes out in Megan's bathroom mid-way through the scene. When he awakens the next morning, his go-to emotions are avoidance and denial: "Perhaps you did not entirely disgrace yourself. Better not to think about it" (145). By contrast, in the film, this scene is much more fully fleshed out, perhaps because the role of Megan would have been otherwise

Even though Jamie suffers the consequences of "his actions" through the loss of his job, the film makes clear from the very beginning that Jamie is not without hope for redemption. This idea is most persuasively conveyed in visual terms with respect to his cocaine addiction. Over the course of the film, for example, the filmmakers go to great lengths to avoid directly showing Jamie snorting cocaine—a decision that might have been driven as much by the star persona of Michael J. Fox as by the conservative ideological spin of the script. After all, at the time, Fox perhaps was best known for playing card-carrying Republican Alex P. Keaton on the hit television series *Family Ties* (1982–1989). Early in the film, viewers see Jamie in a bathroom stall pouring cocaine from a black pouch onto his hand, but the narrative cuts to a flashback before Jamie brings his hand to his nose and ingests the drug. In a later scene, Jamie readies a line of cocaine on his desktop, pulls a straw from his desk drawer, and blows the paper wrapping off from the straw in a dramatic arc. But again before he ingests the substance, the camera cuts to another scene. One of the most obvious examples of the ways in which the filmmakers attempt to sanitize the source text by refusing to show Jamie's drug use is when Tad, Jamie, and two women cram themselves into a public bathroom stall to share a vial of cocaine. Throughout this scene, the camera remains fixed on the group's feet, which are just visible under the bathroom stall partition. At one point, Tad drops the cocaine vial and for a moment his hand comes into view to retrieve the vial. But once again before viewers can witness (or, in this case, hear) drug use, the camera cuts to another scene. What all of these scenes collectively reveal is the film's unwillingness (or inability) to approach the topic of addiction in a direct and explicit manner. Instead, the representation of addiction in the filmic adaptation of *Bright Lights, Big City* is trapped within innuendo and metaphor—always alluding to but rarely giving voice to the enigma that unravels Jamie for the bulk of the film. But this innuendo also serves another purpose: namely, it morally sanitizes the figure of Jamie, identifying him as capable of being redeemed.

In those rare instances when viewers are permitted to witness Jamie's drug use, those behaviors are served up in a rather heavy-handed (ideologically-speaking) fashion. For instance, after Jamie loses his job at the newsmagazine, he stops at the public bathroom for a hit of cocaine on his way out of the

---

unappealing (due to its lack of development and screen time) to an actress of the stature of Kurtz. Nonetheless, this scene marks an important stepping stone on the path to Jamie's eventual realization that he "need[s] some help." Throughout the scene, Jamie is forced to confront his failed relationship with Amanda and the role that he played in the failure of that relationship (i.e., "She wanted to live a magazine ad and I wanted to live a literary cliché") and the need to move on (i.e., "My heartbreak is just a variation on the same old story").

building. This is the first of only two points[5] in the film when viewers are allowed to see Jamie snort cocaine—which perhaps is shocking enough given that, in similar scenes up to this point, the filmmakers have employed not-so-veiled sleight-of-hand maneuvers to conceal these very behaviors. After Jamie ingests the drug, he accidently drops the cocaine vial into the toilet bowl, punctuating the gesture with an expletive. For a beat or two, the camera remains tightly focused on the amber vial that is framed in the center of, and that stands out in stark relief against, the white toilet bowl. This visual could not be more overt in its meaning. For Jamie, who can now count unemployment among the many casualties of his addiction, his life is euphemistically "in the toilet." But this scene also pictures his lifeblood (i.e., cocaine) as being literally in the toilet. In this respect, cocaine is likened to excrement with only a single, albeit significant, difference. Whereas excrement is expunged from the human body in order for it to function properly and remain "healthy," cocaine (at least for Jamie) is purposefully ingested into the body. The waste/excrement that is the drug, then, is visually and causally linked to the waste that is Jamie's life—his lost job, his estrangement from biological family, his failed marriage all offered up as evidence of the ways in which cocaine abuse and addiction will transform an otherwise "normal" human being into a waste of a life.[6]

---

5 The second instance occurs while Jamie's brother, Michael (Charlie Schlatter), is visiting the city. The purpose of Michael's visit is to confront Jamie about his estrangement from their father and the impending one-year anniversary of their mother's death. After Jamie reluctantly agrees to return home with Michael and join their father in spreading the dead mother's ashes, Jamie sits down with the etched wall mirror that he inherited from an aunt and does several lines of cocaine. What is especially interesting about this scene is the way in which it implicitly identifies Jamie's cocaine addiction with a material inheritance from a relative. I am not suggesting that this scene, or the film at large, advocates for genetic predisposition. Instead, I would suggest that Jamie's use of the family heirloom as the surface from which to snort his cocaine at this particular moment in the film functions in two important ways. First, narratively it reinforces the causal link that is reiterated repeatedly throughout the film between the death of Jamie's mother (the family "legacy" that he carries with him) and the escalation of his substance abuse, thereby ultimately identifying an environmental stressor, and not a weak moral constitution, as one of the central obstacles that Jamie must overcome. Second, this scene suggests that if Jamie's problem is an emotional stressor, then he can be more easily "redeemed" within the narrative.

6 The heavy-handed morality of the film also is conveyed in the film's treatment of Tad and Amanda. At the close of the party scene when Jamie finally confronts Amanda, Jamie's final words—spoken to Tad—before exiting the apartment are, "You and Amanda would make a terrific couple." In the film adaptation, this line is allowed to linger without response (from Tad) or commentary (by Jamie) and, as such, it takes on a moral certainty that it lacks in the novel. In the novel, Jamie's line of dialogue immediately is followed by Tad, who quips, "I suppose that means that you get Odysseus

The final scene of the film makes clear the indebtedness of *Bright Lights, Big City* to the tradition of literary realism and also the attitude that the film adopts toward the lived experiences of addiction. The final scene of the novel is riddled with ambiguity and ultimately underscores the unreliability of Jamie's seeming commitment to sobriety. By contrast, McInerney alters Jamie's final monologue quite significantly in the film adaptation; the revised monologue clarifies two important differences between source text and adaptation: 1) Jamie is committed to a life of sobriety and therefore 2) he can be (morally) redeemed within the narrative because the addiction is moralized against and marginalized.[7]

> It's 6 a.m. on the island of Manhattan. In the dawn's early light, you can imagine the first ship from the Old World sailing slowly up the biggest river they'd ever seen. That was almost how you felt the first time you saw the city from the window of a Greyhound—like you were looking at a New World waiting to be discovered. And that's how it looks to you now. But you have to go slowly. You have to learn everything all over again.

In this monologue, Jamie casts himself as an explorer, implicitly likening himself to such historical figures as John Cabot, Christopher Columbus, and Henry Hudson. The analogy alludes to Jamie's newfound commitment to living drug-free, with sobriety cast as the virgin territory (or, the "New World") in which explorer-Jamie now finds himself. This same idea is hinted at earlier in the film when, while on a date with Tad's cousin (Tracy Pollan), Jamie, in voice over narration, notes that he is going to "see if it's possible to get through an evening without chemicals for a change." Further, Jamie alludes to the fact that

---

all to yourself," referring to Amanda's new boyfriend, and the scene ends when Jamie says simply, "Later, Tad." Film Jamie judges Tad (for being a poor friend and exacting peer pressure regarding the use of illicit substances) and Amanda (for being a poor wife and abandoning him without explanation) and the definitiveness of his final line suggests a severing of ties with both friend and estranged wife. And, of course, it is only through the severing of ties with these characters, both of whom exhibit moral weaknesses, that Jamie can emerge reformed and drug-free.

7   Interestingly, McInerney's screenplay also clarifies the bartering of Jamie's Ray Bans for freshly-baked bread that happens in the final scene. In the opening monologue that Jamie delivers at the bar, McInerney adds the following lines: "You're the kind of guy who wakes up early to the smell of bread from the local bakery, goes out, brings back the paper, a couple of croissants to your wife, Amanda." This extended monologue makes clear the symbolic and ideological significance of the bread for which Jamie barters at the close of the film. Here, the bread signifies normality—defined as sobriety, but also as masculinity, heterosexuality, affluence, and, of course, citizenship. Bartering for and then subsequently eating the bread, then, marks Jamie's return to normality in its many forms.

Manhattan has long been regarded by both immigrants and citizens alike as the Gateway to the American Dream. Like the immigrant, or like himself when he first arrived by Greyhound in New York City, Jamie is transitioning from Old World (read addiction) to New (read sobriety). The journey, like the journey to becoming a citizen, will not be easy, but like any Fresh Off the Boat immigrant, the film suggests, Jamie can succeed (in sobriety, in citizenship, in morality) through the application of hard work and determination (that is, by proceeding "slowly" and by learning "everything all over again"). That this monologue is delivered against the backdrop of the Manhattan skyline, as well as echoes language from America's national anthem, only works to reinforce the links that are drawn between sobriety, citizenship, and American nationalism. By the end of the film, then, Jamie's cocaine addiction has been moralized against and marginalized and narrative resolution has been achieved through Jamie's *choice* of sobriety, which has redeemed him as a human being, as a man, and as an American citizen.

Less Than Zero in the Realist Tradition

From its opening frames, *Less Than Zero* immediately announces itself as markedly different from its source text— in terms of both the narrative that it charts and the ideological implications of that narrative. Whereas the novel begins *in medias res*, four months into Clay's first year away at college, the film takes viewers back to Clay's (Andrew McCarthy), Blair's (Jami Gertz), and Julian's (Robert Downey, Jr.) graduation from high school (a scene that the novel never represents). As the opening credits flash (in block-style red text) against a black background, a male voice can be heard in voice over: "One last thought before the bright halls of high school fade into memory. Good luck. Good life. I wish you all the health, prosperity, and happiness you desire." As the speaker lists the three attributes that he associates with a "good life," other voices from the crowd overlap and interrupt his: "We want money!" and "Yeah, we want money!" Next, the shot fades in to an extreme close-up of the American flag rippling in the breeze of a bright California afternoon. Against this imposing visual image, the male voice (still in voice over) says, "Congratulations, Class of '87," at which point cheering and clapping erupts from the off-camera crowd and a sea of mortar boards sails upwards from the bottom of the frame, those caps momentarily juxtaposed against the backdrop of the oversized American flag.

This opening sequence crafts a thematic and ideological framework for the narrative that unfolds over the film—a framework not unlike the one established for John Belushi's biography in the film adaptation of *Wired*, which I discuss in Chapter 1. Here, the opening sequence frames this film as not just a story about American youth culture in the 1980s, but a story about the nation in a moment of moral crisis. Of foremost significance is the fact that the film adaptation identifies the trio's high school graduation as a kind of "origin story" for the narrative of excess, degeneracy, and ultimately waste that it charts. Graduation ceremonies function both symbolically and ritualistically as rites of passage from one point in the life cycle to another. Generally speaking, graduation ceremonies are forward-looking, and as such connote the promise, hope, and opportunity both imbued in and presumably signified by the graduates. This opening sequence implicitly links these somewhat generic symbolic connotations typically associated with the ritual of graduation to the mythos of the American Dream in several ways. First, the speaker's allusion to the "good life" (which he defines in terms of "health, prosperity, and happiness") invites parallels with the national ethos of America. These parallels are underscored quite dramatically by the imposing image of the American flag—arguably the most recognizable icon of American national identity and what Carolyn Marvin and David W. Ingle, in *Blood Sacrifice and the Nation: Totem Rituals and the American Flag* (1999), term "the totem object of American civil religion" (1) and "the ritual instrument of group cohesion" (2).

That this film is about not merely the nation, but the nation in crisis, is intimated by the voices that overlap and interrupt the speaker's. Given the content of the speaker's lines, he is identified as some form of authority within the educational institution—maybe a principal or superintendent. The speaker also is male and presumably Caucasian, given the predominant demographic make-up of the high school graduates that viewers see over the next few scenes, as well as the fact that *Less Than Zero* is a mainstream American film produced in the 1980s. In all respects, then, the speaker is identified as privilege incarnate—an educated Caucasian male of some authority who speaks not merely for himself or for the affluent educational institution for which he is a figure-head, but for the nation at large. The version of the American Dream for which he advocates is, in the mouths of the graduates, perverted—the notion of general "prosperity" conflated, or perhaps even replaced by, the accumulation of material wealth. Thus, these graduates—a group to which Clay, Blair, and Julian belong—represent merely another iteration of the "Greed is good" American yuppie archetype that has been reiterated repeatedly in cultural productions from and about the 1980s, such as *Wall Street* (1987), Tom Wolfe's *The Bonfire of the Vanities* (1987), and Bret Easton Ellis's *American Psycho* (1991). This opening sequence, then, identifies as centrally meaningful to the film an ideological conflict between generations over the shape and meaning of America itself. Ultimately this conflict is played out as a cautionary tale of national proportions—a tale that, in the true spirit of literary realism, both marginalizes and moralizes against the addict as a means of reinforcing the ideal of the "good life" (defined in terms of "health, prosperity, and happiness") that is authoritatively articulated by the male speaker in this opening sequence and that is realized in the character of Clay.

One of the central (moral) agents in the charting of this cautionary tale is the character of Clay, a character that is developed in significantly different ways in the source text than in adaptation. These differences are especially heightened with respect to Clay's addictions to illicit substances. Source-text-Clay exists in a drug-addled haze for the entirety of the novel. By contrast, adaptation-Clay is at "worst" a reformed addict who navigates the film in a perpetual (and perpetually judgmental) state of sobriety. Never once does adaptation-Clay partake of any illicit substance, even though viewers witness both Julian and Blair do so on a variety of occasions, and on only a single occasion very early in the film are Clay's former "habits" even directly referenced. At a party on the night of his return to Los Angeles, Clay encounters Rip (James Spader), a friend from high school and drug dealer/pimp. The following exchange ensues:

Rip (offers Clay a vial of cocaine): You look like you could use a little Christmas cheer.
(Clay considers. Beat.)
Clay: No.
Rip: C'mon, Clay. Old habits never die. They just hibernate. (Tucks vial into Clay's breast pocket.)
Clay: Old dealers?
Rip: They go to jail, right? Play hardball with the Wall Street guys. You don't belong here, man. These people are assholes. Who gives a fuck about these people anyway?
Clay: I don't know. Good customers, though, right?

On one hand, this scene establishes a modicum of fidelity between source text and adaptation by alluding to Clay's former "habit" of drug-seeking and use. In this respect, adaptation-Clay is marginally recognizable *as* source-text-Clay. At the same time, this scene identifies adaptation-Clay as an entirely different character than his source-text counterpart. To be sure, the brief, but perceptible, pause that Clay takes between Rip's offer and his refusal of that offer suggests that while cocaine may be an "old habit," it remains, for Clay, a temptation. Moreover, that the cocaine is visibly tempting implies that Clay suffered from more than a casual "habit," although an actual addiction is never confirmed within the diegesis and never implied again after this single reference. The tempting nature of Rip's offer (and of the cocaine itself) is underscored both here and throughout the film by James Spader's charismatic portrayal of an otherwise despicable character. Yet as tempting as the cocaine is, and as widely available as drugs generally are shown to be throughout the film, Clay refrains from using both here and elsewhere and, in the end, his character is chiefly defined by the twin characteristics of sobriety and morality.

Rip's line, "You don't belong here, man," is of equal importance to understanding the significant ways in which source-text-Clay is altered for the filmic adaptation and how he functions as a chief moral agent in the charting of the film's cautionary tale. In Ellis's novel, Clay returns to Los Angeles after a semester of study at a small New England college only to assimilate fairly seamlessly back into his former peer group and milieus. Adaptation-Clay does not weather this transition so easily; in fact, in the film, Clay perpetually is cast as an outsider—at home (for example, the awkward Christmas dinner with his blended family), among his closest friends (for example, Julian reminds Clay that "You've been away a long time"), and even within his former peer group (as here with Rip). Clay's outsiderhood is born, in part, of his decision to continue his studies in New England rather than remain in southern California; but that outsiderhood, the film implies, also derives from Clay's sobriety—an important difference between adaptation-Clay's former and current selves, as well as the key difference between source-text- and adaptation-Clay. This sobriety locates adaptation-Clay outside of the self-destructive lifestyles in which his friends engage, a point that is underscored by the several scenes in which Clay wanders around at his peers' parties voyeuristically observing the excess (for example, the number of television sets present in these scenes) and the depravity (for example, drug use, promiscuous sex, and so on).

Clay's outsider status in Los Angeles is echoed later in the film when Clay discovers Julian, high once again on cocaine, performing fellatio on one of Rip's friends to pay off some of the money that he has borrowed to bankroll his addiction. As Clay drags a half-naked Julian from the hotel room, he accusatorily barks, "Make me understand, Julian. I really want to understand," to which Julian replies simply, "No you don't." This moment in the film, more so than any other, highlights the way that adaptation-Clay is employed as a moral barometer and often a mouthpiece for conservative Middle America. At this moment, Julian has hit his proverbial "rock bottom," having relapsed after committing to sobriety only days before and having "debased" himself (as implied by Clay's disgusted reaction) by engaging in sexual activity with men. (This final point is particularly interesting given the polyamorous sexuality expressed by Clay, Julian, and other characters in Ellis's source text.) The film's representation of same-sex sexual relations between men remains problematic to the end—casting it as predatory and repulsive—but, at least in this single moment, the adaptation recognizes (albeit uncritically) that it takes a moralistic approach to the source text and its subject matter, and that that approach is incredibly flawed. When Julian forces Clay to acknowledge that he does not want to understand, he simultaneously is indicting Middle America for refusing to understand the experience of addiction and the ways in which addiction has ravaged his life. What Clay cannot, or will not, understand is that Julian is not culpable, at least not wholly, for the "choices" that he has made that brought him to this hotel room. What Clay cannot understand is the nature of addiction itself. Like so many politicians, legislators, and even treatment providers in and beyond the 1980s, Clay erroneously views addiction as a "choice" to which Julian could easily "Just Say 'No.'"

Of course, casting choices for the adaptation of *Less Than Zero* may have played a role in the alterations made to Clay's character, especially given the star persona of the actor who ultimately landed the role of Clay. Prior to being cast in the role of Clay, Andrew McCarthy had almost exclusively played the "passive" but likeable "boy next door" "[h]elplessly sucked down by the undertow of female desire" (Bernstein 117). Hadley Freeman, a contributor to *The Guardian*, provides a more thoughtful overview of the star persona that McCarthy had cultivated prior to *Less Than Zero*, writing:

> [The] time was called the 1980s and a group of twentysomething actors, soon dubbed the Brat Pack, dominated the American youth film market. Each had their cosy and eventually constricting niche: Molly Ringwald was the princess, Rob Lowe was the pinup, Judd Nelson was the bad boy, no one was really sure what Emilio Estevez was—and Andrew McCarthy was the dream boyfriend. His performances in films such as *St Elmo's Fire, Less Than Zero, Mannequin* and, most of all, *Pretty in Pink*, with that puppyish face, those soulful eyes and hesitant but—you just knew—deeply sensitive demeanour, made him the template for the perfect swain for a generation.
>
> McCarthy was the boy for girls who found Judd Nelson too threatening and Rob Lowe too cheesy; in other words, for sensitive girls who would become overly reflective adults who remember those first crushes a little too deeply.

Ensemble casts, like the Brat Pack, typically rely on the perpetuation of recognizable archetypes (note that Freeman refers to McCarthy as a "template") into which their members become typecast. Within the group of up-and-coming twenty-somethings known as the "Brat Pack," McCarthy typically played "the dream boyfriend" and, in fact, on those rare occasions when he did not play this role (for example, *Fresh Horses*, 1988), the films flopped (both financially and critically) among the Brat Pack's target audience and reviewers. In part, McCarthy's boyish and nondescript good looks marked him as the ideal contrast to the more conventionally attractive Rob Lowe and the more hard-edged Judd Nelson. But playing opposite of then-reigning Teen Queen Molly Ringwald in *Pretty in Pink* (1986) truly cemented his "niche" as "the perfect swain" for overly sensitive American teen girls during the 1980s. (It is worth noting here, too, that the original ending of *Pretty in Pink*—in which Ringwald's and McCarthy's characters did not end up together—was changed because test audiences reacted negatively.) The star persona that McCarthy brought to *Less Than Zero* stood in direct contrast to the role in which he had been cast, at least as that role was conceived in the source text. Perhaps the casting decision impacted the way in which the role was re-written; perhaps the script itself determined the casting choice. More than likely, the two variables were mutually generative.[8] Regardless of "which came first," what is clear is that the role of Clay was significantly altered in the process of adaptation and the resulting character bears some striking resemblances to the straight-laced, boy-next-door star persona of McCarthy.

McCarthy's star persona was not alone in influencing the alternative thematic and ideological direction that the adaptation of *Less Than Zero* took. Indeed, much of the film's conservatism where addiction is concerned centers on the figure of Julian Wells and the actor tapped to portray him, Robert Downey, Jr. To understand further how the character of Julian participates in the traffic of the metaphor of waste, readers need first to understand the figure of the scapegoat and the position that that figure occupies within the American cultural imaginary. Folklorist Maria Leach defines the scapegoat as "[a]ny material object, animal, bird or person on whom the bad luck, disease, misfortunes and sins of an individual or group are symbolically placed, and which is then turned loose, driven off with stones, cast into a river or the sea, and so on, in the belief that it takes away with it all the evils placed upon it" (quoted in Douglas 3). From its origins, which Tom Douglas in *Scapegoats: Transferring Blame* (2003) traces (at least etymologically) to William Tyndale's sixteenth-century English translation of the Bible, to its myriad uses in twenty-first-century global culture, the scapegoat has stood as a receptacle of cultural- and temporal-specific anxieties around normality. Onto the scapegoat a community projects its deepest and most profound shortcomings, preoccupations, and fears—the scapegoat's "Otherness" serving as a powerful sign of and an *a priori* justification for its ostracization *as* a scapegoat. The forced expulsion of the scapegoat from a given cultural group is intended to pacify the self-same anxieties (or, in ancient times, alleviate the misfortunes) that initially necessitated the identification and ostracization of the scapegoat.

Less Than Zero charts a causal linkage between addiction and a series of traumatic consequences, especially for the character of Julian who could be read as a scapegoat for Middle America's conservative views on addiction. At

---

8 Aljean Harmetz of *The New York Times* provides a fascinating overview of the process by which Ellis's novel was "sanitized" for the big screen and the kinds of cultural and institutional pressures that were placed on the revolving door of screenwriters tasked with adapting *Less Than Zero*.

his core, Julian (both in the novel and in the film) is a "wasted and self-pitying addict" (Ellis, *Imperial Bedrooms*). In *Imperial Bedrooms* (2010), a strangely meta-fictive sequel to *Less Than Zero*, Clay reveals that Julian is "the only person who expressed any embarrassment or disdain about the novel"; Clay attributes Julian's reaction to the fact that "the author had exposed not only Julian's heroin addiction but also the fact that he was basically a hustler in debt to a drug dealer ... and pimped out to men visiting from Manhattan or Chicago or San Francisco." Both the source text and its adaptation emphasize Julian's heroin addiction as the chief defining feature of his character arc. Both also identify heroin addiction as the chief determinant of Julian's narrative arc—that is, Julian's addiction to heroin stands as the cause of the significant debt which is used by his debtor as leverage to strong-arm Julian into prostitution. However, the novel fails to pass judgment on Julian's actions—both in the terse, disinterested narration through which Clay relates the action and in the resolution (or lack thereof) of Julian's storyline. Specifically, that the Julian of the novel survives his addiction relatively unscathed—neither its victim nor its conqueror—suggests quite powerfully that addiction does not *de facto* lead to self-destruction, moral degradation, and death.

By contrast, minus the disinterested narrative voice of the source text, Julian's behaviors in the film resonate as reckless, self-destructive, immoral. Julian's recklessness is intimated at early in the film. Shortly after Clay, Blair, and Julian reunite at a party, the trio takes to cruising the streets of Los Angeles in Clay's classic Corvette convertible. At one point, Julian, who has been standing up unrestrained and belting out Christmas carols, is nearly thrown from the speeding car and killed—an action that not only marks Julian as reckless, even self-destructive, but also underlines Blair's concern that "Julian's in a lot of trouble." Later in the film, as Julian's behavior becomes increasingly erratic, and as his drug use becomes increasingly severe, the self-destructive nature of his actions begins to manifest itself in a deteriorated physical appearance. One of the most disturbing and illustrative examples of how Julian's descent into addiction is visually underscored occurs in the scenes that immediately precede Julian committing to sobriety. These scenes follow Julian as he stumbles around Blair's loft, so high (literally wasted) he can barely hold his head up, let alone walk. Shot from below with Julian's emaciated face captured in extreme close-up, these shots are startling due to the graphic manner in which they attempt to translate the experience of extreme substance dependence. The shaky, hand-held quality of the camera work only adds to the unnerving feeling that viewers are voyeuristically and helplessly watching as an addict self-destructs. Through each of these scenes, and the many others like them, viewers are encouraged to trace a line of causality between Julian's recklessness, his self-destructiveness, and his abuse of illicit substances; in short, the drugs are chiefly responsible for the waste that has become Julian's life.

However, that Julian commits to sobriety, successfully weathers withdraw, and then eventually relapses suggests that Julian's weak will is also responsible for the waste that his life has become. Indeed, the film charts a very clear and very damning chain of causality that implicates Julian's substance dependence as the single inciting cause in a series of morally (and often legally) problematic *choices*. Because he chooses to snort cocaine, Julian has become estranged from his biological family and has contributed to the disintegration of that nuclear family unit. Because he has become estranged from his biological family, Julian has had to borrow over $50,000 from Rip to support his drug habit. Because Julian has had to borrow over $50,000 from Rip to support his drug habit, he has had to turn to a life of crime (that is, the theft of Clay's mother's jewelry) and degradation (that is, prostitution for Rip's male friends). These are the central plot points that constitute the primary storyline of *Less Than Zero*, leading the viewer from exposition (that is, the graduates' promise and hope for the future) through rising action (that is, Julian's devolution) to climax and resolution.

The climax of the film most clearly and directly illustrates the interrelationship between the metaphor of waste and the realist form. After "rescuing" Julian from a hotel room in which Rip is holding him captive in what amounts to sexual slavery, Clay decides to whisk both Julian and Blair away to a presumed "happily ever after" on the East coast. The trio drives through the night and, by morning, have reached the desert where Clay discovers that Julian has died. The stark, desolate landscape of the desert mirrors the wasteland that is Julian's drug-addled life and underlines the causal linkage that the film draws between Julian's addiction and the ruination of his body, his relationships, and his life. Julian's filmic death is a classic example of the ways in which the ideological operations of the realist form necessitate the excision of the addict-Other. Death silences the addict. Death renders the addict invisible. Death erases addiction from public consideration. But death (at least within literary realism) does more than merely marginalize the addict and the addiction; death also signifies a moral judgment against the addict. That Julian ultimately cannot be redeemed or saved within the narrative of *Less Than Zero* reads as condemnation of and punishment for Julian's abuse of illicit substances. Moreover, that Julian's and Blair's storylines diverge so sharply at the close of the film—when they have paralleled throughout—works to underscore the film's condemnation of Julian. Once Blair commits to sobriety by dumping the contents of her cocaine vial down a bathroom drain, she is rewarded with health (read sobriety), prosperity (read education), and happiness (read heterosexual union)—the very qualities of a "good life" that were promised from the outset of the film, that are achieved through her relationship with Clay, and that are indicative of Reaganism and the 1980s, at least for the privileged class to which Clay and Blair both belong.

Conclusion

As a form, realism promises to make the lived experiences of addiction "readable" and "understandable" to an audience by casting those experiences as an enigma (that is, as the central plot complication) and then exposing and unraveling that enigma as a means of achieving narrative resolution. To achieve the kind of resolution that realism promises, the form charts a narrative explanation for addiction that identifies how the addiction came to be, how it impacts the addict's life (and the lives of those closest to the addict), and why the addict should choose sobriety. (This narrative trajectory serves as a guiding premise in many of the most popular treatment programs in the current moment, as I discuss in Chapter 4.) The film adaptations of both *Bright Lights, Big City* and *Less Than Zero* clearly illustrate the narrative machinations of the realist form. *Bright Lights, Big City*, for instance, advances a plot that is chiefly concerned with uncovering why Jamie is so self-destructive; within the causal narrative that the film charts, it is only after Jamie has been confronted with the denial that he has long harbored about his mother's death that he can acknowledge how that denial contributed to his poor decision-making and can then opt for a life of sobriety. *Less Than Zero* even more overtly expresses an interest in the etiology of addiction; this point is most clearly conveyed through the radical changes that were made to narrative focus in the process of adaptation. In both films, then, etiology makes manageable the chaotic narrative force that is addiction; in other words, causal logic renders the lived experiences of addiction both readable and understandable within a realistic narrative.

In realism, though, the addiction must not only be "readable" and "understandable" to its audience, but those lived experiences also must be made "palatable." Because addiction is cast as an enigma—that is, as a puzzle that complicates and/or disrupts the status quo—it can only ever be recuperated for a dominant culture audience through the assignation of blame. Sometimes the blame for an addiction rests squarely on the shoulders of the addict who is regarded as too selfish, too damaged, or too immoral to cease using. Julian Wells in the film adaptation of *Less Than Zero* certainly fits this bill. Sometimes the blame is assigned to the addict's family and friends, who might enable or exacerbate the addiction. As I discuss in Chapter 1, the film adaptation of *Wired* targets many of Belushi's friends and acquaintances as partially responsible for his overdose and death. Sometimes the blame can be attributed to environmental factors, which includes everything from a high-stress occupation to an emotionally-draining family life. In *Bright Lights, Big City*, for instance, the death of Jamie's mother and his abandonment by wife Amanda are tapped as the key forces that exacerbate his cocaine addiction. And sometimes the blame is cast onto the addiction itself, which is viewed as a "disease"—a genetic predisposition for some, a neurobiological condition for others, but always a disorder that is hardwired into the addict and that adversely affects him/her.

Where the blame for an addiction is placed typically is much less important than the act of blaming itself. To blame is to judge—to assess a person/experience within the rigidly-defined parameters of "innocence" and "guilt," "right" and "wrong," "moral" and "immoral." The act of blaming assumes that the addict *chose* to become dependent on an illicit or controlled substance and therefore must accept the consequences of that choice. Judgment thus presupposes autonomy and demands accountability, and it is squarely within the realm of accountability where addiction becomes palatable for a dominant audience. Stated differently, it is only when the addict is punished for his/her poor choices (whether those choices are cast as "sins" or "crimes" or simply "errors of judgment") that s/he can be (morally? narratively? ideologically?) recuperated for a dominant culture audience. Within the realist form, autonomy and accountability converge on the moment at which the plot achieves resolution and the addict/addiction either is moralized against or marginalized. To paraphrase Dolan, then, the addict most "readable" (and thus palatable) in realism is either dead or aping sobriety. In either case, realism is always and only ideologically punitive for the addict. The metaphor of waste parallels the realist form in its emphasis on an ideologically punitive narrative regarding the lived experiences of addiction. Indeed, the notion that addiction warrants both blame and punishment is a chief animating fantasy of the metaphor of waste—and this is perhaps why the metaphor of waste finds its origins (at least partially) in the evolution and dissemination of literary realism.

Both readability and understandability, though, come at a steep price, particularly for those who exist outside of the representational apparatus but not outside of its ideological reach. For the "real world" addict, realism offers a very limited range of standpoints (that is, dead or sober) from which to experience an addiction. Indeed, in the binary logic advanced through its resolution, the realistic narrative does not even acknowledge being "in recovery" (a kind of interstitial standpoint between death and sobriety) as a legitimate identity construct. A similar kind of "logic" is at work in Alcoholics Anonymous (as well as in other 12-step programs) and, in *The Sober Truth: Debunking the Bad Science Behind 12-Step Programs and the Rehab Industry* (2014), Lance and Zachary Dodes point up one of the most significant potential consequences that such "logic" might have on an addict: "If you are in AA and you slip, you cannot avoid feeling like a failure, because that's exactly what the system is designed to tell you" and "this system can cause a great deal of pain, and the humiliations that come with it can be manifold" (Chapter 8). Of course, the "pain" of personal humiliation can breed a host of other problems for the addict. As a result of such humiliations, the addict can experience low self-esteem and could sink even deeper into a dependence on illicit/controlled substances as a means of coping with his/her poor self-image. In fact, *Psychology Today* contributor Carole Bennett suggests that the "uncertainty, insecurity and confusion" that stem from low self-esteem can be "the perfect, fertile breeding ground for substance abuse." Furthermore, the heavy-handed moralism advanced in realism can be patronizing, even infantilizing, to the addict, especially since realism covers over its ideological operations and therefore its resolution seems not only "right," "just," and "normal," but also inevitable. For those who struggle with sobriety, then, a life of addiction (and perhaps even death) might itself be seen as inevitable. At best, realism identifies addiction as a self-perpetuating cycle from which self-loathing addicts are offered few means of escape. Equally damaging is the impact that such representations potentially can have on how we legislate addiction, how we treat addiction, and even, in the everyday, how we perceive addiction and respond to addicts. This topic of how the metaphor of waste is deeply imbricated in common treatment and recovery programs will be taken up in the next chapter.

Chapter 4

"My name is Jim, and I'm an alcoholic": Peddling the Wasteful Propaganda of 12-Step Treatment in Peter Cohn's *Drunks*

Alcoholics Anonymous was proclaimed the correct treatment for alcoholism over seventy-five years ago despite the absence of any scientific evidence of the approach's efficacy and we have been on the wrong path ever since.

Lance and Zachary Dodes, *The Sober Truth: Debunking the Bad Science Behind 12-Step Programs and the Rehab Industry*, Preface

By the time that the inaugural chapter of Alcoholics Anonymous (hereafter AA) was founded in Akron, Ohio, in June 1935, the metaphor of waste already was firmly cemented within the American cultural imaginary. Indeed, as discussed in the previous two chapters, this metaphor was born of several parallel socio-cultural formations of the nineteenth century, the period during which "the addict" emerged as a recognizable identity construct in the West. Yet the founding of 12-step recovery programs marks a significant milestone in the metaphor's history—not as a site at which the metaphor originated, but as *the* site at which the metaphor gained its greatest foothold in America over the twentieth and into the twenty-first centuries. In "The Impact of Alcoholics Anonymous on Other Substance Abuse Related Twelve Step Programs," Alexandre B. Laudet suggests that "[s]ince its inception in the U.S. in 1935, Alcoholics Anonymous [has] grown to become the largest and most well-known self-help organization for alcohol problems not only in the US but worldwide." Scott O. Lilienfeld and Hal Arkowitz, contributors to *Scientific American*, further illustrate the stranglehold that 12-step programs have over the global treatment and recovery movements, noting in 2011 that AA alone "count[ed] two million members who participate[d] in some 115,000 groups worldwide, about half of them in the U.S." As further evidence of "12-step hegemony," health writer Maia Szalavitz notes that "[b]y 2000, 90 percent of American addiction treatment programs employed the 12-step approach" and that annually "some 165,000 Americans and Canadians ... are court-mandated into the program." In *The Sober Truth*, Dodes and Dodes elaborate more fully on the ways in which "AA and rehab have ... been codified into our legal system." They write, "court-mandated attendance, which began in the late 1980s, is today a staple of drug-crime policy. Every year, our state and federal governments spend over $15 billion on substance-abuse treatments for addicts, the vast majority of which are based on 12-step programs" (Chapter 1). Finally, it is important to acknowledge that the influence of AA extends far beyond the treatment of alcoholics in America. As Laudet explains, *The Big Book of Alcoholics Anonymous* "has been translated in 28 languages," and the recovery model espoused by the organization has been adapted to over 258 fellowships for different behaviors, cultures, and belief systems.

This chapter investigates the role that 12-step recovery programs have played in the widespread proliferation of the metaphor of waste in twentieth- and twenty-first-century American culture. Anchoring this chapter's investigation into the hegemony of 12-step programs in America is *Drunks* (1997), an independent film that has been dubbed by its producers as "the first film to fully portray a meeting of Alcoholics Anonymous" ("DVD/Streaming"). To be sure, by the time that *Drunks* premiered at the Boston Film Festival in 1995, 12-step recovery already was a staple subject of the American cinema thanks to such films as *The Lost Weekend* (1945), *Days of Wine and Roses* (1962), *Clean and Sober* (1988), and *When a Man Loves a Woman* (1994), among many others. However, *Drunks* marks an obvious departure from its predecessors in at least one significant respect: namely, the filmmaker's insistent desire to represent 12-step programs as faithfully (read realistically) as possible. Indeed, director Peter Cohn credits John Cassavetes, a pioneer of *cinéma vérité*, as the chief stylistic influence on *Drunks*. It is the staunch cinematographic verisimilitude of *Drunks* that at once identifies the film as an obvious and ideal site at which to consider not only how 12-step programs are represented within the American cinema, but also how 12-step programs have shaped—and, indeed, continue to shape—our shared perceptions of addiction in the everyday.

From *Blackout* to *Drunks*: A Brief Production History

Drunks began life in the early 1990s as a stage play under the title *Blackout*. Penned by Gary Lennon, who perhaps is most well-known for his television writing credits (that is, *The Shield, Justified,* and *Orange is the New Black*), the play takes place on Christmas Eve in New York City at an AA meeting. (The Christmas Eve setting is one of several noteworthy differences between the stage play and its filmic adaptation.) Through a series of monologues, the cast of nine re-lives the emotionally-overwrought "rock bottom" moments that originally brought them to the 12-step group. The action of the play is continuous, although many of the monologues are intercut by brief blackouts that underscore the title and central subject of the play, and the emotions are unrelenting. The dramaturgy of the play centers on verisimilitude—that is, on representing AA as realistically and as faithfully as possible. The minimalist staging echoes the landscape of the many church basements in which such meetings regularly are held. For example, the opening stage directions indicate: "The stage is bare except for the table and chairs. The twelve steps and twelve Tradition Signs of A.A. are hanging in the back with a Christmas wreath between them." The dialogue mimics the discourse of AA from the initial line of the play, which, perhaps predictably, is "Hi, my name is Jack, and I'm an alcoholic," to its closing, in which the cast stands, holds hands, and in unison intones the Serenity Prayer. Even the temporal structure of *Blackout*, which melds diegetic and extra-diegetic time, reinforces the playwright's commitment to both realism and verisimilitude. The play premiered at the Harold Clurman Theater in New York City on 11 November 1991; it was produced by the Second Generation Theater Company.

Marketed under the tagline "The Groundbreaking Feature Film about Alcoholics Anonymous," *Drunks* is a low-budget independent film adaptation of *Blackout* that premiered at the Boston Film Festival in August 1995. Two years later, *Drunks* would be screened as an official selection of the Sundance Film Festival and, that same year, would earn one of the very first Prism Awards for its realistic depiction of alcoholism and substance abuse. Produced under first-time director Peter Cohn, *Drunks* features an all-star cast including Faye Dunaway, Dianne Wiest, Spalding Grey, Amanda Plummer, Parker Posey, Howard Rollins, Richard Lewis, and Calista Flockhart, among others. Like its source text, *Drunks* centers on a single meeting of a New-York-City-based chapter of AA, beginning with the unfolding of chairs and ending with the speaking of the Serenity Prayer. The bulk of the film is comprised of monologues in which the diverse cast of characters recount some of the most humiliating and humbling moments that they experienced prior to entering treatment, although there is not an emphasis here on either the experiences of blacking out or the moment of absolute "rock bottom." A few of the monologues (for example, Helen's, Tanya's) are lifted almost verbatim from the source text, but most are unique to the film adaptation. Also unique to the film adaptation is a second, parallel storyline that focuses on Jim (Richard Lewis), a character who does not appear in the stage play. At the beginning of the film, Jim is cajoled by mentor Marty (George Martin) into speaking at the meeting, something that Jim has not done since his wife died suddenly several months earlier. From the monologue, viewers quickly realize that Jim is hanging onto his sobriety by a thread. (The monologue builds to a climax, at which point Jim repeatedly admits, "I just want to get high!") After Jim delivers his monologue, he uncharacteristically leaves the meeting and, over the evening that ensues, he relapses.

When *Drunks* opened in limited release in March 1997, the film was widely praised by film critics. Stephen Holden of *The New York Times* lauded the film as "a thoroughly unsentimental group portrait of people in various stages of recovery struggling with the same inner demons that torment all of us." Holden went on to describe Lennon's screenplay as "tough-minded enough to avoid a disease-of-the-week mawkishness that the theme invites" ("Why They Drank"). In his review of *Drunks* for *Variety,* Daniel Kimmel suggested that the film "uses a star-studded cast to overcome the lack of action and narrative drive"; still, Kimmel's review of *Drunks* is, in the end, largely laudatory, concluding that *Drunks* "succeeds in presenting a fictional AA meeting and getting across the idea that alcoholics come from all walks of life." Like Kimmel, noted reviewer for *The New Republic* Stanley Kauffmann also finds the cast noteworthy; however, Kauffmann regards the "star-studded" cast as the film's one deviation from its documentary-like style. Kauffmann writes, "[I]f we didn't see Faye Dunaway or Howard Rollins or Dianne Wiest and other familiar people speaking the words, we might feel we were intruding" on an AA meeting (28). Despite the "star-studded cast" remarked upon by many of the film's reviewers, Leslie Camhi of *The Village Voice* contends that "the film's everyman aspirations" facilitate "a series of funny, moving, and sobering reflections on our consuming needs for things, people, and, most of all, stories." In one of the rare negative reviews of *Drunks,* Lea Russo of *Boxoffice* magazine contends that the film "forgets the most important element of an AA meeting: It's for members, not audiences." Russo describes the film as "whiny" and "caricature-driven" and takes particular issue with the storyline that focuses on Jim: "When his character desperately screams 'I just want to get high!' even Nancy Reagan might want to give him a bong hit, just to shut him up" (56).

Russo's comments here are quite interesting, both in terms of how profoundly she misunderstands *Drunks* and in terms of what those comments reveal about wider American cultural attitudes toward addiction in the late twentieth century when this film initially was released. As a disclaimer, I want to acknowledge that Russo is discussing a fictional character within the context of a film review, and so much of the tact that she might normally reserve for discussions of "real" addicts might be sacrificed here for the eagle-eyed cynicism often expected of a seasoned film critic. Yet one of the central premises of this study—perhaps *the* central premise—is, as I explain in the Preface, that cultural representations of addiction are not innocuous mirrors held up to and reflective of everyday lived experiences. Rather, such representations profoundly matter in the extra-diegetic world. Stated differently, what we read on the page, and/or bear witness to on the stage/ screen, impacts and is impacted by the everyday lived realities of addiction. For Russo to so dismissively disparage Jim could only be possible within a culture that itself so easily maligns, belittles, and even vilifies addicts. Moreover, Russo's characterization of Jim's confession as "whiny" alludes to the double bind within which American addicts perpetually are trapped. At once forced to confess as part of a nationally-sanctioned recovery program and simultaneously derided for doing so, addicts like Jim are coerced into complicity in their own stigmatization and marginalization at the very moment they seek out a 12-step program. Even more disconcerting is the not-so-subtle vitriol that Russo exhibits toward Jim and, I would argue by extension, "real world" addicts. To suggest that Jim's whininess should be met with a "bong hit"—a sentiment that Russo assures readers would be shared by anti-drug crusader and former First Lady Nancy Reagan—is the equivalent of suggesting that addicts are not worth the time and energy that we might expend listening to their experience and contributing to their recovery. In other words, Russo's dismissive comment implies that addicts are little more than waste. Also of note is Russo's profound misunderstanding of the film. By characterizing the film as "caricature-driven," Russo ignores the indebtedness of *Drunks* both to literary realism and to the tenets and practices of 12-step recovery. Lennon and Cohn's strict adherence to verisimilitude both in form and in subject matter may mark the film and its characters as contrived, but certainly not as exaggerated. In fact, in the argument that follows, I suggest that the film constitutes an interesting site at which to examine some of the most problematic practices and wasteful propaganda of extra-diegetic 12-step programs.

Why Jim Just Wants To Get High

The title of the film immediately identifies *Drunks* as deeply imbricated both in the culture of AA and in the metaphor of waste. To be sure, the film's use of this particular term to refer to its cast of addicts (all of whom are, at various times, members of an AA group in New York City) is not particularly surprising since, as Dodes and Dodes explain, the "language is AA's own," adopted as a means to "break down the barriers between group and self and to take down a peg those who come to meetings feeling that they don't really belong lumped in with everyone else" (Chapter 8). Despite the relevance of the term to the primary narrative arc of the film, "drunks" nonetheless gestures toward some of the most problematic assumptions and attitudes that Americans currently hold with respect to addicts. In being saddled with the moniker "drunk," alcoholics, rather than their afflictions, are cast in pejorative terms, identified as ones who are prone to excess (a precursor to waste) and wanton self-destruction (a manifestation of waste). Alcoholics also are wasted in the sense that they are discursively disposed of as mere "trash." The generic moniker, "drunks," is reductive, cancelling out the individual and lumping all alcoholics into a single category that is defined exclusively by a shared affliction (that is, addiction). The discursive operations of the term "drunks," of course, have a material impact on the everyday lived experiences of the alcoholic as well. Like a pariah, the alcoholic is cast out from "normal" society, the term "drunks" simultaneously a precondition of and a justification for the many acts of exclusion and marginalization that the alcoholic must endure. From the sideways glances cast at them to ostracization from family and friends as acts of "tough love," the alcoholic, once rendered a garden variety "drunk"—a term that often is used interchangeably with "wino" or even "skid row bum"—repeatedly and endlessly is reminded that s/he is "somehow different from the rest of us, as if addiction is an innate quality rather than an acquired behavior" (Dodes and Dodes, Chapter 8). By locating the addiction within the individual, as the alcoholic's definitive and exclusive trait, the term "drunks" further suggests that alcoholism is an identity—an innate and therefore inescapable one, at that—rather than a compulsive behavioral pattern. As such, alcoholism cannot be changed or even overcome (as behavioral patterns can); rather, alcoholism can only ever be acknowledged (the first step of any 12-step program) and managed. These ideas, too, align perfectly with the philosophy of AA, which advances the simplistic and problematic notion of "Once an Addict, Always an Addict" (a topic that I take up more fully below).

The predominant narrative form employed in *Blackout* and, less so, *Drunks*—that is, the monologue—echoes these attitudes about the nature of addiction through its emphasis on narrative stagnancy. That these texts employ the monologue as their primary mode of address should not be particularly surprising given that both texts focus on 12-step recovery programs. A cornerstone of any 12-step program is the confession—a discursive act of self-identification by which the individual's identity is indelibly marked and, I would argue, marred by the label "addict." 12-step meetings, for example, largely are comprised of "willingly shared" monologues in which attendees confess their struggles with addiction—past wrongs committed against friends and family while high on their substance of choice, current temptations and worries about relapse, future hopes for continued sobriety and personal growth. Ritualistically such monologues begin with some variation of the statement, "My name is Bill and I am an alcoholic." Fittingly, Lennon's stage play opens with the statement "Hi, my name is Jack, and I'm an alcoholic," and, throughout the play, a similar admission precedes each monologue. In *Blackout*, then, the discourse of AA becomes a leitmotif that lends verisimilitude to the "narrative" that unfolds on stage and transitions (albeit not seamlessly) from one monologue to the next. But those admissions that pepper the scripts of both *Blackout* and *Drunks* also operate ideologically, perpetuating the psychologically harmful cycle of self-shaming that often accompanies membership in a 12-step recovery program.

The addict's confession is reminiscent of J.L. Austin's "performative utterance"—a statement that does not merely describe the world, but performs an action in the act of being uttered. Austin's classic and oft-quoted example of the performative utterance is the statement "I do," spoken by many a bride and groom throughout the world as a means of literally enacting the legal (and, for some, spiritual) ties that bind their matrimonial union. In a similar manner, by describing the self as "an addict," by verbally laying claim to that identity, the individual also and simultaneously *becomes* an addict in the eyes of self and others. Stated differently, within the act of confession, speaking is becoming, whether the individual is copping to a substance abuse problem within the rooms and therefore becoming an addict, or copping to adultery within a church confessional and therefore becoming a sinner. It is, I suspect, also no coincidence that two of the 12 steps (Steps One and Five) to sobriety concern (or, is it demand? coerce?) an act of confession. In this respect, saying "I am an addict" not only creates the individual in that image, but also that utterance constitutes an act of healing and recovery. And, as I discuss below, once an individual is saddled with the identity of "addict," that identity is incredibly difficult to escape, at least within 12-step recovery programs.

Although devout members of 12-step programs insist that all participation at meetings is entirely voluntary on the part of attendees, a critical examination of both the philosophy behind and the day-to-day operations of 12-step programs suggests that coercion sometimes is a necessary prerequisite to the kind of "talk therapy" advocated by such programs. Programs like AA and Narcotics Anonymous stress the importance of fellowship, a pseudo-religious tenet originally borrowed from the Oxford Group, "a religious movement popular in the United States and Europe in the early 20th century" ("Origins") that spawned AA. Within the program, the philosophy goes, an individual's sobriety is predicated on that individual's "willingness" to share openly his/her experiences with other members, to bond with his/her fellow members over those shared experiences, and to create through acts of bonding a community of support that will ensure the individual's sobriety (provided the individual devoutly "works the steps"). Fellowship, then, is the philosophical and pseudo-religious foundation on which the addict's confession is coerced. Interestingly, although *Drunks* is wildly celebratory of 12-step programs, an exchange near the opening of the film implicitly supports my claim here that coercion functions as an important (albeit unwritten) tenet of AA and like programs. As Jim spoons coffee grounds into an urn in preparation for the impending meeting, Marty confrontationally asks, "When was the last time you spoke at a meeting?" When Jim admits that he has not spoken at a meeting in seven months, Marty casts a disapproving glance at Jim and says simply but firmly,

"You need it," as if a failure to disclose and confess is the only obstacle standing between Jim-the-addict and continued sobriety. Coercion here is obvious in the marked distinctions that are drawn between the two men. In age, Marty is noticeably older than Jim. He also is coded as a kind of mentor (maybe even sponsor) to Jim, especially in the paternalistic attitude that he adopts toward Jim in this opening scene. Marty also takes on important leadership roles within the organization: he is the first to arrive, he sets up the chairs, he facilitates the meeting, and later he passes the collection plate and leads the Serenity Prayer. In all of these respects, Marty speaks from a position of authority *over* Jim and, as such, his "suggestion" that Jim "needs" to speak at the impending meeting reads as coercion.

Although the other characters who deliver monologues over the course of *Drunks* and its source text may not be coerced to do so—at least not within the diegesis of the film/play—their monologues contribute to the overarching sense of narrative stagnancy that not only characterizes the stage- and screenplays, but also indicts 12-step recovery programs as deeply flawed. As a form, the monologue does not inherently lack narrative momentum and, in fact, the monologue often has been employed as a device to facilitate the intrapersonal epiphany that precipitates narrative action and character growth, most particularly in literary realism. Whether used as the sole means of storytelling or interspersed with other narrative modes, the monologue constitutes a rich and varied mode of address that can work to advance the plot, develop the characters, and/or underline theme, especially (though not exclusively) in the theater. In both *Blackout* and *Drunks,* by contrast, the monologic form always and only operates as a means of revealing background information, or exposition. As the part of a narrative that introduces backstory for the current narrative action, exposition identifies as its chief concern a sequence of events circumscribed by strict temporal and causal limitations; in Lennon's stage- and screenplays, these limitations are heightened, in large part because of the setting (that is, an AA meeting) and the subject matter (that is, addiction). On one hand, the backstories are bracketed by a finite temporal structure with a distinct beginning and ending (a point that I will discuss in greater detail below). When the events that a monologue rehearses have already occurred and concluded in time, there is no opportunity for change, growth, or even action; rather, all that the monologue can accomplish (much like the confessions at a 12-step meeting) is to rehash endlessly a series of events that already have atrophied in the character's past. At the same time, the characters of *Blackout* and *Drunks* repeatedly employ the monologue as a means of explaining their ongoing struggles, both with addiction and with life more generally—a common rhetorical and ideological motif of 12-step recovery programs. In this respect, the backstory serves as a causal precursor to the current narrative action, albeit a precursor that cannot be altered, ignored, or escaped; after all, in the "logic" of 12-step recovery, "Once an addict, always an addict." Unable to escape the deterministic confines of a perpetual past tense, the addicts in both *Blackout* and *Drunks* fail to experience epiphany, growth, autonomy, or change over the course of their narratives.

Narrative Stagnancy

The stagnancy of the characters is mirrored in the narrative trajectory, a characteristic that both *Blackout* and *Drunks* share. Indeed, the very title of the stage play locates the narrative of *Blackout* in a single moment of (non-)action: a climactic turning point in the addict's journey, but a moment without prelude (that is, exposition and rising action), without resolution (for example, falling action and *dénouement*), and without recollection. This sense of non-action alluded to in the title of the stage play also is incorporated into the dramatic structure. As a series of monologues only loosely connected by topic, *Blackout* focuses on a single meaningful, but isolated, moment in each character's backstory, offering absolutely no narrative momentum precisely because all of the conflict is situated firmly in the past (usually in the form of blackouts and the proverbial "rock bottom") or in the future (usually in the form of a feared relapse). In the much-prolonged opening monologue, for instance, Jack—described in the Cast of Characters as "A man in his twenties. An orphan."—recounts his "last time being drunk," which also happened to precipitate a massive blackout. He recalls waking up in an unfamiliar, "afghan covered bed" to discover a strange (and much older) "Spanish woman" "tugging at [him], down there." Jack paints the Spanish woman in unflattering, borderline stereotypical terms. He describes her as wearing "knee high stockings" and having "her housedress over her head, and it was caught in her curlers and she had egg salad smeared all over her bare breasts." The bedroom is overwhelmed by the "horrifying" smell of the Spanish woman's shoes, the sheets of the bed are adorned with "huge wine stains" that remind Jack of "circus hoops," and the bed itself is drenched from an "accident" that either Jack or the Spanish woman had in the night. For Jack, this blackout represents the final, "humiliating" experience in the downward spiral of alcoholism that prompts him to attend his first AA meeting and, eventually, to tell the tale that he has just narrated to the assembled members (and Lennon's audiences). Jack's monologue reeks of self-loathing and shame, impressions that are reinforced through a variety of sensory details: from the rancid smells of unwashed feet and stale urine, to the sights of egg-salad-covered breasts and wine-stained sheets. Exacerbating Jack's feelings of shame is the marked age disparity between himself and the unnamed Spanish woman, who wears a "housedress" and keeps her dentures in a clear glass on the bedside table. The obsessive need to relive this moment of humiliation is, of course, prompted by Steps 4 (that is, "[We m]ade a searching and fearless moral inventory of ourselves.") and 5 (that is, "[We a]dmitted to God, to ourselves, and to another human being the exact nature of our wrongs") of AA, and therefore the narrative stagnancy contributes to the verisimilitude of the play. However, the fact that neither Jack nor any of the other recovering alcoholics included in the Cast of Characters moves beyond these two steps of the program, at least not within the diegesis of *Blackout*, also points (albeit both implicitly and, I suspect, inadvertently) to two of the most significant forms of stagnancy that unfortunately characterize AA and like 12-step programs: namely, (1) the unwillingness of such programs to adapt to the particular needs of the individual who enters treatment; and (2) the unchanging nature of the organization as a whole over its 80-year existence.

Like its source text, *Drunks* suffers from a lack of narrative momentum, locating most of its action in the (blackout) past or the (relapse) future. Joseph's (Howard Rollins) monologue, for instance, focuses on a blackout moment that occurred several years earlier while he was driving his five-year-old son to spend the day with the child's grandmother. Following the blackout, Joseph recalls, he awakened in a jail cell where a law enforcement officer revealed that Joseph's blackout had resulted in an automobile accident that landed his young son in the intensive care unit at a local hospital. For Joseph, there is no epiphany moment during which he comes to the realization that at a certain point he needs to allow the past to be past. There is no self-forgiveness. There is no growth or change. There is always and only an overwhelming sense of guilt, both for Joseph and, thanks to Rollins' dramatic performance, for the film's audience. Joseph's narrative wallows in that final blackout moment that injured (and perhaps killed—the film is noticeably ambiguous on this point) his son, ultimately trapping Joseph in an unchanging and unforgiving past tense that perpetually condemns him to a state of self-loathing and dread. Joseph hates himself for drinking, a "choice" which, he believes, made him a poor father. But the film suggests that Joseph's only defense against these feelings is to endlessly rehearse the same narrative over and again, telling his story to remind himself of the damage that his drinking has wrought on those he loves. Of course, guilt is not Joseph's only motivation to obsessively relive the blackout-induced accident that harmed his son; rather, Joseph's monologue suggests that he equally is motivated by fear—specifically, the fear that his alcoholism will resurface and cause him to harm more people. As Joseph admits, "I am feeling fucking crazy tonight. I am scared. I'm scared …. I'm afraid I'm gonna do something crazy to somebody or-or-or-or-or maybe to myself." In this regard, Joseph's fear of future relapse keeps him, in the present, firmly stagnated in the past.

Like Joseph, Brenda (Linda Gay Hamilton) is trapped within a perpetual past tense that endlessly haunts her present actions (and the actions of those she loves). In particular, Brenda worries that her former addictions to alcohol and heroin are responsible for her younger brother's current heroin addiction. Like Joseph, Brenda is rendered impotent (a form of emotional and psychological stagnancy) by all-consuming feelings of guilt and self-blame. The younger brother, who years earlier had walked in on Brenda shooting up, has of late developed his own heroin addiction, which Brenda has discovered in the same manner that her own addiction was revealed to the brother—a narrative parallelism that clumsily gestures toward the cyclic nature of addiction in some families. The allusion to the cyclic nature of addiction in Brenda's monologue not only perpetuates a harmful cultural mythos regarding the inevitability and inescapability of addiction, but also underscores the overarching sense of narrative stagnancy in which Brenda and the other addicts are mired thanks to a treatment program that forces them endlessly to repeat those rock bottom moments. To be sure, Brenda's narrative is peppered with hopeful asides that at least momentarily suggest growth beyond the trauma of her past addictions, such as when she reveals that she has started taking singing lessons. But any sort of forward narrative progress and character growth are frustrated by Brenda's somewhat off-handed revelation that she has tested positive for the Human Immunodeficiency Virus (or, HIV). Although Brenda eschews any direct causal link between medical condition and addiction (that is, "I don't know how I got it. It could have been through sex, it could have been through needles, who knows? It doesn't matter."), the film decisively identifies Brenda's diagnosis as punishment for her former moral transgressions by casting that diagnosis, in Brenda's own words, as the harbinger of certain, imminent, and painful death, despite the fact that the film was set and released in 1997, long after a variety of newly emergent medical treatments had rendered AIDS a chronic, but manageable, medical condition. Denied, at least according to her own "logic," any possibility of a future because of her HIV status, Brenda's much-rehearsed and oft-repeated monologue, then, alludes to her entrapment within both an unforgiveable past (morally-speaking) and an unforgiving present.

While both Joseph and Brenda are firmly rooted in an unforgiveable past, other characters are shackled to a future that is as devastating as it is unavoidable. For example, although Helen's (Calista Flockhart) monologue, perhaps in homage to the play's title, offers an obligatory nod to her past, it focuses principally on the anxieties that she feels about her lack of will power. (I reference the play and the film here interchangeably because Helen's monologue is one that occurs in both source text and adaptation.) She admits to a minor relapse the day prior, noting that "I smoked a joint and drank. I had to. I had to get through it. It helped me." She justifies her relapse by explaining that "I'm not like the rest of you. I can't do it. I'm not as strong," and she repeatedly gives voice to the panic and dread that her addiction triggers. Helen confides, "I was gonna drink this afternoon, but I came here instead. I'm trying. I can't keep running here every time I'm gonna use. I can't keep hiding in these rooms [...] it keeps finding me." And she expresses her concern that "when I walk outside this room, I'm gonna walk straight into a bar." Her monologue concludes with the desperate plea: "I'm here because I want you to stop me. I don't think I can do it." For Helen, addiction is a sword of Damocles hanging by a single horse hair over her sober present. It threatens her with a past that she endlessly is doomed to repeat in the future. It stalks her like a former lover[1]—in her words, she runs from it but "it keeps finding [her]." It coerces her into behaviors that, as her guilt-ridden monologue implies, she understands are immoral and self-destructive, at least within the culture of AA and, by extension, late-twentieth-century America. But addiction also renders her impotent in the face of its many temptations (a thematic that is echoed in Jim's parallel storyline). She cannot stop herself from imbibing—note the phrasing "I had to" when Helen references her relapse from the previous day—and her only protection against another relapse is this confined room, this insular meeting, this supportive group of fellow addicts. In this respect, Helen's monologue casts AA as a momentary refuge from the temptations of addiction (another thematic motif that is echoed in Jim's storyline outside of the rooms, as well as in the cinematography, both of which I will discuss in greater detail below), but ultimately identifies the addict as solely responsible for controlling her strong urge to drink. It is precisely this philosophy regarding personal accountability and blame—a philosophy that flies directly in the face of well-established neurobiological research on addiction—that fuels such erroneous and damaging myths as "Relapse means you didn't work the steps hard enough" or "Once an addict, always an addict."

---

1 Indeed, many addicts and persons in recovery discuss their substances of choices in terms that they might otherwise ascribe to a romantic partner and/or lover. In Kristen Johnston's memoir, *Guts*, the actress recounts the physical devastation that her addictions to alcohol and prescription medications wrought on her body. In one particular chapter, Johnston recalls lying in the hospital after her "guts blew up," suffering from terrible pain, and lying to her physician about the extent of her substance use. She writes:

> That's how strong He is. When He's got His evil talons in you, you don't care. You will lie to protect Him, no matter what happens. He's your most devoted better half, your longtime lover. He's adoring and reliable and He's never let you down. It's certainly not His fault that He's killing you. Like a battered wife, you take Him back even though He just knocked out your two front teeth. You lie to your weeping mother even though He's convinced you to steal the painkillers she actually needs after a knee-replacement surgery. You will die protecting Him, no matter what. (Chapter 5)

Interestingly, in the stage play, Helen's final, desperate plea for help immediately is followed by her storming off-stage and a blackout transition into Rachel's monologue. Then, for 14 pages of the play script, Rachel mires in her own alcohol-fueled, past transgressions without a single verbal acknowledgement of Helen's entreaty. At the close of her monologue, Rachel *does* finally address Helen directly, although Helen's actual return from off-stage is not noted in the script until many pages later, making me, as a reader, wonder if the line is spoken rhetorically rather than conversationally. Rachel's response to Helen is terse: "Helen, you say you want us to stop you, but we can't stop you. We can help you, but we can't stop you." Admittedly, *Blackout* is unequivocally celebratory with respect to AA and 12-step recovery; that is, the play repeatedly and uncritically advances the notion that these characters, while deeply flawed and traumatized by their addictions, nonetheless are "better off" for having sought refuge in the fellowship of AA. At the same time, though, the playwright's insistence on verisimilitude, on representing the rooms as realistically as possible, cannot help but implicitly reveal some of the harmful misconceptions that the "real" AA not only labors under, but also peddles to its membership. The abrupt shift from Helen's monologue to Rachel's, simultaneously underscored by and achieved through the simple blackout, identifies AA as a deeply self-interested and problematically contradictory recovery program. The demand for confession and the employment of monologue as the exclusive means through which confession is enacted isolates the individual addict from the group (even as the program maintains the importance of group support) and identifies recovery as a type of monologic performance practice with little more than entertainment value (and even that is questionable).[2]

Furthermore, the anxieties that characters like Helen express over the possibility of a future relapse are born out of a treatment movement that always and only saddles the individual with an inescapable, deterministic, and shameful identity (that is, "addict"). Within the doctrine of 12-step recovery, addiction is regarded as akin to a chronic, but manageable, medical condition (hence, the parallel that Lennon draws between alcoholism and AIDS in the

---

2 A seventh season episode of *The Golden Girls*, titled "Ro$e Love$ Mile$," pokes fun at 12-step recovery programs for the obvious commonalities that they share with more conventional forms of entertainment, like the theater. At the outset of the episode, a frustrated Rose (Betty White) returns home following an evening out with boyfriend Miles (Harold Gould) and confides in Blanche (Rue McLanahan) that, of late, Miles has become "really tight ... with his money." As evidence to substantiate her claim that Miles is "frickin' frugal," Rose recounts a recent date during which Miles "snuck [them] into an AA meeting," which Miles refers to as "Theater of the Living ... with free refreshments after."

stage play); addiction, in this respect, stands as a neurobiological always and already to which the individual endlessly is condemned. This misunderstanding of the lived experiences of addiction gains persuasive force and credibility when advanced by members of the medical profession, as it so often is in twenty-first-century America. In the immediate aftermath of Philip Seymour Hoffman's death by overdose, for instance, Dale Archer, a clinical psychiatrist who regularly contributes to *Psychology Today*, penned an article that sought to explain the actor's "relapse after 23 years of sobriety." Titled "Philip Seymour Hoffman: The Curse of Addiction," Archer's article ultimately offers the following explanation for Hoffman's relapse: "Once an addict, always an addict. Regardless of your sex, race or creed, if you're an addict, you're an addict—for life. Addiction is a brain disease. If you go through rehab, you're not cured. You're clean. But you're not cured." The title of Archer's article alone is quite telling with respect to America's long-standing and problematic relationship to addiction. A "curse" in noun form portends misfortune, doom, and evil. To cast addiction as a curse, then, reinforces limited and limiting cultural narratives regarding what it means to be an addict. If addiction is viewed as an unending "curse," and if the addiction and the addict are regarded as synonymous, then those who suffer from the affliction are condemned to an existence circumscribed by unrelenting shame—a cyclic hell-on-earth in which the traumas and the stigmas of addiction endlessly and inevitably recur, world without end.

The philosophy of "Once an addict, always an addict" pervades both *Drunks* and *Blackout*, in which the characters' past addictions haunt their present and, curse-like, portend certain misfortune for their futures. At the same time, this philosophy alludes to the metaphor of waste that is the central preoccupation and concern of the current study. Within this deterministic philosophy, the addict always is fighting a losing battle, even when the addict actively seeks out a recovery program and faithfully works the steps (as Jim and the other characters do in *Drunks*). In some respects, this philosophy implicitly regards 12-step recovery as merely a stopgap—a necessary, albeit ultimately futile, expenditure of time, effort, and emotion, especially since relapse is viewed as a given for the perpetual addict. And, of course, within the narrative arc of *Drunks*, the addition of Jim's parallel storyline drives home the inevitability of relapse, or, in the language of this study, Jim's sobriety is sacrificed in service of a dominant ideology that will always and only paint the addict as morally corrupt, as shameful, as waste. Thus, whether a relapse occurs 23 days or 23 years after the addict becomes "clean"—itself a problematic descriptor that identifies the person in the throes of an addiction as dirty, diseased detritus—the addiction stands as an *a priori* explanation for the addict's inevitable and wayward behaviors, as the curse that portends the addict's moral and physical demise.

Despite similarly stagnant narratives in both *Drunks* and its source text, *Blackout*, it is important to acknowledge the one significant difference between the two texts: namely, the creation of an entirely new, second storyline revolving around Jim's struggles with sobriety once he leaves the meeting. These scenes, interspersed between the confessional monologues spoken by the meeting attendees, take the viewer to various locales in nearby Hell's Kitchen, including a bar where Jim relapses with a series of drinks, a park where Jim purchases some heroin and steals a syringe from a passed out addict, and an apartment where Jim attempts to have sex with a strung-out prostitute. Reviewer Stanley Kauffmann identifies this parallel storyline as the script's single "flaw," observing that it was "obviously inserted to give the film variety" (28). Daniel Kimmel concedes that the screenwriter's "[a]ttempt to open up the action by having Richard Lewis stalk out of the meeting and go off on a binge provides some dramatic moments," but, like Kauffmann, he ultimately argues that the "excursion seems tacked-on in terms of the narrative."

I agree with Kauffmann and Kimmel that the narrative of *Drunks* feels contrived, but I disagree with their fairly superficial conclusions regarding the cause of that contrivance. Of *Drunks*, Director Peter Cohn once remarked while the film was still in production, "The 12-step movement is growing very rapidly and has permeated our society. Hollywood movies deal with it so formulaically within the context of melodrama without really showing what goes on at a meeting" (quoted in Glucksman). This statement from the director of *Drunks* suggests that, at the forefront of this film's approach to representing AA is an insistence on verisimilitude, a desire to create "a documentary slice-of-life in the tradition of Cassavetes and Italian neorealism" (Glucksman). In *Drunks*, Cohn apes the language, the practices, and even the iconography of extra-diegetic 12-step meetings, and, in doing so, he and screenwriter Lennon inadvertently expose in their realistic and contrived narrative many of the contrivances at the heart of the 12-step recovery movement. In this respect, Jim's seemingly "tacked-on" storyline that takes place outside of AA is, in actuality, the very obvious and very orthodox progeny of the recovery movement that this film uncritically celebrates.

The orthodoxy of Jim's narrative—ideologically-speaking—and the seamlessness with which it is incorporated into the narrative fabric of the film are most pointedly revealed in the reverse success narrative, or cautionary tale, developed around Jim's character across this second, parallel storyline. Outside of the rooms, Jim at once appears unmoored from the stagnancy of AA. His character makes choices in the present moment of narrative action, and those choices produce consequences that reverberate in future scenes. Jim himself undergoes marked and dramatic changes between the opening and closing scenes of the film. For example, not only does Jim relapse over the course of the film, but also his addictive behaviors escalate from imbibing alcohol to (almost) shooting up heroin. He also becomes increasingly disheveled and, by the end of the film, Jim appears to be the physical and moral antithesis of his former self. Yet these changes are deceptive, giving the viewer a sense of narrative progress—albeit narrative progress that is predicated on Jim's intrapersonal regression—even as those changes in Jim's character decidedly, seemingly inevitably, return both Jim and the viewer to the very place (location-wise *and* ideologically) where the film began. Stated differently, Jim's return to an AA meeting at the film's close underscores the narrative stagnancy that characterizes *Blackout, Drunks,* and, indeed, 12-step recovery more generally. His confession to the many transgressions of the previous night, so seemingly different from the confession of "I just want to get high" that opened the film, in actuality casts his relapse (an experience, the reader will recall, that is feared by so many of the other members of Jim's original AA group) as an inevitability. Through a book-end effect whereby the beginning and the ending of the film mirror each other, Jim is revealed to be little more than a sacrificial pawn in the film's ideological crusade to glorify 12-step recovery programs. I would suggest, as many others have before me, that extra-diegetic 12-step programs "use" their members in similar ways—the few success stories becoming poster children for the efficacy of the program; the legions of lapsed addicts serving as proof-positive of the need to "work the steps" harder.

Cinematographic Stagnancy

Cinematography further implies much about the film's laudatory attitude toward AA and 12-step recovery programs; simultaneously, cinematography reveals some of the ideological fault lines shared by 12-step programs and the metaphor of waste. As I note above, the narrative of the film alternates fairly evenly between the church basement (where the AA meeting takes place) and various locales in nearby Hell's Kitchen. The opening frames of *Drunks* capture the film's protagonist, Jim, on the streets of New York City. Clad in all black and carrying two paper grocery bags, Jim strides with purpose down sidewalks that are sparsely populated with other human beings despite the fact that the film is set during early evening rush hour. The many storefronts that Jim passes largely are devoid of either action or distraction. Some already are closed for business, their entryways covered over with corrugated tin that appears freshly painted and is noticeably unadorned with graffiti. The streets, too, are noticeably devoid of litter and random debris. In many of the scenes that take place outside of the AA meeting, the director's use of an uncluttered visual frame alludes to the myriad temptations that exist outside of the rooms, and the potential chaos that those temptations portend. In this respect, the emptiness of the visual frame reflects Jim's boundless freedoms—including the freedom of "choice" to relapse—once he is unmoored from AA, but it also suggests (in line with the unwritten philosophy of 12-step recovery) that everything outside of the rooms is a vast wasteland of temptation, sin, and degradation for individuals who always and only will be "drunks," even when they are "on the wagon." The streets are, after all, the location at which Jim takes his first deep swig of liquor after seven months of sobriety. And the streets are the location at which Jim purchases a hit of heroin and, later, steals a needle from a passed out addict. In the end, the street scenes foreshadow Jim's eventual relapse, thereby confirming the 12-step philosophy of "Once an addict, always an addict" through the equation that *Drunks* draws between the world beyond the rooms and moral depravity.

But the streets also are the site at which the addict can wallow in his/her depravity; indeed, the streets encourage and nurture self-destructive behaviors by supplying the addict with access to illicit substances, and by shielding that addict's behaviors from public view (and scorn), a thematic that is visually reflected in Jim's costuming. On one hand, Jim's nondescript black costume echoes the anonymity prescribed by 12-step recovery programs, allowing him to blend seamlessly into the landscape of New York City without being identified or targeted as an "addict." In the opening credit sequence, for example, Jim is one of five persons captured within the visual frame, yet a first-time viewer would be hard pressed to see this image as anything other than an establishing shot populated by extras, especially since Jim's anonymity is underscored by his displacement from the optical center of the frame. At the same time, later in the film, especially during the park sequence in which Jim purchases heroin from a seedy dealer, the nondescript black costume serves as perfect camouflage, literally enfolding Jim within the shadowy recesses of the visual frame and hiding him both from the police (diegetically) and from viewers (extra-diegetically). However, the visual camouflage at once shields *and* shames. That Jim willingly ventures into the dark night, first when he opts to leave the AA meeting early and later when he seeks to purchase drugs in the park, rehearses the deeply-held (if erroneous) belief that addiction is a shameful choice that addicts make over and again, especially given that darkness itself is a traditional symbol that portends evil, sin, and degradation. The visual camouflaging, then, enacts the ideological shaming that AA and other 12-step programs force their membership to endure. That Jim experiences shame at his relapse is narratively revealed through his avoidance of the telephone calls from his AA peers. Moreover, by hiding Jim within the shadows of the park, *Drunks* underscores the equation that 12-step programs insistently draw between relapse (a fairly common, and not always catastrophic, occurrence among persons in recovery) and moral depravity. But the film also suggests (albeit uncritically) that this attitude toward relapse has been internalized by all of the characters, which is not surprising given that, as Dodes and Dodes explain, "If you are in AA and slip, you cannot avoid feeling like a failure, because that's exactly what the system is designed to tell you" (Chapter 8). Some, like Helen, repeatedly endure acts of self-shaming for minor relapses. Most look to a future of what they perceive to be certain relapse with anxiety and dread. All exist within the shadow of their own "inevitable" failure—a failure that is foretold by the very recovery program through which they hope to maintain their sobriety. It is this defeatist ideology that is visually echoed in the film through the many narrative and cinematographic allusions to anonymity—allusions that suggest that, within the big city, it is so easy to visually disappear and to morally get lost.

By contrast, the scenes that take place in the church basement where the AA meeting is set feel cramped, almost claustrophobic. Generally, the interior set is littered with both stage and hand properties that lend verisimilitude to the film, but also gesture toward the insularity of the world of 12-step recovery. In one of the initial scenes of the film, Tony (Sam Rockwell) talks with his sponsor, Jim, about a recent near-relapse and Jim's failure to provide the requisite support during that difficult time. Taking place in a small, cluttered kitchen adjacent to the basement meeting room, this scene stands in sharp visual contrast to the street scene discussed above. The minimal counter space is consumed by an oversized coffee urn, a plastic dish drainer, pan lids, coffee cans, and kitchenalia. The walls are adorned with cabinetry, a calendar, and other items that fill up the visual frame. Even the window ironically contributes to the sense of claustrophobia invoked by the setting with its opaque glass and its ornate grating. For much of the scene, the characters are captured in medium shot—another visual element that simultaneously lends a sense of intimacy and confinement to the cinematography. Similar cinematographic motifs recur across the church basement scenes—from medium and close-up shots crowded by multiple characters to numerous stage properties littered throughout the set. What such motifs allude to is the presumed intimacy of the 12-step community. The physical closeness of the characters within the visual frame, coupled with the myriad props, suggests the emotional support and the insularity that are both cornerstones and selling points of AA and like programs. At the same time, these scenes reflect a strict adherence to rules and structure, suggesting that 12-step recovery will impose order on the chaos of addiction. From the visual iconography of AA (for example, the neat rows of folding chairs, the 12 steps banner) to the language and protocol of 12-step recovery (for example, "My name is Jim, and I'm an alcoholic," the Serenity Prayer), the extra-diegetic structures of the program and its meetings impose narrative and cinematographic order on *Drunks*.

At the same time, the cramped visual frame employed quite liberally throughout the AA scenes alludes (most likely unintentionally) to the restrictiveness of 12-step recovery—that is, to the many written and unwritten mandates that codify lived experience and dictate behavior of those in recovery. AA constitutes a rigidly codified organization, with the 12 Steps and 12 Traditions representing only a handful of the directives that it issues to its members. With chapters titled "There is a Solution," "How It [AA] Works," "Working With Others," "To Wives," and "A Vision For You," *The Big Book of Alcoholics Anonymous* further illustrates the prescriptive approach that the organization takes to the process of recovery. The meetings, too, follow a common "script" that typically varies only in minor ways from group to group (that is, Welcome, Preamble, "How It Works," "12 Traditions," sharing of stories, Serenity Prayer), and, within the meetings, members are expected to conform to guidelines like: Keep confidentiality; Make "I" statements; Stay in the "here and now"; Share feelings; No fixing, or advice giving; No crosstalk. (In my research for this chapter, I actually encountered a number of web resources that provide a "Meeting Script," including not only a general structure, but also specific "lines" that the Chairperson would deliver to the assembled members.)[3] Newcomers are expected to attend "90 in 90" and can only choose a sponsor of the same sex. And all members are inundated with (and "encouraged" to repeat) pithy, arguably even cult-like, slogans and "prayers" intended to help them and their fellow members in their recovery processes: "Let go and let God"; "But for the grace of God go I"; "I am not unique"; and "One day at a time."

The stranglehold that 12-step recovery programs often have over their members is visually reflected in the claustrophobic visual frames that characterize the AA scenes of *Drunks*. In one particular scene that occurs late in the film, for instance, three characters—Louis (Spalding Gray), Tony, and Shelley (Amanda Plummer)—are seated and captured in medium-shot from the viewer's left; these three characters dominate the immediate foreground of the frame. Visible just behind and above those characters' shoulders are the slightly blurred faces of Jasmine (Fanni Green) and Francine (Laurie Taylor-Williams). This shot is especially interesting for the way that it locates the main characters' knees at the optical center of the visual frame, thereby forcing the viewer's angle of vision dramatically upward from a vantage point below the characters. Through the manipulation of perspective, this shot makes the viewer hyper-aware of his/her own position as an onlooker. At the same time, the jam-packed visual frame, as well as the displacement of the speaker, Louis, to the (viewer's) left of the optical center, complicates the viewer's understanding of the narrative that is unfolding on the screen.

---

3 For an illustrative example of how Alcoholics Anonymous meetings are heavily scripted, see the personal webpage of Dr. Darvin Smith, Director of Addictive Behavior Ministries, International.

In effect, the viewer's focus is divided between these five characters pictured in the shot and we are cinematographically coerced into watching all of the characters on screen for a possible explanation of why our attention is visually being diverted from Louis. I would suggest that these cinematographic techniques constitute an unintended allusion to the centrality of policing and surveillance so common in 12-step recovery. In a program like AA, everyone is under the watchful eye of everyone else. Behavior is severely constrained by rules, dictates, expectations, and "traditions." Recovery is confined to a one-size-fits-all model that, in the end, is successful only for a dramatically small percentage of those who initially enter into the program. Newcomers are trained on how to behave in 12-step recovery, and reprimanded when they violate the rules and order of 12-step programs. Sponsors are responsible for keeping themselves and the newcomers in line, and, again, are reprimanded when they fail to do so. Meetings are scripted, and the process of recovery is pre-planned. In the end, it is no wonder that AA and like programs fail so many of the individuals who come to them in desperate need of help and guidance. What such programs claim to offer their members is a way forward, beyond the shame, embarrassment, and degradation of addiction. What such programs actually offer (as Jim's parallel narrative in *Drunks* reveals) is an invitation down what Dodes and Dodes refer to as "the wrong path" (Preface)—that is, a circuitous way back to the wasteful propaganda of metaphor that has defined America's relationship with addiction for over two centuries.

Conclusion

In 2012, filmmaker Greg Williams turned to Kickstater, "the largest funding platform for creative projects in the world," to raise the final $45,000 he needed to complete his documentary film *The Anonymous People* (2013). Conceived as a response to a national dialogue that persistently sensationalizes drug and alcohol problems, "marginalize[s] people suffering from an illness [that is, addiction]," and casts "the addiction epidemic in America … [as] hopeless," *The Anonymous People* regards addiction as "America's most underfinanced public health problem" (Catsoulis) and poses the question: "Why don't we treat addiction in this country like any other health issue?" ("The Path"). Featuring interviews with a handful of "the over 23 million Americans living in long-term recovery from addiction to alcohol and other drugs" (*Many Faces*), including such recognizable public figures as actress Kristen Johnston, former Miss U.S.A. Tara Conner, and former Congressman Jim Ramstad, the film seeks "to transform public attitudes and policies affecting people seeking or in recovery from addiction" (*Many Faces*) by simultaneously identifying some of the root causes for the prevailing national dialogue on addiction and advancing a way forward that is focused on recovery-based solutions. Over the film, Williams implicates a variety of socio-cultural institutions as responsible for the harmful perceptions of addiction that currently haunt addicts, including "a criminal justice system that chooses incarceration over treatment; a news media that revels in drug-fueled celebrity meltdowns while cold-shouldering the productively rehabilitated; and a populace that, by and large, tends to view dependence as the wages of sin rather than an illness" (Catsoulis). Eventually Williams' project would attract 272 backers and well exceed its creator's initial goal, raising $70,061. The resulting feature documentary film, *The Anonymous People*, opened to limited release on 15 August 2013 and opened in New York City on 14 March 2014.

In its very title, the film identifies itself as a direct response to 12-step recovery programs, which insistently assert as one of their foundational tenets the need for secrecy and anonymity in the recovery process. The film's generic and reductive title is employed ironically as a kind of mock homage to the secrecy surrounding 12-step programs that *The Anonymous People* and the recovery programs that it supports refuse to perpetuate. Indeed, from its opening frames, *The Anonymous People* insistently identifies its featured performers by name and advocates a more humane attitude toward addicts. Early in the film, for instance, the "narrative" builds to a climactic moment during which Kristen Johnston (Person in Recovery, Est. 2006) reads from her memoir *Guts: The Endless Follies and Tiny Triumphs of a Giant Disaster* (2012) to an assembled audience. Johnston recalls that once she became sober after a decade of battling a "terrible, terrible, chronic addiction to painkillers and alcohol," a friend from Los Angeles took her aside and warned her to "stop telling everyone that you're sober" because "[the admission] makes people uncomfortable." Johnston's response not only is characterized by the wry wit that pervades Johnston's memoir, but also reflects one of the key philosophies behind the recovery-based treatment movement documented in *The Anonymous People*:

> I left seething. And feeling as if my hand had been slapped, as if he would have *preferred* it if I had gotten trashed and puked on his shoes. As if I was *supposed* to be embarrassed that I was sober. As if I should keep my mouth shut like a good little sober girl.
> It made me feel like a Freak. That's when I remembered that comments like that are the entire reason I wrote *GUTS* .... I refuse to feel ashamed of who I am. I most certainly won't be embarrassed that I'm an addict. So screw my career or my privacy or other people's sensibilities. I'll tell whomever I damn well please. (261–2)

The refusal to "keep [her] mouth shut like a good little sober girl" harkens (at least most recently) to the 1980s when "naming names" through a grassroots political/creative endeavor like the NAMES Project AIDS Quilt was regarded as an anti-establishment political act in the culture of secrecy and hatred that Ronald Reagan helped to build around the newly-emergent medical crisis. In a similar way, the insistence on speaking the truth of one's addiction without fear or embarrassment serves as a powerful contemporary illustration of the enduring legacy of silence and shame in this country, as well as a powerful reminder that, in twenty-first-century America, silence still equals death. As Johnston writes, "[Addiction] is *our* black plague … It is destroying people by the untold millions. And I believe, without a doubt, that the shame and the secrecy that shroud the disease are just as deadly as the disease itself" (262).

The Anonymous People suggests that, in a relatively small way, the rhetoric around addiction in twenty-first-century America is shifting toward a less restrictive, less deterministic understanding of the condition. To self-identify as a "person in recovery," as opposed to "an addict," or "a drunk," marks an important conceptual and temporal break between addiction and sobriety that is unprecedented, at least in America. The moniker "person in recovery" unsettles the cycle of shame that casts addiction as an inescapable curse and, unlike 12-step programs, it insists on a present and a future unencumbered by an addicted past. To be sure, the recovery movement is not about denial, as some of its detractors would have us believe, and neither does it misunderstand the nature of addiction (another common counterargument raised against the movement). Instead, the recovery movement is centrally concerned with empowering the person in recovery, with offering hope for a future lived outside of the "curse" of addiction. No longer an "addict" divested of self-authority because of his/her "immoral choices," the "person in recovery" is recognized first and foremost *as a person*—a flawed and deeply human person, to be sure, but a person with autonomy, with self-respect, and, finally, with hope. And *The Anonymous People* is, without question, hopeful. In contrast to decades'-old attitudes that regard addiction as an albatross around the neck of the morally corrupt, the film suggests, quite simply, that recovery is possible, not as a momentary pause on the circuitous path toward inevitable relapse (the very path that the protagonist of *Drunks,* Jim, follows), but as a stepping stone on the journey elsewhere, perhaps even beyond the metaphor of waste. Certainly, the recovery movement takes us, as a culture, beyond the Draconian dictates that advance abstinence (a virtually impossible goal for many persons in recovery) as the only moral and healthy route to sobriety. It circumvents the wasteland of shame and blame that America has built on the backs of addicts at least since the nineteenth century and erects in its stead a foundation of self-respect, community support, and visibility-as-empowerment. It demands that individuals take ownership of their histories, of their addictions, and ultimately of their futures and, in doing so, to refuse to be saddled with a one-size-fits-all identity that always and only leads to moral degradation, self-destruction, and waste. It refuses to accept shame and embarrassment as the inevitable consequences of addiction and empowers the addict to assert the terms and conditions of his/her own sobriety. It teaches us to persevere. It encourages optimism. And, finally, it adamantly rejects anonymity and silence—both as a prerequisite to recovery and as a practice of sobriety.

In the next part of *Wasted*, I turn my attention to an examination of some of the ways in which the metaphor of waste has impacted and continues to impact how twenty-first-century Americans perceive, legislate, treat, and experience addiction. In Chapter 5, I suggest that contemporary anti-drug campaigns often target already disenfranchised groups as both their subject matter and their primary viewing audience, thereby producing a "boomerang effect" that potentially can intensify deeply-entrenched forms of institutionalized oppression, can inhibit an addict's willingness to seek and/or ability to complete treatment, and can exacerbate other related social problems facing such risk groups (including poverty, homelessness, increased incidence of depression and suicide, and/or increased rates of sexually-transmitted infections). The final chapter of this study returns to some of the issues around American nationalism introduced in the first chapter of *Wasted*, most particularly the idea that addiction constitutes a locus of social control by which American citizenship is regulated and the "nation" itself is imagined, demarcated, and contained. Through a reading of the life, celebrity persona, and death of pop icon Whitney Houston, I suggest a set of consequences of the metaphor of waste that extend beyond the individual to the collective.

PART III
Performing Wasted Lives

Chapter 5

"Real People With Real Stories":[1] Anti-Drug PSAs, the Propagation of Stereotypes, and the Boomerang Effect[2]

It has long been assumed, of course, that guilt and shame were ideal ways of warning of the dangers associated with binge drinking and other harmful behaviors, because they are helpful in spotlighting the associated personal consequences. But … [v]iewers already feeling some level of guilt or shame instinctively resist messages that rely on those emotions, and in some cases are more likely to participate in the behavior they're being warned about.

Jeremy Mullman, *Advertising Age*

Often alternatively referred to as "the theory of psychological reactance," boomerang effect theory maintains that forms of persuasive communication sometimes can result in unintended attitude and behavioral changes in the message recipient, depending on the audience, purpose, tone, and content of the communication. Boomerang effect theory dates at least to the 1953 publication of *Communication and Persuasion* and, in subsequent decades, has engaged the intellectual interest of all manner of social and behavioral psychologists, communication scholars, and marketing professionals. Many of these scholars widely believe that anti-drug PSAs are particularly likely to produce a boomerang effect among their target viewers. In "Social Marketing Messages That May Motivate Irresponsible Consumption Behavior," Cornelia Pechmann and Michael D. Slater examine what they term the "'dark side' to social marketing campaigns," noting, "social marketers often try to alter major lifestyle decisions, which may increase the potential for adverse effects"

---

1 This phrase is taken from a March 2013 statement made by Dr. Tom Frieden, Director of the U.S. Centers for Disease Control and Prevention. In the statement, Frieden discusses the effectivity of the CDC's *Tips from Former Smokers* campaign, which he declared an unequivocal success *while* the advertisements were airing primarily because the advertisements feature "real people with real stories" (quoted in Koch).

2 A previous version of this chapter was presented at the Global Queerness conference at The College of Wooster in October 2012.

(185). This claim is echoed by Jason T. Siegel and Judee K. Burgoon, who, in their co-authored article "Expectancy Theory Approaches to Prevention: Violating Adolescent Expectations to Increase the Effectiveness of Public Service Announcements," suggest simply that "[t]he wrong advertisement at best will be ignored and at worst will cause a boomerang effect" (177). And writing about a 2010 study conducted at Northwestern University's Kellogg School of Management, *Advertising Age* contributor Jeremy Mullman suggests that anti-drug PSAs that rely on the use of scare tactics are especially prone to the boomerang effect, noting that while "[i]t has long been assumed that guilt and shame were ideal ways of warning of the dangers associated with binge drinking and other harmful behaviors," "[v]iewers already feeling some level of guilt or shame instinctively resist messages that rely on those emotions, and in some cases are more likely to participate in the behavior they're being warned about."

While the operations of the boomerang effect are fairly well-documented, the reason why certain messages have this effect and certain other messages do not is open for some debate. Some attribute the effect to simple curiosity. As *Popular Science* contributor Shaunacy Ferro explains, "When anti-drug ads say 'don't do drugs,' they inherently bring up the implicit question 'Should I do drugs?' The ads can draw attention to a gap in what the viewer knows about drugs, making them more curious." Others attribute the effect to the attitude that a particular message adopts toward its receiver. For instance, Nidhi Agrawal, a marketing professor at Northwestern University, suggests that "people who are already feeling guilt or shame resort to something called 'defensive processing' when confronted with more of either, and tend to disassociate themselves with whatever they are being shown in order to lessen those emotions" (Leah). For other audience members, such ads can seem condescending. Richard Todd Aguayo of Razorsharp Creative explains, "You can speak words of wisdom to someone, but unless they feel you understand where they're coming from, they'll just tune you out" (quoted in Leah). In addition to the tone of the advertisements, the audience and the content also are likely candidates for why some messages boomerang. Michael Slater of The Ohio State University regards resistance to anti-drug scare tactics as sometimes indicative of where an audience member is (developmentally and chronologically) in his/her life cycle. Of teenagers, who constitute some of the most resistant receivers of anti-drug advertisements, Slater asserts, "Research shows that at least half of teens are sensation-seeking. Taking chances is exciting. It's developmentally part of being a teenager to buck adult rules and take moderate risks. Drug use is implicitly seen as a way to become autonomous and independent from your parents and everybody else" (quoted in Ferro). Finally, in some of the earliest research conducted into this topic, Jack W. Brehm and Sharon S. Brehm contend that persuasive messages that seek to restrict an individual's autonomy can result in acts of resistance—especially among an American audience that regards "freedom" as an inalienable entitlement of citizenship.

This chapter is centrally concerned with the concept of the "boomerang effect" and its potential to disrupt the intended messages of contemporary anti-drug PSAs. Here, I examine Public Service Announcements (or, PSAs) from two different anti-drug campaigns produced and "marketed" in the United States over the past decade: *Faces of Meth* (2004, hereafter *Faces*) and *Tips from Former Smokers* (2012, hereafter *Tips*). While these two campaigns alone could not sufficiently represent the entire genre of anti-drug PSAs, they do constitute a fairly diverse cross-section of that genre. *Tips*, for example, is a national campaign conceived and disseminated by the foremost public health agency of the United States government (that is, the Centers for Disease Control and Prevention, or CDC), whereas *Faces* derives from, focuses on, and serves a more local community. Together the campaigns focus on two different addictive substances—methamphetamine (that is, *Faces*) and nicotine (that is, *Tips*)—and target two different audiences—high schoolers in Oregon (that is, *Faces*) and a national audience of smokers aged 18 to 54 (that is, *Tips*). Finally, the campaigns differ in terms of production and distribution. *Tips* includes print, television, internet, and radio advertisements, and *Faces* is disseminated in non-traditional formats (for example, posters, web-based slideshow).

Despite these differences, both campaigns share at least two significant commonalities. First, in purpose, such advertisements seek to prevent, or curb, the use of controlled/illicit substances among a specific subset of the American populace. Second, in form, these advertisements rely on the graphic presentation of the consequences of substance abuse as a means of scaring their viewers "straight."

More speculative than certain, this chapter nonetheless paints a not-so-hypothetical portrait of the ways in which scare tactic PSAs, or what has commonly been termed "health terrorism," potentially can impact the lived experiences of twenty-first-century American addicts. My argument here is grounded in two foundational claims: 1) that such PSAs so often are premised on and unproblematically reinforce the metaphor of waste; and 2) that, in so doing, such PSAs not only are likely to be ineffective at curbing drug use, but also possibly could have precisely the opposite effect of what was intended. Throughout the chapter, I discuss and explore the kinds of devastating consequences that this "boomerang effect" potentially can have with respect to the treatment and recovery of addicts who self-identify with one or more historically "marginal" groups.

On Being a White Trash Meth Head in Oregon

Faces of Meth is a community-based, grassroots, anti-drug campaign that, in its original iteration, strived to educate Oregon teens about the devastating physical consequences of an addiction to methamphetamine. (Although the campaign remains firmly grounded in and targeted to Oregonians, its educational materials have been adopted in middle and high school curricula across the county.) The name of the project alludes—whether self-consciously or no—to the 1978 mondo film, *Faces of Death*, a controversial "shockumentary" that allows its viewers to "bear witness to death in its many forms—even visiting a debauched death cult that mixes the ecstasy of sex with the sweet release of that final moment" (Buchanan). The mondo film typically "consist[s] of compiled camera footage of murders, suicides, accidents, assassinations, and other real-life disasters" (Brottman 167); as an exemplar of that genre, *Faces of Death* compiled both stock footage of real deaths (for example, Vietnam being bombed with napalm and seals being clubbed) and fabricated death scenes into a exploitative mélange of guts, gore, and gruesomeness. While *Faces* avoids some of the more sensational flourishes (both stylistically and content-wise) of the mondo film, the project shares with its filmic namesake a commitment to raw and gritty verisimilitude as the central means through which to shock its audience into a shift of perspective or mindset. The project began in 2004 when Bret King, a Deputy Sheriff in Oregon's Multnomah County, and his colleagues in the Classification Unit were sorting through arrest records "to identify people who had been in custody more than once" for methamphetamine use (*Faces of Meth*). In an interview with Carl Quintanilla of NBC News, King recalls that during this process, he began to notice a disturbing trend in some of the repeat offender mug shots: "There were a few cases where the changes that had taken place due to the methamphetamine use were so extreme, that we didn't realize the person was who they were." Through a juxtapositioning of Before and After mug shots of persons repeatedly arrested for methamphetamine use, King says, he sought to "create a realistic presentation about methamphetamine"—not "something that made people curious about a drug" and not "a scared straight program," but a factual account of the ravages that methamphetamine exacts on a person's body (*Faces of Meth*). The project was first publicized in a 28 December 2004 article that ran in *The Oregonian* and subsequently has spawned a poster and a video slideshow that has been used in high schools throughout the country to educate teenagers about the potential dangers of using methamphetamine.

The central conceit of the *Faces* campaign is the use of time-lapse photograph pairings to document in graphic visual form the physical changes that prolonged methamphetamine use exacts on a body. This pairing of Before and After photographs constitutes a fairly common form of visual argument that is employed throughout a wide variety of advertising genres but that is especially prevalent in advertisements for health and beauty products and services. From Jenny Craig and Weight Watchers to Rogaine and Proactiv Plus, such advertisements "sell" their services and products through an implicit (or, sometimes, explicit) causal narrative that documents the "improvement" of the "character" or spokesperson featured in the advertisement as a result of engaging the featured service or using the featured product. The earlier, Before photograph identifies the human subject as flawed in some manner. Given that such photographs typically must convey the entire (usually harrowing) backstory of the character/spokesperson, the "flaws" of the person often are accentuated, if not exaggerated. This strategy not only allows a reading audience to quickly grasp the narrative being built across the Before and After photographs, but also dramatically heightens the contrast between the two photographs, thereby suggesting that the product is even more effective than it perhaps actually is. The later, After photograph pictures the human subject in a much improved state. When juxtaposed, the Before and After photographs put forth a Pygmalion narrative and their effectiveness in persuading viewers to engage the featured service or purchase the featured product turns on the believability and desirability of the subject's transformation.

In anti-drug campaigns like *Faces*, this Pygmalion narrative is reversed. Instead of offering viewers a promise of self-improvement and personal happiness (both iterations of the classic American Dream mythos that necessitates progress in myriad forms as an *a priori*), *Faces* offers viewers a warning, or, more precisely, several interrelated warnings. To understand the kinds of messages that such advertisements communicate about drug use and addiction, and why they have the potential to produce a boomerang effect, I want to look specifically at the poster that the Multnomah County Sheriff's Office has produced and disseminated widely to educators, parents, and other interested parties by way of its website. The poster measures 17" x 22" in size and is visually anchored by four sets of Before and After mug shots of varying sizes. The viewer's eye immediately is drawn to the title "the faces of meth: before and after," which is printed in large, block letters just above the optical center of the page. The word "meth" is the only part of the title that is printed in bright red—the remainder of the title being printed in muted grey—and this use of selective color very effectively works to identify the central concern of this anti-drug PSA. The term "meth" sits atop two large mug shots of a woman who, over a period of "3 years, 5 months," as indicated by the photograph caption, is much altered in appearance. Adjacent to the large mug shot pairing that comprises a significant portion of the center of the poster is a block of red text that reads: "One addict said it's the closest thing to becoming a living zombie. 'I can't stand to look at myself in the mirror,' she says." Although the quotation here is not attributed to the woman whose much-altered appearance stares out through dead eyes in the mug shot directly to the right of the quote, the dotted vertical lines that section off this quote and the large-scale photographs from the other mug shot pairings in the poster encourage viewers to make this leap. At the top of the poster, in smaller font than the poster title, is a block of text that reads: "Methamphetamine destroys the mind and body. Jail photos show only a hint of the drug's devastation. Meth eats away at brain tissue, accelerates blood pressure, creates psychosis and causes the body to overheat. Teeth fall out. The body stops craving food, and only wants the drug." These statements take on even greater menace given that all but the second sentence is printed in bold red font. Along the left-hand side of the poster is a thin column that runs from the middle of the poster (just under the title) to the bottom of the page and contains one mug shot pairing, much smaller in size than any of the three other pairings included on the poster, and a series of web addresses and telephone numbers for addiction treatment services, all of which are printed in the same bold red as the word "meth." Along the right-hand side of the poster is a thin column that contains, from top to bottom, *The Oregonian* logo, an acknowledgement of a partnership between the newspaper and the Sheriff's office, and two mug shot pairings, much smaller in size than the one included in the center of the poster, but slightly larger than the one included in the thin left-hand column.

That this poster is intended to serve as a warning to its viewers is instantly conveyed through the color scheme chosen by its designers. The severe red stands out in sharp contrast against the neutral black background, thereby accentuating and immediately drawing the viewer's attention to all of the text that is printed in that color, but especially to the word "meth," which is overwhelmingly the largest of any printed text on the page. By printing the word "meth" just above the optical center of the page in large, block red letters, the designers immediately identify and draw the viewer's attention to the subject matter of the poster as well as the attitude that they adopt—and that they hope their viewers will adopt—toward that subject. The color red typically is associated with objects that warn (for example, stop signs), that signal danger (for example, fire trucks), and/or that symbolize intense emotional investment (for example, roses). Here, viewers see the word "meth" and instantly (though probably subconsciously) identify it as a threat, a menace, a danger simply because of the size and color of that text. That the word "meth" is linked (both by size and by visual adjacency) to the two largest and most graphic photographs on the page is not a coincidence. This Before-and-After pairing that runs down the very center of the poster documents in stark detail the dramatic transformation of one woman who has been arrested on multiple occasions for methamphetamine use. In the Before photograph, the woman appears youthful, vibrant, "normal." Her complexion is ruddy, her eyes are alive, and her hair is well-groomed and shiny. By contrast, in the After photograph, which, according to the caption, was taken "3 years, 5 months later," the woman from the earlier photograph is virtually unrecognizable. Her complexion has taken on a deathly pallor. Her face is etched with deep lines around her mouth and above her eyebrows. Her hair is unkempt and her eyes are dull, near lifeless. The causal link that this poster encourages its viewers to draw between the drug and its effects is underscored by the reverse Pygmalion narrative that vividly demonstrates the physical devolution of this methamphetamine addict. This reverse Pygmalion narrative is rendered even more compelling through the allusion that this campaign makes to its mondo film namesake—an allusion that poetically and causally links "meth" and "death." Of course, the equation drawn between methamphetamine use and death reiterates a deeply-entrenched cultural narrative that, for American audiences, is at once hauntingly familiar and deeply frightening in its familiarity, which supposedly only works to heighten the intended effect of scaring viewers into sobriety.

Although the "Meth = Death" thematic recurs in a variety of ways throughout the poster, it is perhaps most noticeable (and, arguably, impactful) in the rhetoric that is used to contextualize and explain the photograph pairings. Here, the designers employ emotionally charged terms and phrases (for example, "psychosis" or "eats away at brain tissue" or "living zombie") to heighten the intensity of the message and to produce an even greater fear-effect for the viewer. The active verbs (for example, "destroys," "accelerates," "stops") coupled with the clipped, simple sentences underline the urgency of the message and, again, heighten the fear-effect for the viewer. Of equal importance is how ambiguity is employed as a scare tactic. In the text box included in the upper-left-hand quadrant of the poster, the designers note: "Jail photos show only a hint of the drug's devastation." Tellingly this statement is printed in muted gray text, which has the effect of de-emphasizing the visual and rhetorical impact of its subject—an unusual choice for a campaign that supposedly finds its persuasive momentum in the contrast that is drawn between the Before and After mug shots. The implication here is that the photographs, while perhaps shocking and disturbing, offer only a glimpse into the "devastation" that methamphetamine use exacts on the human body. In other words, the designers want viewers to conclude something like: "If you think methamphetamine is bad for your physical appearance, you should see what these mug shots cannot show you." The ambiguity here is in many ways more compelling than the explicit display of physical deterioration because its fear-effect turns on the unknowable and the unshowable.

The threat of imprisonment also is central to the *Faces* campaign's persuasive appeal, serving as the intended moral and legal deterrent for developing or sustaining an addiction to methamphetamine. That the campaign is visually focused on police mug shots ideologically reinforces the equation between working-class whiteness, addiction, and criminality, and the stereotypical take-away message appears to be that working-class whites are *de facto* methamphetamine addicts and criminals. The arrest and imprisonment of the featured addicts (consequences implied by the very existence of these mug shots) clearly identifies some of the unseemly effects of addiction; at the same time, the very public revelation of both the addictions and the subsequent arrests is employed as a shaming device. In other words, the act of making an addict's transgressions visible to a national audience works to humiliate the addict (both ones featured in the campaign and ones who are not) by reinforcing an implied standard of normality with respect to American citizenship—a standard that is predicated on sobriety, affluence, Puritanical morality, and legality. Furthermore, there is even a suggestion, subtle though that suggestion may be, that prolonged methamphetamine abuse can lead to other legal infractions: namely, sexual immorality/impropriety. On first glance at the After mug shot located in the upper-right-hand corner of the poster, the female addict appears to be nude—an observation that, at least for me, was strengthened by the marked contrasts between the Before and the After photographs. In the Before shot, which was taken at a slightly greater distance away from the woman than the After shot, viewers see the left and right neckline of what appears to be a black mesh jersey. In the extreme close-up After shot, only a sliver of what might be fabric is visible in the bottom-most right-hand corner of the mug shot, and this sliver of possible fabric is not immediately noticeable. The suggestion of nudity in what is obviously a police mug shot alludes (whether intentionally or not) to the long-held stereotype that female addicts engage in prostitution and returns viewers to the nineteenth-century notion (as discussed in Chapter 2) that addiction "leads to neglect of duty, moral degradation and crime."

The *Faces* campaign, however, does not merely peddle predictable warnings regarding the dangers of prolonged drug use, though; it also trades in the traffick of stereotypes, identifying working-class whiteness as synonymous with methamphetamine addiction and casting both as abjections. Of course, stereotypes are quite common in advertisements generally and PSAs specifically, in part because they allow for the kind of rapid exchange of information that is a prerequisite of the genre. Citing psychologist Gordon W. Allport, cultural critic Duane Carr in his book *A Question of Class: The Redneck Stereotype in Southern Fiction* (1996) notes that "[t]he function of a stereotype ... is to justify or rationalize our acceptance or rejection of a particular group. It also acts as 'a screening or selective device to maintain simplicity in perception and in thinking'" (8). According to this logic, the stereotype constitutes an ideally suited rhetorical device for advertisements, a kind of visual shorthand that allows narratives, themes, and persuasive appeals to be conveyed to viewers in the two seconds or fewer that they typically spend engaging with a print advertisement (Sutherland). Moreover, because stereotypes typically are grounded in controversial oversimplifications and/or -generalizations about a group of people, they can serve as the necessary "hook" needed to draw the viewer into the advertisement within the initial 0.3 seconds of engagement (Grimm) and potentially can keep the viewer looking at the advertisement for a longer period of time, which can lead to greater recall of the message ("Make Ads 'Stick'"). The stereotypes being trafficked in the *Faces* campaign center on a particular class-based identity construct that, in the vernacular of American English, is commonly termed "white trash." In *Not Quite White: White Trash and the Boundaries of Whiteness* (2006), Matt Wray examines the "disturbing liminality" of working-class whiteness, suggesting that it constitutes "a monstrous, transgressive identity of mutually violating boundary terms, a dangerous threshold state of being neither one nor the other" (2). Wray specifically focuses his attention on the moniker "white trash," an identity construct that, he argues, speaks to the tension between race and class in America. He writes, "[S]plit *white trash* in two again and read the meanings of each: *white* now appears an ethnoracial signifier, and *trash*, a signifier of abject class status. The term conflates these two aspects of social identity into an inseparable state of being, suggesting that if we are to understand *white trash* and the condition it names, we must confront the multithreaded nature of social inequality" (3). The moniker "white trash," then, enacts a devaluation of the typically privileged signifier "white" by its coupling with the term "trash." "Trash," in this iteration, not only refers to, but also derives from, a low socioeconomic status. Thus, class renders "whiteness" as marginal, as Other, and ultimately as abject in a culture where the presumed and privileged median in terms of socioeconomic status is "comfortably middle-class." It is this "disturbing liminality" of working-class whiteness, a liminality that is conflated with methamphetamine addiction, that is exploited as a potentially persuasive scare tactic in the *Faces* campaign.

The *Faces* campaign repeatedly references deeply-entrenched stereotypes not only of methamphetamine addicts, but also, and perhaps quite coincidentally, of working-class whites (aka "white trash"). Of course, I am neither the only nor the first critic to observe the simultaneous vilification of the working class and methamphetamine addicts in cultural representations about addiction generally, or in the *Faces* campaign specifically. In their co-authored article, titled "'This is your face on meth': The Punitive Spectacle of 'White Trash' in the Rural War on Drugs," Travis Linnemann and Tyler Wall seek to "unpack the popular 'white trash meth head' trope" employed in a variety of anti-drug PSAs, ultimately arguing that "the Faces of Meth campaign powerfully demonstrates how images and visuality are key features of contemporary punishment" (317). For Columbia University researcher Carl Hart, the vilification of methamphetamine in twenty-first-century

America represents only the most recent iteration of America's long-standing problematic relationship with illicit substances. Hart suggests that, much like crack in the 1980s, methamphetamine has become the scapegoat drug for Americans (and, more specifically, the American media) in the current historical moment. He goes on to argue that "the dangers of meth are exaggerated today just like the dangers of crack were blown out of proportion three decades ago" (Short). Of particular concern to Hart is the way in which media reports about the drug, buttressed by so-called "scientific evidence," consistently stigmatize and vilify two groups of people that are most likely to develop an addiction to the drug: the poor and gay men. Hart's report cites as context for his conclusions a comment by former Oklahoma Governor Frank Keating in 1999: "It's a white trash drug—methamphetamines largely are consumed by the lower socio-economic element of white people and I think we need to shame it …. Just like crack cocaine was a black trash drug and is a black trash drug" (quoted in Short).

The *Faces* campaign underlines the equation that often is drawn between working-class whiteness and abjection by visually highlighting a variety of unseemly aspects of the addicts' physical appearances. On first glance, all four of the Before and After mug shot pairings advance the idea that methamphetamine abuse alone causes the premature aging of the addict, even though the actual chronological ages of the featured addicts are not revealed to the viewer. From the first mug shot to the second, all of the featured addicts visually age, some (like the woman at the optical center of the poster) quite dramatically. Hair becomes more unkempt and gray. Wrinkles accumulate and are etched even more deeply in the gaunt faces of the addicts. And, of course, the juxtapositioning of the Before and After mug shots only works to accentuate the dramatic weight loss that all of the featured addicts experienced in the time that lapsed between the earlier and the later photographs. The implication is that the physical wasting, or deterioration, of the addict's body is the direct result of drug use—a not-unsurprising observation given that this drug, "like other stimulants, suppresses appetite and can lead to undernourishment … Over time, the body begins consuming muscle tissue and facial fat, giving users a gaunt, hollowed-out appearance" ("Why Meth Users Have Sores"). Interestingly, physical emaciation also and simultaneously references stereotypes of working-class whiteness, an identity construct that, in media representations, often is linked to poor lifestyle (in this case, dietary) choices. But what the *Faces* campaign neglects to reveal is whether other environmental or lifestyle conditions might have contributed to the emaciated and prematurely aged appearance that is exploited for fear-effect in all of the After mug shots. Viewers simply and uncritically are supposed to accept the equation implicitly drawn between methamphetamine use, working-class whiteness, and bodily aging/wasting—and, of course, many viewers will do so because that kind of stereotypical misunderstanding of class and oversimplification of addiction is so deeply ingrained in the minds of twenty-first-century Americans.

All of the featured addicts, too, suffer from obvious dermatological issues, with two of them sporting the bright red facial blemishes that have become a kind of visual shorthand for the "formication" (or, a tactile hallucination of bugs crawling beneath the skin) that often accompanies that addiction; these blemishes are intended to serve as a confirmation of a methamphetamine addiction. I would suggest that it is not a coincidence that the creators of this campaign selected mug shots that highlight a skin condition linked to insect infestation (albeit an imagined one). The presence of formication in these mug shots underlines the wide-spread cultural belief that addicts are "dirty" or unclean (literal white *trash*) in both a physical and a moral sense. But it also reinforces certain class-based stigmas that identify the working class (also commonly, though erroneously, conflated with "white trash") as lacking good hygiene. In the *Faces* campaign, then, the metaphor of waste simultaneously manifests itself in a variety of interesting forms. On one hand, the metaphor becomes an identity construct that at once implicates an individual's addiction and class status. At the same time, the metaphor is made manifest in both the narratives that this campaign spins about its subjects and in the ideological reverberations of those narratives. *Faces* encourages viewers to see the real addicts who are featured within its campaign not as human beings who are struggling with a very real and very serious mental illness, but as mere pedagogical props to be used and then discarded (that is, thrown in jail, tossed back onto the street without being given access to treatment, and so on) once their use-value has been served.[3] There is no follow-up to the

---

3 When actor Philip Seymour Hoffman died of acute mixed drug intoxication on 2 February 2014, his death initially registered shock in mainstream and social media and many were quick to reminiscence about the man's life, celebrate the actor's body of work, and speculate about his enduring legacy. But very quickly—within hours, in fact—Hoffman was transformed into one of these pedagogical props to which I refer above, his death-by-overdose becoming a touchstone for a myriad of conversations that had little actually to do with the man himself. Many of these conversations focused on a new, deadly strain of fentanyl-laced heroin that, at the time of Hoffman's death, was responsible for the deaths of over 80 Americans, even though all of these articles concede that "[i]nvestigators in New York tested the heroin found in [Hoffman's] apartment for fentanyl, but found that it did not include the additive" ("Lethal New Mix"). Some journalists questioned whether Hollywood should "do more for troubled stars" (Kendall), while others mined Hoffman's death for "Lessons in Struggles with Mental Illness, Addiction" (Cocca). Later, following the suicide of comedian and fellow addict Robin Williams in August 2014, some reporters used the deaths of both men as a platform for initiating a conversation about why some people "grieve dead celebrities" (Murphy, Tim). And, in what is perhaps the strangest example of how Hoffman, in

narratives that are glimpsed in snapshot form in the *Faces* campaign. There is no concern registered or encouraged for what happens to the addicts once the mug shot is captured. There is always and only just that single moment of despair, humiliation, and degradation. *Faces*, then, is an anti-drug campaign that exclusively focuses on exploiting the "rock bottom"—a narrative trope manufactured and peddled by 12-step programs—as a shaming device. In this respect, the addicts featured in the *Faces* campaign represent just another disposable commodity in the river of trash that is America's consumer culture. And it is precisely this underlying attitude toward addicts—and toward those, like the poor and gay men, who are most likely to develop a particular addiction—that marks this campaign as especially likely to boomerang.

What the *Faces* campaign implicitly conveys to its viewers is a paternalistic narrative that regards white, working-class methamphetamine addicts as an object lesson in enforced sobriety. At its core, the campaign speaks from a position of knowledge and authority, deriving as it does from a law enforcement agency, and it seeks to protect viewers from the horrors of addiction that the speaker (that is, the Multnomah County Sheriff's office) has seen; in this respect, the paternalistic tone that the campaign adopts initially seems well-suited to its speaker and message. But paternalistic messages rarely are received as pure altruism and often register as condescending. In the case of *Faces*, the campaign condescends to the viewer first by building its argument on unsteady logical grounds. Missing from the poster are vital pieces of information that would help the viewer to determine the validity of the argument. How old are these subjects? Might the physical aging that is depicted in the mug shot pairings be the result of "natural" aging processes, rather than drug use? Might there be other health, environmental, or lifestyle factors that contributed to the physical deterioration of the subjects? Moreover, are these subjects representative of methamphetamine users? Or are they "worse case scenarios" who erroneously are being exploited as typical? By withholding this (and other) information, and presenting the faulty argument as "fact," the *Faces* campaign identifies the viewer as either stupid or gullible, neither of which is a particularly flattering or

---

death, metamorphosed into an educational prop at the mercy of the mass media, his "tragedy" was used to "Shine a Bright Light on Estate Planning" (Lacey). What all of these examples illustrate is a particular manifestation of the metaphor of waste by which the addict (whether celebrity or not) is divested of autonomy and identity and rendered an object to be exploited for "educational" ends. As such, the addict is worthless (trash, garbage, refuse, waste) except as a vehicle through which to convey a message. A similar rhetorical strategy is at work in the *Faces* campaign, whereby the "Just Say 'No'" message is privileged over the "speakers" whose lives and addictions convey that message.

desirable identity to inhabit, if only for the two or so seconds it takes to engage with the PSA.

Not only does the campaign demean the viewer through its touting of a markedly flawed argument as fact, but also it imposes limits on the viewer's autonomy—a gesture that actively challenges some of the core tenets of American citizenship. The desire to protect, so central to the *Faces* campaign, typically is predicated on the imposition of limits. States, for example, limit the conditions under which teenagers can operate a motor vehicle as a means of protecting them from their own potential for reckless boundary-pushing, as well as the inherent risks in operating a two-ton machine in the absence of significant prior experience. Parents, too, often impose a curfew (a temporal limit) as a means of teaching self-discipline, but also as a means of protecting their progeny from the myriad dangers associated with "things that go bump in the night." In a similar manner, scare tactic anti-drug campaigns like *Faces* place demands (read limits) on the viewer's behavior as a means of protecting that viewer from the ravages of addiction. In this poster, for example, the mug shot photographs convey an implied warning regarding the impact (both health-wise and legal) that prolonged methamphetamine use will have on an addict; in doing so, the mug shot becomes an edict against a limit that must not be transgressed: "Do not smoke meth unless you want to end up like these addicts." While this message certainly is well-intentioned and makes more logical sense than some of the proffered claims in the *Faces* campaign, it nonetheless can register as patronizing precisely because it prescribes a behavior and an attitude for the viewer and demands that the viewer accept that behavior and attitude without question or consideration. In so doing, the PSA installs the collective at the helm of personal choice while stripping the individual of sovereignty. In other words, *Faces* privileges the institution over the individual, homogeneity over diversity, conformity over autonomy. The scare tactics employed throughout the PSA serve as a means of strongarming the viewer into acquiescence of what is revealed to be a very *un-American* Dream. Both of these tactics, then, ultimately undermine the long-standing spirit of American individualism and self-reliance and suggest why this campaign not only might not have its desired effects, but also might encourage viewers to engage in precisely the behaviors that it seeks to curb.

On Being a Terminally Ill Former Smoker in America

Tips From Former Smokers is a national anti-smoking campaign launched (and funded) by the Centers for Disease Control and Prevention (CDC) in March 2012, the first-ever paid national tobacco education campaign. To date, the CDC has produced two waves of advertisements in the campaign—first for

12 weeks in 2012 and then again in 2013—and has spent over $100 million in its efforts to convince current smokers that smoking causes severe and long-term health effects on the body and now is the time to quit ("Anti-Smoking Activist"). Featuring "real smokers" telling their "real stories" about "living with serious long-term health effects from smoking and secondhand smoke exposure," the campaign strives to reach an audience of smokers ages 18 to 54 and boasts of three interrelated goals. First, *Tips* seeks to "[b]uild public awareness of the immediate health damage caused by smoking and exposure to secondhand smoke." Second, the campaign strives to "[e]ncourage smokers to quit and make free help available." Finally, the campaign "encourage[s] smokers not to smoke around others and nonsmokers to protect themselves and their families from secondhand smoke" ("Campaign Overview"). Primarily distributed on television and online as 30-second PSAs, the campaign spots focus on all manner of smoking-related health issues, from cancer, to heart disease, to stroke, to chronic obstructive pulmonary disease (or, COPD), and Buerger's disease. The CDC maintains that the campaign has been incredibly effective at achieving its stated goals. It was reported in the 9 September 2013 issue of *The Lancet* that "[a]n estimated 1.64 million Americans tried to quit smoking because of the campaign" and "[a]t least 100,000 smokers are expected to stay quit for good" ("Frequently Asked Questions"). The CDC also cites as evidence of the campaign's "effectiveness" the fact that during the same 12-week period that its first wave of PSAs ran in 2012, "the national quit-line featured in every ad … received about 365,000 calls, more than twice the number of calls in the same period the previous year" (O'Connor).

Although *Tips* features many individuals in its PSAs, Terrie Hall quickly became "America's Face of Smoking Cessation." Hall began smoking at the age of 17, due largely to peer pressure, and she soon advanced to a two-pack-a-day habit that she maintained for 22 years, until, in 2001, at the age of 40, Hall was diagnosed with oral cancer and underwent a laryngectomy. Over the remainder of her life, Hall was diagnosed with cancer on 11 separate occasions, endured 48 radiation treatments and almost an entire year's worth of chemotherapy, and lost her upper palate, teeth, voice box, and part of her jaw. Hall's initial foray into anti-smoking advocacy occurred in 2006 when she was featured in one of the PSAs produced by *Tobacco Reality Unfiltered*, a North Carolina-based anti-smoking campaign. In August 2011, Hall filmed her first *Tips* PSA in which she walks viewers through her daily personal beauty rituals—from inserting a set of false teeth to adjusting her wig and fitting a small speaker inside her stoma. As of this writing, her first *Tips* video has received nearly 3.7 million views on YouTube and, according to Tom Frieden, Director of the CDC, "has inspired more comments than any other CDC video." Only weeks before the second wave of *Tips* videos began airing in 2013, Hall's "doctors found her smoking-caused cancer had spread to her brain." Two days before she died in September

2013, Hall shared "the final effects of smoking on her body" from her hospital bed in Winston-Salem, North Carolina (Frieden).

The final "Tips" PSA featuring Hall was shot on 14 September 2013, just two days before Hall died at the age of 53 in a Winston-Salem, North Carolina, hospital. Like other installments in the series of PSAs, this one opens with a title slide announcing the central conceit of the campaign—"A Tip From A Former Smoker"—in white text against a black background. The next shot is a still photograph of an attractive, smiling young woman posing in a graduation cap and gown. In her signature mechanically-raspy voice, Hall narrates in voice over, "I had a lot of friends." (All of Hall's voice over narration is "translated" via subtitles for the audience.) Before the PSA advances to the next still image, viewers hear the distinctive whir of Hall's electrolarynx—a kind of mechanical punctuation mark that reminds viewers that Hall lost her voice box to cancer many years earlier. The next slide features another still photograph, this one presumably taken a few years before Hall's high school graduation. In the second photograph, a slightly younger version of the same young woman is wearing a cheerleading uniform and is captured mid-cheer, smiling at the camera. In voice over narration, Hall reveals, "I was a cheerleader," a statement that, once again, is punctuated by the whir of Hall's electrolarynx. The next still photograph pictures the young woman arm-in-arm with a male peer, both decked out in their 1970s finest. Hall narrates, "I was on the homecoming court." Her electrolarynx sounds. The scene shifts one final time, in this instance to a school yearbook photograph of Hall, a goofy smile plastered on her youthful face. Against the backdrop of this image, Hall narrates, "It breaks my heart to see teenagers smoking." Again, the electrolarynx sounds. The next cut takes viewers to an extreme close-up profile shot of current-day Hall, who is sitting upright in a hospital bed. Her head is shaved save for a thin line of sparse brown hair just below the base of her skull and suture scars, suggestive of fairly recent neurosurgery, are clearly visible a few inches above Hall's ear. Her face appears markedly gaunt, her skin stretched tight around her skull as if to accentuate the scars and facial disfigurement that resulted from a surgery, done many years prior, to remove a portion of Hall's jaw. Still in voice over, Hall explains, "Because I started smoking when I was a teenager," a revelation that is twice punctuated by the whir of the electrolarynx. Through a cut to blackout, the scene shifts to a black title slide against which, in stark white text, the following statement appears: "CANCER FROM SMOKING KILLED TERRIE." Following a beat, "She was 53." appears below the all-caps statement. A quick cut to another title slide reveals the CDC logo and URL. In voice over, an authoritative male speaker announces, "You can quit. For free help, visit CDC.GOV/Tips." A variation of this PSA features Hall again seated in her hospital bed and delivering the following narration in voice over: "My tip to you is, don't start smoking. And if you do smoke, quit. And don't give up at one try. Keep trying until you succeed. I don't want anybody to have to go through what I'm going through." Throughout the narration, the camera travels along Hall's scarred countenance in extreme close-up, pulling back only at the end to a long shot of Hall staring through downcast eyes at the camera. This PSA concludes in the same manner as the other.

Highlighted in all of the *Tips* PSAs, but especially the ones that feature Hall, are the physical ravages of addiction. The scars on her head and jawline visually echo the many surgeries and medical treatments that Hall underwent as a result of her 22-year addiction to nicotine. Hall's material body, then, serves as a powerful reminder of the ways in which addiction compromises the body's ability to maintain itself, necessitating the removal of certain "diseased" parts and the replacement of certain others. In some respects, Hall's material body no longer is even recognizable *as a body*; instead, like Mary Shelley's graveyard creation, addiction has rendered Hall a grotesque *assemblage* of miscellaneous components—part human, part "monster," and part machine. The mechanization of Hall's body—the rendering of human form *as machine*—is reinforced by the close-up shots that highlight the stoma in her throat as well as the soundtrack that is repeatedly punctuated by the whir of her electrolarynx; all of these elements underscore the myriad ways in which the addict's diseased body repeatedly, seemingly inevitably, betrays itself.

Of course, Hall's body is not the "human-machine coupling" (Balsamo 18) that "disseminates new hopes and dreams of corporeal reconstruction and physical immortality" (2) once imagined and celebrated by critics like Donna J. Haraway (for example, *Simians, Cyborgs, and Women*) and Anne Balsamo (for example, *Technologies of the Gendered Body*). For such critics, the cyborg stands as a "contemporary cultural conjunction" where "the 'natural' body has been dramatically refashioned through the application of new technologies of corporeality" (Balsamo 5), "where machines assume organic functions and the body is materially redesigned through the application of newly developed technologies" (2–3). Through an engagement with what Balsamo terms "techno-science" (for example, bodybuilding, cosmetic surgery, cyberspace), the "natural" body is rendered "healthy, enhanced, and fully functional—more real than real" (5). This "human-machine coupling" that is the eponymous "cyborg" not only alters "the dimensions and markers of what counts as a 'natural' body," but also "enables a fantastic dream of immortality and control over life and death" (2). Like the cyborg, Hall's body has been "dramatically refashioned" through its engagement with traditional medical science and the product of this dramatic refashioning of materiality stands as a challenge to what constitutes a "natural body." However, the coupling of human and machine within the confines of Hall's material body marks the "natural" body as diseased, diminished (both in functionality and in morality)—less real than real, more abject than natural. In other words, to re-work Balsamo's phrasing slightly, as techno-science provides the realistic possibility of replacing/removing body parts, it also and simultaneously serves as a profound reminder of the materiality and mortality of the addict's body.

This theme is further reinforced through the disembodiment of Hall's voice in the final two PSAs that she shot for the campaign. For the entirety of both 30-second spots, Hall is divested of the authority to speak on camera, her voice noticeably disembodied in voice over narration, most especially once current-day Hall appears in the live action shots that comprise the final moments of the photo collage PSA. (In the PSA that I did not describe at length, Hall is always physically present, even though the physically-present Hall remains mute throughout.) The absence of Hall's voice in these particular PSAs is especially haunting given that it was precisely that disease-ravaged voice that became her most recognizable "feature," her signature as an anti-smoking advocate. Indeed, in Hall's second *Tips* PSA, she laments that her grandchild has never heard her "natural" voice, and the social media content produced to correspond with this PSA simplified Hall's sentimental message as, "Record your voice for loved ones while you still can." In another social media .jpeg, a close-up photograph of Hall appears beneath the tagline, "After Terrie lost her voice, she found an even stronger one." Ironically, in these final two PSAs, the woman without a voice box who, in the twenty-first century, became one of the most vocal advocates for America's anti-smoking crusade is stripped of the very voice that was both her trademark and her stock-in-trade. In this respect, Hall's signature raspy voice functions as a conspicuous and intrusive absent-presence, her enforced silence reminding viewers of the often violent, and always devastating, ways in which addiction robs the individual of health, autonomy, identity, and, finally, life. Also ironic (although not especially surprising) is the fact that always the "stronger" voice (both in tonal quality and in overall "importance" to fulfilling the purpose of the PSA) is that of the male narrator who, also in voice over, delivers the final lines of the PSA. In speaking for the CDC, the male voice takes on the institutionalized authority of the medical profession, a stand-in for the institution from which his directive is issued. Addiction, then, is not the only force that, in these PSAs, robs Hall of her voice and renders her mute within what is supposedly her own life story; the genre of the PSA, as well as the institutions of health and medicine that originally gave rise to that genre, also are implicated in Hall's silence.

In this way, these *Tips* PSAs implicitly rehearse the classic relationship between the body of the female patient and the institution of Western medicine. Within this power dynamic, the patient's body—always cast as unruly, pathological, hysterical—must be subjected to endless acts of surveillance by agents—usually males—of the institution of medicine as a means of controlling and subduing that body. (Charlotte Perkins Gilman's

"The Yellow Wallpaper" traces this narrative trajectory perfectly, as does the section of Bram Stoker's *Dracula* that focuses on the metamorphosis and death of Lucy Westenra.) These medical authorities probe the female body, both literally and intellectually, laying bare its secrets and, in doing so, rendering that body a known, docile, and ultimately disciplined object stripped of both agency and autonomy. The voice constitutes one (perhaps *the primary*) locus of both agency and autonomy. It functions as a site at which the individual fabricates him-/herself into existence. To articulate the self as a singular "I" is to acknowledge the self as an autonomous entity separate from and unique when contrasted with other such entities. The voice is not only the site at which individuals acknowledge and reinforce their selfhood, but also the site at which that selfhood is self-consciously crafted and maintained. It is, in other words, the site at which my saying "I am Heath" brings the "Heath" to which I refer into existence. This perhaps is why, within the fields of health and medicine, the patient (especially the female patient) must capitulate to male authority if she hopes to understand her own body and ultimately improve her health. But that act of capitulation also demands the surrender of the patient's voice, which is simultaneously a surrender of identity, knowledge, and authority. In the *Tips* PSAs, the disembodiment of Hall's voice signifies the loss of her authority over both the "text" (that is, the PSA) and her own image, which is an extension of her identity. In this way, the *Tips* PSAs featuring Hall remark, albeit in an uncritical manner, on the myriad ways in which the woman's ailing body is disciplined and controlled by the institution of medicine. Like so many addicts before (and since), but especially those addicts featured in anti-drug PSAs, Hall appears most "useful" when disciplined into an inanimate object, a mere stage property in the drama that plays out on the small screen, little more significant than the generic hospital bed on which she sits. Here, as elsewhere, Hall is an exemplar of a moral point. Hall is a symbol of consequence. Hall is a vehicle for emotional appeal. But Hall is not "Terrie" any longer.

One of the primary reasons why this series of PSAs has the potential to boomerang is that the campaign at large is characterized by hyperbole and therefore its claims lack both credibility and believability. To be fair, some of the former smokers featured in the *Tips* PSAs suffer from fairly common afflictions, such as Shawn who suffered from "throat cancer" and whose advice is: "When you have a hole in your neck, don't face the showerhead, keep your stoma covered when you're outside, be very careful shaving, get used to eating only soft foods, [and] clean out your speech valve twice a day." But most of the former smokers who lend their "real stories" to the CDC constitute worst case scenarios that are as shocking and as devastating as they are rare. For instance, one PSA features Brandon who, at the age of 18, was diagnosed with Buerger's disease, "a disorder linked to tobacco use that causes blood vessels in the hands and feet to become blocked and can result in infection or gangrene" ("Brandon's Biography"). Eventually, both of Brandon's legs were amputated at the knee, as were several of his fingers at the tips. Despite the fact that Buerger's disease is an incredibly rare medical condition, and that "[t]he prevalence of the disease is decreasing in developed countries" (Scott and Knott), this PSA fails to acknowledge the rarity of the condition that it spotlights and, instead, presents Brandon as a kind of former smoker Everyman (which, of course, is one of the central conceits of the campaign). But Brandon looks nothing like the garden variety smokers that Americans see lingering outside of public buildings every day. Neither, for that matter, does Terrie, whose body records an exaggerated and traumatic accumulation of loss that is difficult to comprehend as "real" (and therefore as a possible consequence of the viewer's own smoking) even when viewers bear witness to that loss with their own eyes. In the end, these PSAs constitute the equivalent of the "hard sell" and they have the potential to boomerang for precisely the same reason that other such marketing techniques fail. The voices of the speakers are too insistent that their experiences are "real" and "genuine" and "representative." The central message of the campaign is too aggressive. And the commonality that all of the *Tips* PSAs share is a penchant for exaggeration, hyperbole. The fact that the CDC misleadingly presents these worst case scenarios as "real" (meaning both "likely" and "representative," and not necessarily "genuine") undercuts the authority and credibility of the message and ultimately could fuel a smoker's denial of the health risks of smoking, thereby potentially prolonging the very addiction that these PSAs were designed to curb.

Also at issue here is the disingenuousness of the campaign. While the campaign does, as promised, feature "real people" sharing "tips" derived from their former addictions, the CDC does little to mask the fact that these individuals' "real stories" are carefully orchestrated and highly standardized by Arnold, the advertising agency responsible for the *Tips* campaign. Like all PSAs, the *Tips* advertisements are stylized, the "real stories" expertly abridged and carefully scripted to achieve maximum emotional impact on the target viewer. In this respect, the "real" smokers are rendered mere mouthpieces for the "stories" that some advertising executive has crafted to fulfill the goals that the CDC has established for its campaign. When a message that is designed to alter behaviors rings false among target listeners, it not only is more likely to be ignored, but also might produce the very behaviors that it seeks to curb precisely because the "authority" warning against the supposedly "bad" behaviors has been exposed as a charlatan.

In a similar manner, the *Tips* campaign repeatedly enacts a violation of the viewer's confidence by undercutting one of its central premises. To bill the PSAs of this campaign under the tagline "Tips From Former Smokers" is to imply an intimacy between the speaker (that is, the spokesperson and the CDC) and the target audience. A "tip," after all, constitutes a piece of advice shared in confidence between intimates. Often born of the speaker's first-hand experience, the "tip," shared out of genuine concern for the listener, is itself intended to help the person to whom it is directed by pointing out potential problems that could result if the listener persists in a given behavior pattern or makes a certain choice. In this respect, the *Tips* campaign fails to deliver on the promised "tips" and, instead, offers up a healthy dose of shame and guilt for its audience of smokers. Undergirding virtually every single "tip" offered to smokers through the *Tips* campaign is not sincere concern for the target audience and its health, but is the implicit, condescending message, "You have to be stupid to smoke cigarettes." Bill's PSA, for example, begins with the statement that smoking and diabetes are "a bad combination"; then, Bill goes on to advise diabetic listeners that if they are going to smoke, then they should "[m]ake a list. Put the people you love at the top. Put down your eyes, your legs, your kidneys, and your heart. Now, cross off all the things you're okay with losing because you'd rather smoke." In most of these PSAs, the "real person" who shares his/her "real story" with the viewer is not a confidant, but is a moralistic didact admonishing the listener for engaging in precisely the same behaviors that have wrought such devastation on his/her own body and delivering a punitive message that undermines the listener's intelligence. Moreover, because such PSAs tend to emphasize (albeit implicitly) the shame and guilt that viewers should feel for smoking (for example, Bill casts himself as selfish vis-à-vis his family and children), there is a strong likelihood that target viewers will engage in "defensive processing," "disassociat[ing] themselves with whatever they are being shown in order to lessen those emotions" (Leah). As a result of this disassociation, the smoker can spiral into a "cycle of shame and blame" that begins with an increase in the addictive behavior as a means of "escape," and then is followed by a decrease in self-esteem as a result of one's perceived lack of self-control, followed by a further escalation of the addictive behavior to cope with the self-hatred. In other words, the belittling tips offered by the CDC's *Tips* campaign potentially can fuel precisely the feelings of shame and guilt that often perpetuate an addiction.

Conclusion

Throughout this chapter, I have speculated some of the messages that select anti-drug PSAs convey—messages that, I argue, might trigger a boomerang effect. For the addict, the boomerang effect typically occurs when PSAs exacerbate feelings of self-hatred by casting the metaphor of waste as Truth.

Some campaigns assert their central message as fact directly (for example, the American Legacy Foundation's *The Truth*), while others attain a sense of verisimilitude through the exploitation of real people telling real stories about their struggles with substance dependence (for example, *Faces* and *Tips*). Regardless of how such PSAs achieve their "truth effect," all such advertisements repeatedly and unequivocally assert a series of interrelated narratives that always and only characterize the addict as sick, degenerate, pathological. Addiction erodes a person's morals, such PSAs claim. Addiction disintegrates interpersonal relationships, leaving the addict degraded, wasted, alone. Addiction squanders personal talents, leading to the loss of a person's livelihood, self-respect, and ultimately use-value. And finally, addiction wastes the material body, leading inevitably to the untimely and painful death of the addict. For addicts, these oft-repeated "truths" can seem as inevitable as their next fix, and the desire (even a subconscious one) to hasten a foregone eventuality can fuel increasingly risky behaviors, overdoses (both accidental and otherwise), and even death.[4]

To be sure, this chapter might appear to be too narrowly-focused on single PSAs, or even a single approach to anti-drug PSAs, to make significant contributions to ongoing conversations regarding the lived experiences of addiction. The *Faces* campaign, for instance, enjoys a significantly more limited audience base than the *Tips* campaign, despite its incorporation into both middle and high school health studies curricula in isolated schools across the country. And while the *Tips* campaign theoretically has the wide, national reach that *Faces* lacks, the infrequency with which Americans currently view television advertisements thanks to devices like Tivo and DVR, as well as a general desensitization to such ads, suggests that its reach and impact may be no more expansive. Furthermore, the PSAs that I have discussed focus on only two of the myriad audiences to which such campaigns historically have been addressed, although I would counter that point by suggesting that such advertisements have been less attuned to target audience needs and expectations than they should be and generally exhibit a profound sense of sameness across campaigns, audiences, messages, and even historical moments. Finally, both of the campaigns that I chose to discuss within this chapter offer examples of "health terrorism," or the scare tactic approach to anti-drug advocacy. No mention is made of other approaches to anti-drug advocacy (for example, the social norms approach) and therefore the observations that I make within this chapter are, admittedly, limited.

---

4 Researchers at the University of Florida, for instance, have suggested that anti-drug PSAs that attack the addict's self-esteem "[produce] higher emotional responses toward drug use" (Orr), thereby contributing to greater and more frequent use, which can, of course, trigger a series of boomerang effects that are devastating for the addict.

However, the very kinds of observations that I have made here regarding these select PSAs reflect thematic and ideological threads in the larger, ongoing conversations about how addiction is framed in the rhetoric of American public policy, how addiction is lived in the spaces of our everyday lives, and how addiction is perceived within twenty-first-century American culture at large. Specifically, in these PSAs, as in most cultural representations of addiction, drug use "is seen as an irrational behavior that serves no useful purpose and can only be explained in terms of pathology" (Keane 122). *Faces*, for example, references the cultural mythos of the American Dream, and specifically its twin foundations of progress and material success, as a moral measuring stick to condemn the addict as both "irrational" and "pathological." Both physical devolution and criminality point decisively to the fact that these addicts "serve no useful purpose." Within the cautionary tale that this campaign spins, then, it is a series of short and problematic cognitive leaps from white trash to criminal to methamphetamine user. An equally short cognitive leap would cast the addict as *un-American*, a topic that I took up in Chapter 1 and to which I will return in Chapter 6. Finally, the *Tips* campaign turns on the conflation of addiction and chronic/terminal illness. Against the backdrop of a culture that is perpetually obsessed with appearance, youth, vitality, and fitness, these PSAs encourage viewers to perceive addicts as actively, even willfully, destructive of their physical health and, ultimately, in the *Tips* campaign, it is a short and all-too-familiar cognitive leap from physical ailment to moral sickness.

Of course, these PSAs do not merely peddle misinformation and stereotypes regarding the addict. Rather, these PSAs which purport to convey to their viewers the Truth about addiction tell us significantly more about the culture within which these PSAs were produced than they do about the addict, the experiences of addiction, or even the substances that the PSAs were designed to combat. These PSAs, like so many before them, adopt "a totalizing, ready-made narrative" that is "concerned not with the experience of this [addiction], but with reproducing the calculus of conservative morality in a deeply puritanical culture" (Patton 25). Founded on the metaphor of waste, this "totalizing, ready-made narrative" has the potential to not only implicate, but also impact, virtually every arena of private and public life through a kind of ripple effect. Historically, that narrative has been used—both implicitly and explicitly—to justify the "tough love" paternalism, or the acts of shaming and blaming, that Americans so frequently target at addicts. Certainly, it provides a compelling justification for the Draconian legislation that, over the past four decades, has unilaterally doled out overly severe punishments for drug offenders of all stripes, regardless of the severity of their offenses. Beginning in January 1973, when Nelson Rockefeller, then Governor of New York, "called for ... mandatory prison sentences of 15 years to life for drug dealers and addicts—even those caught with small amounts of marijuana, cocaine or heroin" (Mann), excessive incarceration has been the preferred punishment for offenders convicted of making "bad choices" with respect to illicit substances. Writing in July 2010, a reporter from *The Economist* brought this devastating trend into sharp perspective by pointing out that "[t]he number of drug offenders in federal and state lock-ups has increased 13-fold since 1980" ("Too many laws"). But the unequal application of criminal law is not the only possible consequence of the endless funneling of resources into prevention efforts that are significantly less effective than most Americans believe them to be. According to the American Civil Liberties Union (ACLU), "There are 2.3 million people behind bars in this country—that is triple the amount of prisoners we had in 1987—and 25 percent of those incarcerated are locked up for drug offenses. Taxpayers spend almost $70 billion a year on corrections and incarceration" ("Drug Sentencing and Penalties").[5]

At the same time that this narrative renders our system of jurisprudence both Draconian and wasteful, it simultaneously reifies differences between addicts and non-addicts, perceived as "natural" and "innate," and implicitly justifies and, indeed, enables a system that discriminates against certain individuals because of those perceived differences. As the Drug Policy Alliance reports, "The drug war has produced profoundly unequal outcomes across racial groups, manifested through racial discrimination by law enforcement and disproportionate drug war misery suffered by communities of color." These writers go on to concede that "rates of drug use and selling are comparable across racial lines," but point out that African Americans and Latinos generally suffer higher arrest and incarceration rates, as well as stricter sentences, due to "law enforcement focus on urban areas, on lower-income communities and on communities of color" (*Race and the Drug War*). In fact, as the ACLU reports, "African-Americans are incarcerated on drug charges at a rate that is 10 times greater than that of whites" ("Too many laws"). Finally, this totalizing, ready-made narrative serves to justify the perpetuation of a largely ineffectual one-size-fits-all treatment model based on the

---

5 It is important to note that in April 2014, President Barack Obama announced that he was "prepared to use his pardon power to grant clemency to 'hundreds, perhaps thousands' of people who have been jailed for nonviolent drug crimes." The previous December, Obama had "commuted the sentences of eight federal inmates convicted of non-violent drug offenses involving crack cocaine," explaining that those individuals "had been sentenced under an 'unfair sentence'" ("Obama Plans Clemency"). Representatives from the Drug Policy Alliance, the "nation's leading organization promoting drug policies that are grounded in science, compassion, health and human rights" (*About the Drug Policy Alliance*), called the efforts a "positive step," but suggested that comprehensive sentencing reform was necessary in order to avoid "more mass injustice" ("Obama Plans Clemency").

12-step philosophy and founded squarely (and erroneously) on the principle of "choice"; this same treatment model has, within the American criminal justice system, become an often mandatory add-on to a drug offender's sentence. One source, for instance, suggests that "[e]ach year, the legal system coerces more than 150,000 people to join AA, according to AA's own membership surveys" (Glaser).

Ultimately, what is wasted in the production and dissemination of "health terrorism" anti-drug PSAs is the opportunity to assist real addicts with the long and arduous journey toward sobriety. Time and again, we needlessly expend valuable material and human resources under the banner of altruism, ignoring the questionable track record of the scare tactics approach while simultaneously telling ourselves that we are doing "important work" in America's War on Drugs. In favor of tradition and the status quo, we squander a valuable opportunity to intervene in the ongoing conversations regarding addiction and to alter the nature, direction, and stakes of that debate. The result is a cultural legacy of waste that we have labored under since the nineteenth century. We choose to shame and blame, rather than to help and heal, and, in doing so, we condemn the addict to a dichotomy of degradation: to be waste or to be wasted. We choose to scapegoat the weak, the vulnerable, the powerless in a vain attempt to shield ourselves from the devastating fact that no one is immune to addiction. We erode the addict's sense of self-worth, just as surely as the addiction itself destroys the addict's health and material body, leaving him/her guilt-ravaged due to what s/he is coerced into perceiving as a chronic and inevitable series of immoral choices. And, finally, the greatest waste of all are the addicts themselves—those who needlessly suffer because they "refuse to seek help," those who endure grossly inflated prison sentences because they made "bad choices," those who relapse because they "didn't work the steps hard enough," and, sadly, those who succumb to their addictions and leave this world too soon because they "selfishly chose the drug over everything else."

Enter Whitney Houston.

Chapter 6
"Didn't [She] Almost Have It All?": Being Whitney Houston/Performing Addiction/Imagining America[1]

Was my life not enough of a cautionary tale for you?

Emma (Whitney Houston), *Sparkle*, 2012

When Whitney Houston died at age 48 on 11 February 2012, her final feature film, a re-make of the 1976 period piece *Sparkle,* was in post-production and set to be released on 17 August 2012. Set in Detroit, Michigan, in 1968, the film—which was inspired by The Supremes—focuses on the rise from obscurity of a three-sister "girl group" fronted by Sparkle (Jordin Sparks). Whitney plays the three women's mother, Emma, a character that *The New York Times* reviewer Stephen Holden describes as "a former entertainer turned prim, disapproving church lady." Holden begins his review, which was published the day before *Sparkle* hit American theaters and six months following Whitney's death, by noting that "[i]t is impossible to watch *Sparkle* and not relate its story to the life of Whitney Houston," and this kind of "20/20 Hindsight (Pseudo-)Wisdom" dominates the critic's review of Whitney's performance. Holden explains, for instance, that "Emma forsook show business after nearly succumbing to the same excesses that caught up with Houston" and, later in the review, Holden suggests that "[a]s Emma talks in clipped, accelerated sentences, you sense the same fierce defensiveness Houston often put on like armor in interviews during her career." In the end, Holden concludes simply, "Houston's presence makes [the film] a cautionary tale."

Holden's conclusion here is not particularly original, or even surprising, as similar sentiments have been uttered with respect to virtually every celebrity who has ever succumbed to an addiction. But what is interesting about this statement, at least in Whitney's case, is the way that it was so seamlessly and strategically employed (by Holden, by marketers for the film, and so on) as a means of blurring the lines between fact and fiction—one of the more prominent and often insidious machinations of the metaphor of waste and one that I discuss at some length with respect to the biopic *Wired* in Chapter 1.

---

1 A previous version of this chapter was presented at the Ray Browne Popular Culture conference at Bowling Green State University in February 2015.

The sentiment is lifted directly from the script of *Sparkle*, in which Emma, after discovering that her daughters are pursuing the same dreams that once almost ruined her life, paternalistically asks, "Was my life not enough of a cautionary tale for you?" This same line was featured prominently in the first trailer for the film that hit the airwaves very shortly after Whitney's death. Given the similarities shared between Whitney and her on-screen character, this line specifically and *Sparkle* more generally offered many a filmgoer and critic a convenient, if flawed, means of making sense of Whitney's off-screen death, ultimately encouraging them to see that death as a cautionary tale about the excesses of celebrity, the immorality of addiction, and the inevitability of a shameful and punitive death.

Indeed, in the immediate aftermath of her death, Whitney was widely and repeatedly mythologized as a tragic figure who wasted the "God-given gifts" that had marked her not simply as a legendary singer, but that had sedimented her place in the annals of history as The Voice. Journalists from media as diverse in quality and reputation as *The Guardian*, *The Washington Post*, Fox News, and *The National Enquirer* issued the same lament: What a waste. What a waste of talent. What a waste of fortune. What a waste of a voice. What a waste of life. Music journalist Paul Gambaccini, in a statement given to the BBC News only hours after the singer's death, illustrates this trend quite clearly. Gambaccini begins his statement by admitting that "while we're shocked by the timing of the tragedy, in a case like this, [we're] not surprised that a tragedy has occurred because her decline was played out publicly. We all saw her behavior under the influence of drugs and we all heard the terrible damage that had been done to her voice." Gambaccini concludes his nearly four-minute lament about the tragedy of Whitney's death with the predictable and predictably problematic statement, "This is the kind of self-administered decline that we've seen through the years ... I saw it first with Judy Garland and then we've seen it recently with Amy Winehouse and it's always a tragedy. It's a life lost. It's a great talent squandered" (quoted in "Whitney Houston: 'A great talent'").

To characterize the years of drug use leading up to Whitney's death as a "self-administered decline" casts addiction as a fault or wrong for which an addict can and must be held accountable through the punishment of death. In this case, Gambaccini places the blame for her death squarely on Whitney's own shoulders, thereby characterizing addiction as a disease of the will, rather than a disease of the body and mind. The "how" and the "why" of Whitney's death, in other words, serve as an indictment against her moral failings, erroneously suggesting that Whitney could have avoided her seemingly inevitable tragic fate if only she had exercised self-control and just stopped using drugs. (Here, readers should hear distinct echoes of the moral condemnation leveled against comedian John Belushi in the texts discussed in Chapter 1, as well as of the blame attributed to addicts who fail to persevere in 12-step programs discussed in Chapter 4.) These ideas are reinforced by the way in which Gambaccini describes Whitney's attitude toward her unparalleled talents. His employment of the term "squandered" casts Whitney not only as one who was prone to wastefulness, but also as one whose penchant for "spend[ing] (money, goods, and so on) recklessly ... extravagantly, profusely, or wastefully" ("squander, v.") was solely responsible both for her wasted voice (something that many lay persons and professional music critics echoed over the years), and for her tragic (but not surprising) demise. Moreover, the surprise that Gambaccini fails to register at the announcement of Whitney's death echoes the deterministic causal narrative that Americans have long drawn between addiction and death and, in many ways, alludes to the stranglehold that nineteenth-century attitudes toward addiction continue to have on twenty-first-century Americans. After all, Gambaccini's statement has traveled very little distance—both ideologically and in subject matter—from the nineteenth-century etching that I discuss in Chapter 2 (that is, "DRINKING LEADS TO NEGLECT OF DUTY, MORAL DEGRADATION AND CRIME.").

This chapter engages the basic question: What does it "mean" to locate Whitney's biography within the narrative framework of the cautionary tale? In *The Greenwood Encyclopedia of Folktales and Fairy Tales*, Ülo Valk defines the "cautionary tale" as "a narrative that demonstrates the consequences of wrongdoing and thus reinforces moral and behavioral norms" (170). Often used interchangeably with other literary genres, such as the "fable," the "exemplum," or the "didactic tale," and witnessed in slightly modified form in the modern "urban legend," the cautionary tale typically follows a three-part narrative trajectory in which a character is warned of a danger, the character "disregards the warning and performs the forbidden act," and "the violator comes to a grisly and unpleasant fate" ("A Cautionary Tale?").

The cautionary tale that is Whitney's biography (or, I would assert, that is the biography of any addict—celebrity or otherwise—who succumbs to an addiction) typically demands the addition of a fourth act to this classic tripartite narrative structure. This fourth act, which serves as a necessary prelude to the cautionary tale proper, locates the addict's origin story within the mythos of the classic American Dream. (Readers will recall that a similar narrative strategy was discussed in relation to episodes of the A&E series *Intervention*, which I examined in Chapter 2.) Whitney, of course, was no stranger to the privilege conferred and the demands exacted by this mythos, and her backstory gave journalists and laypersons much fodder for building this particular narrative around her addiction in the later years of her career. Born into an impressive musical pedigree, plucked from relative obscurity by music industry mogul Clive Davis, and boasting of an unparalleled talent, Whitney enjoyed a meteoric rise to superstardom during a moment in America's history that was characterized by staunch classism, misogyny, and racism. She overcame many obstacles in her path to superstardom and, at the height of her career, seemed to "have it all." Many events from this early period of Whitney's career allude to the prosperity that, at least according to our shared national mythologies, *necessarily* derives from simple hard work, dedication, and know-how, though perhaps none so compelling as her performance of "The Star Spangled Banner" at Super Bowl XXV in Tampa, FL, in 1991.

This performance demonstrates Whitney's virtuosity quite vividly, but it also serves as a compelling point of contrast for the post-addiction Whitney who regularly cancelled performances, whose voice was marked by an addiction-fueled decline, and whose erratic behaviors inspired a treasure trove of tabloid headlines. Whitney's later struggles with addiction often are refracted through this performance, and, indeed, the entirety of Whitney's early career, which is so steeped in the mythos of the American Dream. These two periods of Whitney's biography are cleanly divided by Whitney's marriage to bad boy Bobby Brown in 1992—a man who metonymically represents the "danger" against which Whitney, the good Christian girl who was raised in Newark's New Hope Baptist Church, repeatedly was warned. Even as late as Whitney's funeral in February 2012, her estranged ex-husband Bobby Brown was identified by many as the primary causal factor that contributed to Whitney's decline and death. Whitney's marriage to Bobby Brown signified her "disregard" for the warning and suggested, as is typical of the metaphor of waste, that Whitney's addiction was a choice, akin to the choice that she made in marrying Brown (which has come to embody the temptation of the very addiction that ultimately killed Whitney). It is precisely this death that represents the "grisly and unpleasant fate" of the American addict's cautionary tale.

1991: Singing "The Star Spangled Banner" in Tampa

Although Whitney's career began many years prior, and those years were marked by countless professional milestones that give shape and meaning to her later descent into addiction, her performance of "The Star Spangled Banner" at Super Bowl XXV in 1991 is, for me, most illustrative of the heights to which Whitney soared at the apex of her career. The origin story for "The Star Spangled Banner" is well-established in America, although its history as an institutionalized component of American sporting events perhaps is more obscure. Originally penned by Francis Scott Key in 1814 "after he witnessed the 25 hour bombardment of Fort Henry by the British" (Macko), the anthem celebrates an underdog nation that perseveres and prevails in the face of adversity. This nation symbolically is represented within the lyrics of the song by the flag that "yet wave[s]." Luke Cyphers and Ethan Trex, writers for ESPN, also regard the anthem as principally "a battle song," and these authors go on to claim that it is precisely the link between the anthem and war that ingratiated it into American sports. Cyphers and Trex write:

[The anthem is] a taunt, a lyrical grenade chucked at a defeated opponent .... That's why, in a country that loudly lauds actions on the battlefield and the playing field, 'The Star Spangled Banner' and American athletics have a nearly indissoluble marriage. Hatched during one war, institutionalized during another, this song has become so entrenched in our sports identity that it's almost impossible to think of one without the other.

At the heart of the American nation are the values of competition, perseverance, and dominance. These values are shared by the institutions of war and sports and suggest why, since World War I, the national anthem has served as a prelude to both amateur and professional sporting events. War protects the boundaries, the ideologies, the resources, and the people of a nation, at least in its ideal, theoretical form. Sporting events symbolically rehearse the nation's preoccupation with territorial and ideological dominance. To sing the national anthem at sporting events, then, is to acknowledge the ways in which national identity is predicated on repeated and ritualized public performances of patriotism.

Whitney was tapped to perform the national anthem at Super Bowl XXV in 1990, the same year that she would release her third studio album, *I'm Your Baby Tonight*. In mid-January of the following year, Whitney recorded the vocal track for her performance in a Los Angeles studio while the Florida Orchestra recorded the instrumental track separately. The performance took place on 27 January 1991 at the Tampa Stadium in Tampa, Florida, just prior to the kickoff of the game between the Buffalo Bills and the New York Giants. Houston's performance was preceded by the following announcement to the 73,000-plus assembled spectators (and an at-home global television audience of 750 million): "And now to honor America, especially the brave men and women serving in the Persian Gulf and throughout the world, please join in the singing of our national anthem." The announcer continued, "The anthem will be followed by a flyover of F-16 jets from the 56th Tactical Training Wing at Macdill Airforce Base and will be performed by the Florida Orchestra under the direction of Jahja Ling and sung by Grammy-Award-winner, Whitney Houston."

From its very beginning, this performance was dramatically marked by understatement, as well as a reverence for the anthem and the nation for which it stands. Before introducing Whitney, the announcer makes specific mention of no fewer than four different groups of people, none of which would ever attain the kind of national visibility and prominence that Whitney already had attained by that relatively early point in her lengthy career. After all, by the time that Whitney delivered the most memorable rendition of the national anthem in recent (and arguably distant) memory in 1991,[2] she already was a much-decorated recording artist and was soon to embark on filming *The Bodyguard* (1992), Whitney's first feature film whose soundtrack would, in many important ways, come to define her as an artist throughout the remainder of her life and career.[3] Yet in the opening remarks that frame this performance, Whitney's celebrity is stripped down to its barest of essentials (that is, "Grammy-Award-winner") and Whitney herself plays a supporting role to America, to "the brave men and women serving in the Persian Gulf," to "the 56th Tactical Training Wing," and even to the Florida Orchestra and its conductor. Instead of insisting on the top billing that she arguably deserved, Whitney humbles herself for the assembled audience by downplaying the remarkable celebrity that she already had attained by age 27. For her performance of the anthem, the opening comments suggest, Whitney is no longer the headliner, but has become merely a supporting player in a drama of national proportions and import. In other words, the Whitney who appeared in Tampa on that day in 1991 asserted, in Lauren Berlant's terms, "a patriotic view of national identity, which seeks to use identification with the ideal nation to trump or subsume all other notions of personhood" (27).

For the two minutes and fifteen seconds during which Whitney performed "The Star Spangled Banner," spectators were repeatedly—albeit implicitly—asked to forget her celebrity and to focus their attention on the song, its message, and its larger significance. This idea at once is visually underscored by the wardrobe choices that were made for the pop diva. The Whitney who appeared on that stage in Tampa was simply clad in an oversized white track suit largely unadorned with other color or detail aside from a thin checkerboard pattern circling her right sleeve and black piping trailing along the side of the pant leg. Her hair was styled in a short, curly bob that was pushed back from her face with a white fabric headband. In her right ear, she wore a crucifix earring—a visual nod to church that nurtured her talents from an early age; her right wrist was encircled by a simple watch and her left wrist was adorned with a thin gold bracelet. On her feet, she sported white Nike tennis shoes with a distinctive red swoosh. Whitney's physical appearance at this event can most

---

2 It is, for example, quite telling that the Wikipedia page for "The Star Spangled Banner (Whitney Houston Recording)" is significantly lengthier and more thoughtfully researched than the Wikipedia page for the anthem itself.

3 After all, it was the signature track from the soundtrack to *The Bodyguard*, Whitney's cover of "I Will Always Love You," that Jennifer Hudson sang at the Grammys during the opening "In Memoriam" tribute to Whitney one day after Whitney died; "I Will Always Love You" also was the final song that was played at Whitney's home going service as her casket was carried from the sanctuary and to her final resting place.

accurately be described as simple, unadorned, humble. The track suit not only alludes to the sporting event for which all of these spectators had assembled, thereby deemphasizing Whitney's celebrity allure, but it also curbs the artist's usual sex appeal. In both ways, the costume deflects attention away from the performer and the performance, redirecting that attention to the subject of the song (that is, patriotism) and the historical context of the performance (that is, America's most anticipated annual sporting event that was taking place, in 1991, only 10 days into the Persian Gulf War).

Vocally, too, Whitney's performance of the national anthem was markedly understated, especially when viewed in light of the complexity of the song and the signature performance style that had come to metonymically stand in for Whitney. In the first place, America's national anthem is notoriously difficult to perform. In May 2012, *New Yorker* columnist Reeves Wiedeman likened "successfully performing the anthem" to "an athletic feat," noting that the anthem "is not only one of the most difficult songs in its genre but also one of the hardest songs to sing, period." Following a particularly "screechy" performance of the anthem by Aerosmith frontman and *American Idol* judge Steven Tyler at the 2012 NFL playoffs, Brian Zeger, the Artistic Director for Vocal Arts at The Julliard School, described the anthem as "fiendish" to *The Los Angeles Times* (quoted in Wiedeman). What makes "The Star Spangled Banner" so challenging to perform is its "very wide range," according to Kenneth Slowik, Director of the Smithsonian Chamber Music Society (quoted in Macko). The one octave and one-fifth range of America's national anthem essentially demands that artists be capable of signing both very low and very high notes, sometimes in rather rapid succession.

Of course, for a talent like Whitney—who was equally comfortable and equally capable of belting out pitch perfect upper-, middle-, and lower-register notes—a song like "The Star Spangled Banner" offered the perfect vehicle through which to showcase her vocal virtuosity. Yet, in virtually every way possible, Whitney's performance of "The Star Spangled Banner" concedes the stage both to the anthem and to America itself, a concession that is obvious from the very first syllable that the artist intones. Although former New York Giant (1952–1964) Frank Gifford once described Whitney's performance of the anthem as "the most electric moment that I've ever seen in sports," Wiedeman has noted that "there's nothing especially revolutionary about her interpretation: it's just an incredible voice throttling an incredibly difficult song." Wiedeman's use of the term "throttle" to describe Whitney's performance of the anthem is, in actuality, a bit of a misnomer, although that term would quite accurately describe the bulk of Whitney's other live performances. In common usage, the verb "throttle" typically denotes the experience of "stop[ping] the breath of by compressing the throat," of "strangl[ing]" or "kill[ing] in this way." The editors of the *Oxford English*

Dictionary go on to suggest that "[t]he original meaning may have been 'to take or seize by the throat'" ("throttle, v."). By employing the term "throttle," Wiedeman likens Whitney's performance of "The Star Spangled Banner" to an act of violence perpetrated by one entity (in this case, Whitney) against another (in this case, the anthem) as a means of subduing, controlling, and/or dominating the latter. Yet the performance more accurately can be described as restrained, subdued. Throughout the performance, Whitney uncharacteristically sings within the confines of the vocal score, paying meticulous attention to the lyrics, the phrasing, and the musicality as they are transcribed onto the page. There is strength in her vocal performance, to be sure, and perhaps that raw, uninhibited strength is what inspired Wiedeman's choice of the term "throttle," but there also is an overarching reverence for the lyrics, the song, the occasion. In other words, Whitney's performance of the song, while arguably the most accomplished and unforgettable in both recent and distant memory, is noteworthy and special precisely because it lacks the stylistic flourishes that elsewhere serve as Whitney's unique performative signature.

As an artist, Whitney regularly delivered vocal performances that showcased the unique melismastic gymnastics that many an *American Idol* hopeful have attempted to ape, but have not even come close to approximating. Indeed, in the immediate wake of the artist's 2012 death, *BBC News Magazine* writer Lauren Everitt lauded Whitney as "a master of melisma." Dating to "Gregorian chants and the ragas of Indian classical music," melisma constitutes a vocal technique through which a performer "packs a series of different notes into a single syllable" (Everitt). For Everitt, Whitney's cover of the Dolly Parton classic "I Will Always Love You"—a song in which "[a]n early 'I' ... takes nearly six seconds to sing"—"pushed the technique into the mainstream in the 90s." Within America, melisma boasts of an even more specific subcultural heritage. In *Idolized: Music, Media, and Identity in* American Idol (2011), for instance, Katherine Meizel characterizes melisma "as both a national American and specifically African American (religious) musical practice." Meizel writes, "Melisma highlights the importance of vocal expression outside of textuality, exposing the voice as ... a 'summarizing symbol of identity'" (64). In effect, melisma connotes (at least in the very capable vocal cords of an artist like Whitney) virtuosity. It is the artistry of expression that exists beyond the textual score and that distinguishes a "good singer" from a "legendary artist." It is one site at which an artist can differentiate herself from her contemporaries and/or her forbearers and establish her star persona; after all, as Meizel notes, melisma constitutes "a summarizing symbol of identity." Melisma also alludes to innate talent by highlighting the artist's ability to riff; at the same time, melisma points decisively to the artist's practiced skill by demonstrating a heightened level of vocal and breath control that few performers possess.

Although Whitney was "able to sing complex melisma in all registers" ("Vocal Range"), her performance of America's national anthem in 1991 provided only a brief glimpse into those stylings and the massive talent undergirding them. Across the two-minute-fifteen-second performance of the anthem, Whitney employs her signature melisma quite sparingly. On three occasions—that is, "by the dawn's early *light*," "Whose broad stripes and bright *stars*," and "O'er the ramparts we *watched*"—the syllabic stretching is so truncated and brief that it easily could be audibly "overlooked." On the other two occasions, though, the melisma is pronounced and worthy of some consideration in the context of my argument here. The first instance of pronounced melisma occurs at the end of the line "O say does that Star Spangled banner yet *wave*." Lasting nearly five seconds, the ornamental phrasing employed for the word "wave" alludes to the American flag, which constitutes a visual leitmotif throughout the cinematography of the edited and aired version of this performance. Only seconds into the performance, for example, viewers witness an interesting use of conspicuous camera position. Along the left-hand-side of the visual frame, in the immediate foreground, Whitney is captured in medium shot. But the Grammy-award-winning performer is not identified as the focal point of this particular shot. Instead, the camera is angled diagonally to direct the viewer's gaze past Whitney to a line of uniformed servicepersons, one of whom is brandishing an American flag. Due to its positioning within the frame, color contrast, and depth of field, the flag is identified as the focal point of this particular shot, thereby reiterating the primacy of the nation and, at least visually, relegating Whitney to a background singer. At other points in the performance, the director makes liberal use of an elongated dissolve as a means of identifying Whitney both literally with the flag, and ideologically with the nation. In the initial moments of the performance, for instance, the director employs a three-second partial fade against the lyric "by the dawn's early light," superimposing briefly an extreme close-up of a waving flag against Whitney's body. Toward the end of the performance, as Whitney belts out the lyric "that our flag was still there," the director similarly employs an elongated dissolve, this time from an aerial shot of the American flag standing sentinel over the Tampa Stadium to an extreme close-up of Whitney's face. In each of these examples, the cinematography underscores the idea that in this place, at this moment, Whitney *is* the nation. Against the backdrop of an incredibly complicated musical challenge like the anthem (which symbolically also might stand for the politically embattled Persian Gulf War in which the American military was then embroiled), Whitney/America not only perseveres, but excels. In this respect, the unparalleled talent that marks her as The Voice and that enables her to "throttle" the anthem symbolically stands for the militaristic dominance and ideological might of America.

The other instance of prolonged melisma occurs in the final bars of the anthem, at the end of the lyric, "O'er the land of the *free*." The vocal ornamentation that highlights the word "free" implicitly references the war that, only 10 days earlier, had been declared against Iraq. The previous August, Iraqi President Saddam Hussein had "ordered the invasion and occupation of neighboring Kuwait" ("Persian Gulf War"). In mid-January 1991, after Hussein had "defied United Nations Security Council demands to withdraw from Kuwait," and around the time that Whitney was recording the vocal track for her performance of the anthem, then-President George H.W. Bush initiated "a massive U.S.-led air offensive known as Operation Desert Storm" ("Persian Gulf War"). Hussein's acts of aggression and despotism were, both in America and abroad, widely cast as a threat to the national sovereignty of Kuwait, but also to any nation that permitted Iraq's continued occupation of that country by failing to hold Hussein accountable for his actions. (These acts also constituted a very real threat to other nations' access to Kuwait's once readily available, and relatively inexpensive, supply of oil, although, in 1991, this causal narrative rarely made front-page headlines.) At the same time, Hussein's refusal to comply with the demands of the U.N. Security Council was regarded as a danger to international political relations and intergovernmental cooperation. The elder Bush's declaration of war, then, once again asserted America's militaristic, political, and historical dominance on the global stage. In this conflict, Hussein represented the egomaniacal force that threatened global freedom; Bush, by contrast, represented freedom's greatest champion: the aged, but still vibrant white knight (racial/ethnic differences have long factored into public perceptions of America's conflicts in the Middle East) who confronted the wavering of freedom with a swift execution of justice (the war lasted a scant 42 days). Against the backdrop of these historical events, Whitney's employment of melisma on the word "free" might be read as an acknowledgement of the larger cultural mythos then being circulated regarding why America went to war against Iraq, and perhaps even as a justification for the Persian Gulf War.

This interpretation is reinforced by Whitney's delivery of the final lyric of the song: "and the home of the brave." Despite the fact that Whitney regularly used melisma as a kind of punctuation mark for her songs—her many performances of "I Will Always Love You" offer an excellent example of this trend—here, the lyric is sung precisely as written. Pitch perfect as usual, Whitney's voice, unadorned here even by a vibrato, tunnels into the very core of the note, serving up a rich and expansive sound that fills the open-air auditorium, energizes the crowd, and dramatically punctuates the performance. The power of that concluding note, and the strength of Key's lyrics, are further underlined by Whitney's physical gesture. On the word "free," the singer extends her arms into the air in a wide "V," perhaps an unintentional, but very impactful homage to Americans' appreciation of competition and dominance, or victory. (The gesture is rendered all the more impactful given the virtual absence of hand gestures throughout the rest of the performance.) On the most literal of levels, the celebratory gesture foreshadows the elation that the New York Giants would feel later that day for having defeated the Buffalo Bills in the only Super Bowl ever won by a single point. On a more symbolic level, the gesture takes on a heightened significance in light of the recently declared Persian Gulf War, offering a visual assurance that America, like its flag, would prevail through even the most difficult of conflicts and reign victorious over any threats to its freedom and sovereignty.

Through her performance of "The Star Spangled Banner" in 1991, then, Whitney not only spoke *of* America's embattled struggle for "freedom" in its myriad forms, but she also spoke *for* the nation itself. More specifically, she spoke of The American Dream—a national fantasy that has shaped The American Experience and American national identity since well before this country had a definitive geopolitical and geospatial identity. Unlike John Belushi in *Wired*, Whitney's relationship to America is cast not in allegorical terms, but rather in metonymic terms. That is, Belushi's story was, at least according to screenwriter Eric Mac Rauch, "the story of America." Whitney, by contrast, *was* America—at least at that moment in January 1991. Of course, as a substitute, or stand-in, for the nation itself, Whitney also tells a tale about America—through her wardrobe, through the performance apparatus, through the arrangement of the song, through the editing of the segment, and so on. And the tale that Whitney (as America) tells is a familiar one about a nation of promise, opportunity, possibility, and advancement. The many years of hard work and dedication to her craft—alluded to in the brief mention of Whitney's Grammy-award-winning credentials—reference the Puritan work ethic on which this nation and its most ubiquitous national fantasy, The American Dream, are founded. That nose-to-the-grindstone commitment to excellence, underscored by Whitney's incomparable talents, afforded Whitney the opportunity to kick off the penultimate display of America's greatest pastime by singing the national anthem—and the mention of her hard work and professional accomplishments sedimented the causal link so often drawn between a strong work ethic, personal opportunity, and professional advancement. But as an African-American woman, Whitney-as-America also charted a narrative of social advancement so integral to more recent iterations of The American Dream. The pre-Bobby-Brown Whitney was the prodigal daughter of Clive Davis, who crafted for Whitney a star persona that would be ideologically and visually palatable to a nation that so desperately wanted to believe that it had come a long way with respect to its many systemic and historical prejudices. And, indeed, that an African-American woman, even one who boasted of such an impressive musical pedigree as Whitney, could, in the immediate aftermath of one of the most politically and socially conservative eras of American history,[4] be invited to sing the national anthem at the Super Bowl certainly seemed to bespeak precisely the type of social change for which Civil Rights and feminist activists had long been fighting. Standing on the makeshift stage that day in Tampa, then, Whitney not only represented a talent that before and since is simply unmatched, but she also stood (in) for "a land in which life should be better and richer and fuller for everyone, with opportunity for each according to ability and achievement" (James Truslow Adams 404). The Whitney of 1991, in short, symbolized the American Dream: "a dream of social order in which each man and each woman shall be able to attain to the fullest stature of which they are innately capable, and be recognized by others for what they are, regardless of the fortuitous circumstances of birth or position" (Adams 404).

1991–2012: Blaming Bobby Brown

The cautionary tale proper begins with a warning and a transgression. Within Whitney's biography, those two narrative elements most often have been conflated in the figure of Bobby Brown, whom Whitney married in 1992 following a three-year engagement. From almost the very beginning of the couple's relationship, many people (from some of Whitney's die-hard fans to members of her home church and media personalities) repeatedly and unequivocally blamed Brown for Whitney's career derailment and drug abuse. In her Biography entry, for example, the author notes that "[w]ith her marriage to singer Bobby Brown in 1992, Houston's career got off track," and later goes on to summarize the couple's marital relationship as follows: "By 1992, Whitney Houston was on top of the world, but her life was about to get very complicated very quickly. That year she married the R&B singer Bobby Brown … At first the marriage was passionate and loving, but things turned sour as the decade progressed and both Brown and Houston battled substance abuse and increasingly erratic behavior" ("Whitney Houston"). For this author, and for many others as well, Brown represented a bad choice who single-handedly triggered, avalanche-like, a "complicated" series of events that caused Whitney's life not merely to "g[e]t off track," but also to "[turn] sour." To be sure, this author attributes some responsibility and even blame to Whitney herself, noting that both artists "battled substance abuse and increasingly erratic behavior" over their 14-year marriage; however, regardless of what role Whitney played in her own devolution, or how much

---

4 See, for example, Ian Haney López and Dedrick Muhammad.

blame is heaped onto her shoulders, this writer and many others like him/her consistently return to that moment in 1992—the moment when Whitney and Brown married—identifying it as the turning point of her life.

Of course, such claims seemed even more justified when the Bravo series *Being Bobby Brown* (2005) premiered in June 2005; although the series was short-lived, lasting only a single season of 11 total episodes, it revealed some harsh (and, at least to that point, somewhat latent) "truths" about the abusive, dysfunctional, and enabling relationship between Whitney and Brown. Considered by many to be Whitney's "darkest public hour" (Juzwiak, "The Strangest Love of All"), *Being Bobby Brown* was supposed to be his comeback, not hers. It bore his name. Yet one of the recurring conceits of the program was how the public failed to recognize Brown's celebrity—and how Brown consistently had to introduce himself as "Whitney Houston's husband." And the entertainment rumor mill has, on more than one occasion, insisted that the program, which earned "incredible ratings," was cancelled midway through production of a second season because Whitney refused to be involved in additional seasons beyond the first (Letslk). That Brown's "comeback" project further contributed to Whitney's fall from grace, then, only added momentum to the claims that Brown was to blame for everything immoral, illegal, and disastrous in Whitney's life. Michael Arceneaux, Opinion contributor to *The Grio*, suggests that Brown was such "an easy target" because "people didn't like their princess being with a sinking R&B star known for arrests, lewdness and everything else antithetical to what made Whitney Houston such a global celebrity." *The Root* columnist Demetria Lucas D'Oyley echoes Arceneaux's claims, noting, "Houston's marriage to Brown didn't jibe with the branding. It was jarring, that first time she didn't seem to be in lockstep with the reigning perception of her, and we keep going back to that moment because it was pivotal *for us.*"

In the end, though, knowing with certainty who is to blame for Whitney's drug problems is significantly less important (if, indeed, the issue is important at all) than understanding why the revelation of an addiction is almost always closely followed by the desire to lay blame. The impulse to hold someone (usually the addict) accountable for an addiction boasts of as lengthy a history in American culture as the metaphor of waste itself; indeed, the two are, as I have shown time and again over the pages of *Wasted*, intimately intertwined. Waste implies an expenditure of resources committed by an agent who acts with purpose and intention. It is an act of destruction. It is a flagrant disregard for well-being—of self, of others, of community. It of necessity demands the identification of a culprit on whom to pin the responsibility for actions that are deemed dangerous, immoral, and/or illegal. But within the cautionary tale, the causal agent (whether a person, a drug, weak will, and so on) always and already exists in an unchanging and unchangeable past that serves, perhaps merely so, as a precursor (or, in classic realist terms, exposition) to the narrative high point. Stated differently, the cautionary tale turns on the consequence, not the causal agent. It derives its narrative force and ideological momentum from the "grisly fate" to which its protagonist (often, though not always, re-cast by the metaphor of waste as anti-hero) inevitably must succumb. As such, the cautionary tale always and only casts its attention onto the addict herself because it is at the site of the addict—within, on, and through her body—that the consequences of addiction are embodied and performed. It is to those consequences that I turn my attention in the final segment of this chapter.

2012: Saying Goodbye

In the final narrative segment of a cautionary tale, the protagonist "comes to a grisly and unpleasant fate" as a result of choosing to participate in the "forbidden act" about which s/he has been forewarned. For Whitney, the forbidden act was drug use—a taboo that, as I discussed in the previous section, was always and only made manifest in the figure of Bobby Brown. In the wake of her death on 11 February 2012, the "grisly" nature of Whitney's fate repeatedly was writ large across American popular culture. From news media reports detailing which drugs (and in what quantities) were found in her hotel room, to offensive "jokes" that I reference briefly in the Preface to this study, and the widespread internet release of Whitney's full autopsy report, virtually every nuance of the years, months, weeks, and even hours leading up to her death was documented in meticulous and sometimes unpleasant detail.[5] One especially illustrative example is the television program *Autopsy*, a British import which premiered in the United States on Reelz in June 2014. Masquerading as "real science" under the narration of world renowned forensic pathologist

---

5 This type of public disclosure is a particularly American response to what is perceived as a moral failing and/or transgression. I am reminded, for instance, of McCarthyism in the mid-twentieth century and the acts of coercion (chief among them the very public "naming names") that were used against American citizens as a means of ferreting out any individuals who had participated in "Un-American Activities." I also am reminded of the ways in which American newspapers during the same period would print names, addresses, and license plate numbers of individuals arrested for (or suspected of participating in) same-sex sexual activity in public bathrooms, a practice thoughtfully documented in Laud Humphreys' seminal work *Tearoom Trade: Impersonal Sex in Public Places* (1970). More recently, I am reminded of the practice of "slut shaming." In these and countless other ways, Americans historically have held up to intense public scrutiny those individuals whose actions or beliefs challenge the moral status quo as a means of simultaneously shaming and blaming the individuals for their failings/transgressions.

Dr. Richard Shepard, *Autopsy: The Last Hours of Whitney Houston* dramatizes the findings of the official autopsy report, taking viewers on a private tour of the bathroom (re-created, of course) at the Beverly Hilton Hotel where the legendary singer died. Throughout the hour-long episode, Shepard describes, sometimes in quite graphic detail, the ravages that years of drug use exacted on Whitney's body (a narrative that calls to mind the autopsy scene from *Wired* that I discuss in Chapter 1); Shepard also devotes much time and attention to identifying and describing the precise manner in which Whitney died. What this program and the multitude of similar news articles underscore is the idea that addicts in America not only must be publicly shamed and blamed for their transgressions (a common narrative trope that I discuss at length in chapters 4 and 5), but also must succumb to a "grisly and unpleasant fate." In many ways, this fate constitutes the unraveling of enigma and the imposition of narrative closure that, as I examine in Chapter 3, is integral to the realist form. But it also and simultaneously serves as a form of ideological and, in Whitney's case, tangible punishment.

While any number of artifacts could serve as a useful springboard for my discussion of the final act in Whitney's personal cautionary tale, I want to look specifically at what has been billed as Whitney's "Last Photo." Published in *The National Enquirer* only four days after Whitney's funeral on 23 February 2012, the "Last Photo" pictures Whitney lying in repose in a viewing room at the Whigham Funeral Home in Newark, New Jersey. Reportedly shot by family friend Raffles van Exel during one of two private viewings held on 18 February 2012 (Atlien), the photograph allegedly was worth a payout of somewhere in the mid-six figures. Although Denise Warner, Executive Editor of Hollywoodlife.com, has unequivocally said that "[n]o one needs to remember Whitney preserved in formaldehyde. And it's certainly not an image that is necessary in the discussion of her life and death" (quoted in Piazza), I would beg to differ. Indeed, I would argue that Whitney's "Last Photo" not only is necessary, but also is integral to understanding her life and death. As one of the most memorable punctuation marks that, at least within the popular imaginary, concluded Whitney's very public biography, that photograph so powerfully conveys much about celebrity, addiction, citizenship, and death in twenty-first-century America, and, for that reason, is very worthy of consideration.

First and foremost, the publication of Whitney's "Last Photo" constitutes an act of mourning and a public expression of grief—one that boasts of a lengthy and interesting history in America. Indeed, as Stanley B. Burns notes in the Preface to *Sleeping Beauty: Memorial Photography in America* (1990), "Postmortem photography, photographing a deceased person, was a common practice in the nineteenth and early twentieth centuries" and, in fact, Burns goes on to explain that "postmortem photographs make up the largest group of nineteenth-century American genre photographs" (Preface, n.p.). During the Victorian period in America, the memorial photograph served as an important visual marker of the decedent—or, as Ben Mattison describes in *The Social Construction of the American Daguerreotype Portrait*, it "often helped to create the presence of the absent—in this case, the dead." As a sort of visual simulacrum of the individual whose likeness it captures, the memorial photograph stands in for the decedent—a copy of the "original" that, through the acts of reproduction and representation, is altered by generation loss, but that nonetheless partially fills a physical and an emotional void that is left by death. As time passes, thereby precipitating acts of misremembering and forgetting, the memorial photograph remains fixed, tangible, present. In this respect, the memorial photograph constitutes a means of suspending the decedent in both space and time. It is simultaneously a commemorative gesture that expresses an individual's desire to remember the decedent, as well as a physical memorial to the decedent, not unlike a traditional headstone or a monetary donation to a favorite charity.

Like more traditional memorial photographs, Whitney's "Last Photo" reflects the American public's need to pay its respects and bid farewell to a celebrity with whom they felt a particular affinity. In this way, the photograph might be understood as an example of what Graham Huggan, in his book *Saviours: Celebrity Conservationists in the Television Age* (2013), terms "mediated grief." Huggan defines "mediated grief" as "a highly visible form of public grief which, channeled through the increasingly wide variety of available media outlets, has the additional capacity to attach itself to an equally wide variety of objects so that the 'original' object of mourning, while not necessarily forgotten, is repeatedly displaced" (123). Huggan goes on to explain that "[m]ediated grief manufactures affection for that which it mourns whether or not that which is mourned was previously known to or experienced by the griever" (123). For centuries in the Western world, displaying bodies in repose—or, more formally, in state—has constituted a ritualized public performance of grief and mourning. To visit the body is to pay respect to the individual whose body is being displayed. Visiting the body also allows the mourner to remark upon the relationship that s/he shared with the decedent, even (and perhaps especially) if the mourner was not intimately associated with the decedent (as typically is so between fan and celebrity). In the case of a deceased celebrity, acts of mourning foremost remark upon the respect and adoration that the mourner holds for the decedent and his/her body of work; a powerful example in recent memory is the spontaneous memorial to British singer-songwriter Amy Winehouse that sprang up on the lawn outside the artist's London flat following her death in July 2011. At the same time, acts of mourning a deceased celebrity also can indicate the intensity of the mourner's fandom: the longer and more intense the mourning, the greater the fandom.

Because Whitney's viewing hours and funeral were closed to the public, the "Last Photo" became a vehicle through which that mourning public could bear witness to the singer's death and pay respect to a life lived.

Psychologically, too, Whitney's "Last Photo" operates very similarly to more traditional memorial photographs, which pacified Victorian fears of death with the comforting promise of an escape from earthly suffering and the achievement of spiritual salvation. The practice of memoralizing the recently deceased through the medium of photography emerged in an historical moment during which death carried very different cultural connotations than it currently does. Burns explains, for instance, that "[w]hat emerges from these images is a vivid visual history of … the change in death concepts and funerary practices, from the image of death as a stark Puritan journey for a sinner to the late Victorian beautification of death and its interpretation as a restful sleep for a redeemed soul" (Preface, n.p.).[6] The practice of mortuary science has long been founded on the premise that death of necessity must be beautified in order to be made aesthetically and psychologically palatable to an audience of mourners. The process of beautification principally implicates the body of the decedent, which must be flushed (of blood, and so on), cleansed, made up, and costumed for public display. But the practice of beautification also involves the entire performance apparatus that frames the viewing, funeral, and burial processes. From the muted pink lighting employed in funeral homes to give the corpse the soft glow of "a restful sleep" to the officiating of funeral services by members of the clergy, most funerary practices are designed to suggest that the decedent has crossed over to another state of existence—symbolized as deep sleep—and signifying grace, salvation, redemption. Whitney's "Last Photo" perfectly captures the ways in which the ravages of death (and the addiction that preceded, and in some ways, precipitated it) are sanitized, rendered visually palatable, for a viewing audience. From the subdued lighting in the viewing room, to the positioning of the body, to the angle of the camera's gaze (which captures Whitney in side profile), and the simple purple dress that adorns the body, Whitney's "Last Photo" is the portrait of serenity and peace. The "Last Photo" is rendered even more tranquil by the implicit contrast that was drawn in the media between it and photographs of Whitney and daughter Bobbi Kristina

---

6 While death in the Western world currently is regarded in much different terms than during the Victorian period that spawned the practice of memorial photography, a newly emergent entrepreneurial venture (that is, remembrance photography) suggests that some of the earlier attitudes toward death, memory, and grief remain, at least where the deaths of infants and children are concerned. One such venture, for instance, aptly named Now I Lay Me Down to Sleep, promises to "Provide the gift of remembrance photography for parents suffering the loss of a baby."

emerging from Tru Hollywood, taken only two days prior to her death. Even before her death, these photographs from Tru Hollywood—which capture a disheveled Whitney, blood running down her leg, cursing at assembled club-goers—were widely disseminated across mass and social media. Staff writers for Bossip, for example, ran the photographs under the headline "Houston, We Have a Problem ... Again! Whitney Leaves Hollyweird Nightclub Lookin' Cray," and captioned one of the photographs with the following: "We're not saying no names, but somebody needs to go back to rehab. Whitney Houston was spotted leaving Tru Hollywood Nightclub last night looking a hot mess." The photographs snapped outside of Tru Hollywood, then, stand in sharp visual and ideological contrast to Whitney's "Last Photo," providing almost a causal context for the narrative after-effect of death captured in the latter.

Memorial photographs generally, and Whitney's "Last Photo" particularly, further work to psychologically pacify an audience of mourners by combatting a wide range of cultural taboos that, within Western culture, have long been associated with death. In *Over Her Dead Body: Death, Femininity and the Aesthetic* (1992), Elisabeth Bronfen explains, "the fear of death is so strong that European culture has made the corpse into a taboo. It sees decomposition as the body's most polluted condition, so that touching and seeing a corpse can be dangerous, and requires subsequent purification" (60). Death constitutes the process by which the body is rendered taboo in part because it signifies the individual's failure to control the material body. In this respect, death has come to symbolize absolute submission to a force more powerful than humanity itself and, as such, it serves as a daunting reminder of our subservient position within the "natural order" and the great chain of being. Death also and simultaneously represents the absolute decimation of the individual, the self. Psychologically the thought of one's own extinction, of ceasing to exist, is inconceivable to the ego and is, according to *Psychology Today* contributor Karl Albrecht, one of "only 5 fears we all share." (Albrecht notes, for instance, that "The idea of *no longer being* arouses *a primary existential anxiety* in all normal humans.") In the first place, the fact that Whitney's corpse was (re-)presented in the form of a photograph helped to pacify, if not nullify, the fears of contamination and pollution that typically accompany the touching of a corpse by locating the viewer at a "safe" remove from the body. Additionally, the viewer's "existential anxiety" around death is curbed in this instance through the inane suggestion that Whitney's death was unnatural ("untimely" was a word often employed in media accounts) and avoidable (a result of her addiction, which she "easily" could have "just stopped").

Although Whitney's "Last Photo" shares some important similarities with conventional memorial photographs, it also differs quite markedly from that tradition. Most significantly, Whitney's "Last Photo" was never intended to serve as a private memorial to the late artist; rather, it was always and only regarded as a commodity for public consumption and individual profit. In this way, *The National Enquirer's* publication of Whitney's "Last Photo" reveals the insidious machinations of capitalism and the ways in which that system often is generative of the metaphor of waste. At its core, this system is exploitative in nature, encouraging individuals to capitalize on the human tragedies of addiction and death as a means of "earning" a profit or an advantage. Within this system, one person's gain is always and only predicated on the objectification of the individual, the commodification of her addiction, and the peddling of that addiction's presumed consequences—a narrative trajectory built squarely on the ideological and literal jettisoning of the addict's right to privacy. Indeed, within the operations of capitalism, at least as the system is practiced by tabloid "journalists" like those employed by *The National Enquirer*, the addict's right to privacy is rendered little more than a waste product in the quest for the almighty dollar. Within this representational economy, Whitney herself was rendered an object: degraded to the status of possession (of the photographer, of *The National Enquirer*, of the American public); denied both autonomy (self-definition and -determination) and subjectivity; and used as a "tool," or instrument, for the purpose of another person's gain or advantage. Personal relationships and lived experiences are rendered commercial through the enactment of a financial exchange that foregrounds the values of competition, self-interest, and profit while simultaneously de-emphasizing the values of compassion, empathy, and altruism. At the same time, the packaging of Whitney's death in the form of the "Last Photo," and the assignation of an economic value to that photograph, commodifies not only Whitney-the-individual, but also Whitney-the-addict. To commodify the addict is to identify her private struggles and tragedies as fodder for public spectacle. The spectacle itself constitutes and is constituted by a pre-packaged set of cultural narratives that are saleable to the American public (and therefore desirable by a parasitic publication like *The National Enquirer*) precisely because they are recognizable, as well as psychologically and ideologically palatable.

Whitney's "Last Photo" further differs from traditional memorial photography because it constitutes a marker of punishment, and it is here that we can begin to see quite clearly the intersections of the cautionary tale genre, the metaphor of waste, and American nationalism. On one hand, the photograph serves as a visual record of the (divine?) punishment inflicted on Whitney as a consequence of her (moral?) transgressions. In this regard, death stands as a "natural"—even inevitable—enactment of retribution against Whitney for her repeated drug use and for her seemingly wanton disregard for her unparalleled talent. In fact, in 2009 upon the release of Whitney's "comeback album" *I Look to You*, self-described "Pop Music Critic" Ann Powers of *The Los Angeles Times* ruminates at length about the tragedy of "Houston's voice [falling] into disrepair." Powers unselfconsciously asserts that Whitney's many "excesses trashed her instrument" and, in a passage that was quoted to Whitney in her by-now infamous interview with Oprah Winfrey that same year, Powers laments Whitney's "seemingly careless treatment of the national treasure that happened to reside within her." Less album review than morality tale, Powers' article is laced with one irresponsible and erroneous comment after another regarding Whitney's addictions. To begin with, the word choice often is quite telling with respect to Powers' attitude toward and misunderstanding of addiction. To assert that Whitney "trashed" her instrument, or that she treated it carelessly, is to assign a degree of agency to the addict that simply does not exist, especially in someone who had nurtured and had been enabled in her addictions for decades. But this word choice also and simultaneously works to shame and blame the addict—a common rhetorical move that, as readers have seen in previous chapters, occurs across temporal, geographical, historical, and generic contexts. What is being "trashed," then, by Powers' review is Whitney herself—rendered a mere waste product at the hands of Powers' own "professional credentials" (after all, she self-identifies as a "Pop Music Critic" in her byline) by the very discourses of shame, blame, and waste that have circumscribed the lived experiences of addiction at least since the addict emerged as a recognizable identity construct in the nineteenth century. Her review is at best irresponsible in its peddling of misinformation about the nature and trajectory of addiction, but it powerfully reinforces the final act moral of the cautionary tale: namely, that "the violator comes to a grisly and unpleasant fate." The photograph not only reminds us of Whitney's "trashed" voice (for example, Whitney in death is silenced),[7] but it also visually drives home the long-standing equation that culturally has been drawn between addiction and certain death, which becomes perhaps the most grisly and unpleasant fate of all.

At the same time, the very nature of tabloid journalism suggests that Whitney's "Last Photo" not only serves as a visual *record* of the punishment inflicted on Whitney for her addictions, but also constitutes a form of punishment in itself. In *Newzak and News Media* (1997), Bob Franklin

---

7   In this regard, Whitney's "Last Photo" calls to mind Coco Fusco's mixed media performance installation *Better Yet When Dead*, in which the performance artist considered "why Latino cultures in the north and south are so fascinated with female creativity once it has been forever silenced" ("Better Yet When Dead"). For this installation, Fusco "converted galleries into funeral parlors and held a series of wakes" for Latina artists like Selena, Ana Mendieta, Sara Gomez, and Eva Perón. In blurring the boundaries between reality and fiction, Fusco hoped that "all the feelings of the uncanny that direct encounters with the dead often produce would become the starting point for an emotional and intellectual exploration of the issues [she] raise[s]" ("Better Yet When Dead").

describes tabloid journalism as "scandal and sensationalism, too frequently masquerading in perverse guise as human interest" (3). Karin E. Becker regards tabloid journalism in a similar way, and she goes on to identify a precondition and an effect of its sensationalist nature: "a component common to the various constructions of the sensational is that attracting attention takes precedence over other journalistic values, including accuracy, credibility and political or social significance" (84). In her prime, Whitney graced the covers of *Jet, Ebony, People, Essence, Rolling Stone, Vibe, Bazaar,* and many other popular and credible entertainment periodicals—her mere presence on the cover enough to ensure excellent newsstand sales. As her troubled private life surfaced and began impacting her professional life and celebrity persona, tabloid journalists declared "open season" on virtually every aspect of Whitney's life, but especially her addictions. In March 2006, *The National Enquirer* promised its readers a "World Exclusive" look "Inside Whitney's Drug Den!" In July 2010, Whitney once again made the cover of *The National Enquirer* for her alleged "$6,300 A Week Drug Habit!" And less than four months before her death, *The Globe* reporters pondered "Whitney Houston Goes Berserk: Is She Back on Drugs?" (These headlines represent only a handful of the many sensational tabloid stories devoted to Whitney over the years, but especially following her marriage to Brown.) The relegation of Whitney's private life—whether fact, fiction, or some manufactured reality in between—to tabloid fodder constitutes a kind of "rock bottom" for a celebrity of her stature. It suggests quite compellingly the fall from grace that she experienced within the American popular imaginary and it identifies quite incontrovertibly her weak will and, less so, her addictions as responsible for that fall. In this respect, the tabloids suggest, Whitney not only "trashed" her instrument, but also wasted her career and, indeed, her life—an all-too-common refrain that was echoed time and again in the years following Whitney's marriage to Brown, but especially in the hours, days, weeks, and so on following her death.

This iteration of Whitney's biography echoes the victim-obsessed "view of national identity" that Berlant describes in *The Queen of America Goes to Washington* (1997), except here the addict becomes the victimizer, and the nation itself becomes the unwitting victim. It is important first to recall that Whitney's vocal talent was cast as a "national treasure"—a point that was reiterated for a wide audience in the very credible voice of Oprah Winfrey during her 2009 interview with Whitney. Implicitly likened to artifacts like *The Declaration of Independence,* locations like Yellowstone National Park, and animals like the bald eagle, Whitney's voice becomes a cog in the machinery of nationalism, a shared cultural legacy that reinforces community (in the form of the nation-state) as an integral building block of social life. Because the nation itself only ever enjoys a tenuous temporal and spatial existence, artifacts like "national treasures"—or, as I discuss in Chapter 1, cultural mythologies like The American Dream—are integral to maintaining the necessary fiction that the nation is inviolable, coherent, permanent. Such artifacts and mythologies, indeed, sustain the nation. They lend to the nation and its citizens a shared sense of cultural identity that geospatially demarcates the nation and socially differentiates its citizens from those who would self-identify with another nation-state. (In doing so, these artifacts also fuel the us/them binary that has dominated international politics and relations for time immemorial.) Such artifacts and mythologies also are generative of the fervent patriotism necessary to defend the ever-permeable and -unstable boundaries of the nation against internal and external criticism, political corruption, and physical conflict. Such artifacts and mythologies, in short, render the intangible nation tangible, giving citizens something larger to identify with, to believe in, to die for. To lay waste to one of our shared "national treasures," then, is to lay waste to the nation itself. It is to unsettle the very foundations of American nationalism and to call into question the geospatial and ideological boundaries of the nation. In the end, Whitney was a woman who seemed to "have it all," and then she seemed to squander her talents, her privilege, her national treasure on an addiction. For wasting the national treasure that "reside[d] within her," Whitney not only could not be forgiven, but also had to be publically exposed and, as a result, humiliated for the very moral transgressions that supposedly had contributed to her wastefulness. Such is the cultural work of Whitney's "Last Photo." And such are the deadly operations of the metaphor of waste.

Conclusion
On Being Wasted
in America—Redux

The body is never only what we think it is (dancers pay attention to this difference).
Illusive, always on the move, the body is at best like something, but it never is
that something. Thus, the metaphors enunciated in speech or in movement,
that allude to it are what give the body the most tangible substance it has.
Susan Leigh Foster, "Choreographing History," p. 4

We live, dream, love, work, and, eventually, die in metaphor. Indeed, the very language through which we communicate our ideas, our experiences, our aspirations, and our fears is steeped in metaphor. To lay claim to a "broken heart" at the end of a relationship with a significant other is to metaphorically allude to the intense sadness that a person is emotionally experiencing. To refer to a college education as the "Holy Grail" is to metaphorically identify that goal as especially desired, highly sought after, even ideal. And to describe someone as having a "heart of gold" is to metaphorically point out that person's kindness, generosity, altruism. Examples of metaphoric language—the phrase itself a redundancy since all language is, to greater or lesser degrees, metaphoric—abound in American English, occurring in (or, as) virtually every part of speech.

At a base level, all metaphors are descriptive, offering an accessible account of the appearance or experience of something else. However, metaphors not only can determine how we think and perceive, but also can shape—sometimes quite profoundly—how we behave. Throughout the pages of *Wasted*, I have concerned myself with a similarly controlling metaphor—the metaphor of waste—and the ways in which that metaphor not only vividly (albeit problematically) describes the experiences of addiction, but also shapes how Americans perceive, respond to, and live through their addictions. As I have discussed in previous chapters, the metaphor of waste determines to greater or lesser degrees how addicts navigate the world and perceive themselves within that world. The blame that this metaphor attributes to the addict manifests itself in the addict's psyche, perpetuating a deterministic and damaging cycle of self-loathing that ultimately enables the addict to sink increasingly deeper into the ravages of his/her addictions. This metaphor also shapes how others perceive addicts. It is responsible, if not wholly then in large part, for the sideways glances directed at an addict who bravely has given voice to his/her addiction. It encourages non-addicts to patronize and condescend to addicts—to view them as victims of their own bad choices and broken moral compasses. It sometimes generates pity, but more often vindicates the frustration, the anger, and ultimately the resignation that non-addicts express toward addicts. It enables non-addicts, under the guise of "tough love," to justify the abandonment of the addict and the denial of access to emotional support, as well as to the very material and financial resources that s/he needs possibly to break the cycle of addiction (itself a metaphoric buttress for the metaphor of waste). Because this metaphor casts addiction as a willful choice and a wanton disregard for personal and public health, it also shapes public policy, justifying Draconian legislation that unilaterally criminalizes all acts of drug use and possession. Finally, that this metaphor is premised on the addict's unwillingness—rather than inability—to stop using contributes to the widespread propagation of self-help rhetoric and 12-step recovery programs as normative in the rehabilitation of addicts. It supports treatment options that are, at best, ineffectual for the vast majority of addicts, and it then insinuates those treatment options into the system of jurisprudence as mandates of a convicted addict's sentence. It blames addicts when these treatment programs fail and simultaneously denies those addicts access to other, more effective forms of treatment through highly regimented insurance policies that limit the type, quality, and duration of treatment programs available to policy holders. In short, the metaphor of waste time and again locks the addict into a deterministic, oppressive, and quite often fatal cycle of abuse in which rehabilitation and respect are, at best, pipe dreams. The above examples constitute only some of the most visible ways that the metaphor of waste impacts the lived experiences of addicts and non-addicts alike, but collectively they offer a powerful reminder that the influence of metaphor extends well beyond the realm of mere language.

Metaphor itself is inescapable. It both circumscribes and animates our epistemological, ideological, and ontological beings in both explicit and implicit, tangible and intangible ways. While we perhaps cannot deny the pervasive influence that metaphor generally exerts over our ways of thinking, living, and being, we can challenge the influence that certain metaphors have over us. We can, in short, begin to untangle, if not entirely liberate, ourselves from the deleterious effects of metaphor and we do so, at least initially, by identifying what these harmful metaphors are and what specific dangers they pose. Throughout the pages of *Wasted*, I have labored in this endeavor, reading "against interpretation" as a means of rendering the metaphor of waste "exposed, criticized, belabored, used up" (Sontag 182). But exposure and critique are only one phase of the process of reading "against interpretation"; such a project also of necessity must involve the imagining and the promoting of alternative metaphors that challenge the representational and ideological status quo. Such is the focus of my endeavors in this final, concluding chapter.

Here, I turn my attention away from the metaphor of waste and toward one of these alternative metaphors that might begin to unsettle the stranglehold that the metaphor of waste has had over the American cultural imaginary since the nineteenth century. Specifically, this chapter concerns itself with a dance routine about addiction that was choreographed by Mia Michaels and that was featured on the fifth season of FOX's *So You Think You Can Dance* (2005—present). Set to Sara Bareilles' "Gravity," the piece premiered during the 8 July 2009 episode of the program and features dancers Kayla Radomski and Kupono Aweau. The style of the dance is contemporary and, as is characteristic of that genre, the choreography borrows quite heavily on both classical ballet and modern dance, as well as on other forms of non-dance-related movement practices like yoga, Pilates, the Feldenkrais Method, and corporeal mime. The "narrative" that unfolds over the one-minute-forty-five-second routine casts Kayla as an addict who is controlled and ultimately consumed by her addiction (that is, Kupono). As the addict, Kayla appears vulnerable, even, at times, broken. Her movements often are jerky and tentative—a sharp contrast to what viewers of the program had, by season five, come to expect not only of contemporary dance generally, but of Mia Michaels's choreography particularly. Kayla's hair is tousled, even wild, and her wine-colored costume is "shredded" across the torso. By contrast, Kupono plays the addiction as mesmerizing, seductive, predatory. He is clean-cut—his hair is closely cropped, and his slacks and vest (both in neutral shades of grey) are crisp, freshly pressed. His movements are fluid. His physicality is commanding. And his presence dominates both Kayla and the performance space.

Although this routine was created and produced for a mainstream television program of some popularity and acclaim, it nonetheless poses significant challenges to the metaphor of waste, ultimately encouraging viewers to "change the way [they] look at [addiction]" (Wayne Dyer quoted in Ford 20) so that our shared cultural perceptions of addiction can themselves change. In this respect, I look to this dance as a case study in what might lie just beyond the metaphor of waste. Within the apparatus of dance, the body becomes a site of near infinite possibilities. It is, as dance historian Susan Leigh Foster explains, "always on the move"—both literally and metaphorically. As the dancers' bodies traverse the stage, tracing in both time and space Mia Michaels's intricate choreography, those bodies suggest a range of subject positions, lived experiences, and cultural narratives that "deprive" the metaphor of waste both its authority and its meaning. At its core, dance is a form that demands complete commitment by and engagement of the body—to the choreography, to each other, and to the spectators. The reciprocity, cooperation, and collaboration witnessed between Kayla (the addict) and Kupono (the addiction) runs counter to the dominant cultural narrative that historically has shamed and blamed the addict for her broken moral compass while, at the same time, acknowledging through Kupono's characterization, the hypnotic, even seductive nature of an addition—that is, the ways in which it robs the addict of autonomy and lures her into a destructive behavioral cycle. Driven neither to conserve nor to squander, this dance expends, even exhausts, every resource on which it draws, at least in its original, live iteration. The dance drains the creativity of its choreographer. It taxes the bodies of its dancers. And it exhausts the emotional storehouses of its spectators. But like all genres of live performance, this dance adamantly resists the compulsion to waste. In fact, within the representational apparatus of this dance, and for the duration of its live performance, the addict is not deterministically circumscribed by a pre-existing meaning, but rather is momentarily saturated in an abundance of significations. Within the "maniacally charged present" (Phelan 148) that is the domain of live performance, the bodies of these two dancers acknowledge "the very real consequences" (Sontag 102) of metaphor. As these bodies sweat and labor under the exacting demands of the choreography, they remind us of the intimate (albeit often ignored) link between metaphor and materiality. And, at the close of the dance, as the music ends, the performance begins to fade into memory, and the dancers reemerge as mere contestants on a reality television program, we are powerfully, even painfully, reminded of the many losses engendered by metaphor, of the ways in which, as Sontag writes, metaphor "kills." In the pages that follow, I engage with the possibilities that this dance suggests—the many ways in which it encourages its spectators to read "against interpretation" and thereby works to unsettle, challenge, expose the metaphor of waste.

The routine opens with Kupono standing at center stage, his left arm extended at a right angle, perpendicular to his torso, as if summoning someone into an embrace. From stage right, Kayla runs barefoot to him, snaking under Kupono's extended left arm and stopping abruptly in side profile to the audience, almost like she is stunned or hypnotized. As Sara Bareilles' voice intones, "Something always brings me back to you," Kupono's left arm encircles Kayla's shoulders while his right hand, snake-like, traces an exaggerated, mesmerizing "S"-shape that extends far above his frame. In the next moments, Kupono side bends left, his right arm sweeping in a wide, fluid arc over his head and toward the floor, simultaneously guiding Kayla's body through a back bend and then immediately into a series of torso convulsions that are perfectly timed to the down beats of the musical score. These opening bars of the routine establish quite vividly the power dynamics between the pair and some of the larger themes at work within the piece. As the embodiment of addiction, Kupono physically dominates the performance space. He is taller and more visibly muscular than Kayla. He occupies center stage for much of the routine. And his movements often guide and direct hers. In the opening sequence described above, for example, Kayla's back bend and torso convulsions seemingly are initiated and controlled by Kupono's seductive hand gestures. He is the puppet master, she the marionette. Later in the piece, Kupono throws Kayla's body across the performance space, the integrity of the choreography and, indeed, Kayla's very safety almost entirely dependent on his training, strength, and skill. And toward the end of the routine, the pair executes a series of movements, apart and in unison; yet even here, Kupono appears to lead his partner, largely because he visually is positioned in front of Kayla.

Immediately following the opening sequence, Kayla—arms outstretched in what could be interpreted as complete abandon—free falls forward into Kupono's arms, which he snakes around her body in a kind of lover's embrace. From this position, Kupono maneuvers Kayla's body around the performance space and through a series of movements, including a turn sequence and a lift; during this segment of the choreography, Kayla's body remains limp, doll-like. She is not merely led around the performance space, as is typical in a variety of partner dances; instead, she is rendered an object, a hand property, whose entire being is controlled by Kupono. Yet spectators would be remiss to forget that the sequence is initiated by an act of submission in which Kayla falls into Kupono's arms. At the most basic level, the gesture suggests the trust that is shared between two dancers, and specifically Kayla's faith in the ability and the strength of Kupono to execute the choreography successfully. But the gesture also and simultaneously alludes to the addict's utter dependence on and obedience to her addiction. To some spectators, then, the sequence might suggest that Kayla eventually could come under the complete influence and control of her addiction, but her possession as an object of the addiction is the direct result of a choice that she initially made (and, of course, the chronology is of vital import to American audiences).

Certainly this interpretation of the opening moments of the choreography has some compelling support to recommend it. However, there also are a number of subtle details that this interpretation overlooks. To begin with, the song lyric that serves as a backdrop for the stage action subtly alludes to the idea that the addict is not wholly in control of her actions when under the mesmerizing psychological and physiological spell of an addiction. "Something" is an indefinite pronoun that points (albeit ambiguously) to an unspecified noun as the cause of Kayla's addiction. *Something* always brings the addict back to her addiction, although whether that "something" is her own poor choices (represented by Kayla's running with reckless abandon?) or the relentless coercion of the addiction itself is decidedly unclear. Furthermore, that lyric renders the addict a direct object—"something always *brings me* back to you"—a recipient of the active verb, rather than an actor in her own right. The very grammatical structure of the lyric, then, resists the notion that addiction is a conscious choice, even if that lyric fails to pinpoint exactly the root and source of addiction. Finally, that Kayla's initial movements are initiated by the music—indeed, that the music plays for a fraction of a second *before* Kayla breaks into the run—suggests that she is being prompted, directed, even led by a force external to herself. In short, the moment poses a subtle, but compelling, challenge to the metaphor of waste by refusing to shackle only the addict with blame for her addiction.

Furthermore, Kayla's free fall into Kupono's arms initiates a sequence of give-and-take movements in which it is sometimes difficult to determine who leads and who follows, thereby making it equally difficult to determine a chain of causality and blame for Kayla's addiction. Of particular note is the series of movements that occurs immediately following the turn and lift sequence that I describe briefly above. Throughout the turn and lift sequence, Kayla's body is limp, near-lifeless, mimicking the ways in which addiction strips the addict of autonomy. From the lift, Kupono plants Kayla onto the dance floor immediately in front of him. Here, Kayla attempts to steady herself, striking a shaky, pseudo chair pose: her arms outstretched away from her body (a steadying gesture), her knees bent, her feet more than hip-distance apart. The posture that Kayla momentarily strikes is, in part, an empowering tableau, suggesting that the addict is capable of breaking the spell of her addiction and "standing on her own two feet." At the same time, the choreography reminds viewers quite persuasively that this autonomy is temporary and conditional. Perched unsteadily on the balls of her feet, Kayla falters in this position, but remains upright, a visual reminder of the razor-thin line that the addict often walks between sobriety and addiction. This idea is reinforced by Kupono, who looms in the immediate background, an omnipotent and domineering figure ready to catch her should she fall. In the next moments of the piece, Kupono once again manipulates Kayla's actions, initiating, in his character's signature puppetmaster-like fashion, a pair of upper-body side bends/convulsions—first left, then right—that culminates in the equivalent of a standing full-body stretch. With arms extended upward at awkward angles, Kayla stands frozen in open-mouthed panic as Kupono sidles closer to her and snakes his right arm around one of her extended arms. The power dynamic between the pair as they execute this series of movements is, at best, ambiguous. Kayla stands apart from Kupono—the addict physically free from her addiction—and yet she perpetually is watched over, sometimes controlled, and eventually possessed by him—a powerful reminder that while addiction is at the very least initially predicated on an autonomous choice, its power eventually overcomes the addict in ways that render her "choices" virtually unrecognizable as such.

Perhaps the most evocative of these gestures of possession occurs about 30 seconds into the routine, immediately following the sequence of steps in which Kupono maneuvers Kayla's body around the stage, rag-doll-like. During this sequence, Kupono, in smooth but rapid succession, manipulates Kayla's body into two successive leg extensions. In the second of these extensions, Kupono holds Kayla's legs in a perfectly perpendicular position to the dance floor as he traces the line of her torso and her upstretched leg with the side of his face. Eyes closed, mouth slightly agape, Kupono's expression is sexually charged, if not orgasmic. It is a gesture of complete and utter possession, signifying the all-consuming way in which addiction so thoroughly arrests the addict's autonomy and power of choice. Like a puppeteer, Kupono manipulates Kayla's body through a series of invisible strings and wires, his sweeping gestures serving as a kind of physical manifestation of Mia Michaels's hypnotic choreography. However, unlike a traditional puppeteer, who encourages the audience's suspension of disbelief through masterful (albeit hidden) manipulations that seemingly breathe life into an inanimate object, Kupono not only reveals to the audience his "working" of the puppet, but also renders Kayla increasingly more inanimate as the piece progresses.

At the same time, for Kayla, it is a gesture of complete surrender—to the addiction, to her partner, to the choreography, and to the live moment of performance. Her body becomes little more than a hand property for Kupono, at least that is the implication of his guiding her into various postures throughout this sequence of movements. Without the ability to ward off the addiction, Kayla tosses her head back, as if simultaneously in a state of pure ecstasy and absolute resignation, and obediently follows the lead of her partner. In some respects, this section of the choreography so beautifully—and simultaneously hauntingly—captures the way in which, for some addicts, their go-to drug, and even their addiction, becomes like a lover, a point that I touch briefly on in Chapter 4. The dance, after all, is incredibly intimate, even sensual, in nature, especially when compared to the stiff and lifeless reboot of the routine performed by Lindsay and Cole several seasons later. Much of the dance is performed with the dancers positioned in close proximity to each other. The curves and lines of the dancers' bodies are visually alluring, and the movements at times are suggestive of various sexual acts. In fact, the positioning of Kupono behind and (seemingly) in possession of Kayla reinforces conventional sex role stereotypes for males and females that often are fetishized in the American popular imaginary and that continue to be the lifeblood of much of the mainstream pornography industry. In the interplay between agony and ecstasy, between pain and pleasure, between dominance and submission, the dancers strike a series of tableaus that powerfully expresses how it feels to be in the throes of an addiction: the utter ecstasy of the high; the self-alienation that results from both physiological and psychological possession; and, finally, the complete and absolute surrender to the power of an all-consuming force external (and antithetical) to the self.

By rendering Kayla a possession of her addiction, the choreography also illustrates rather evocatively the ways in which addicts in the throes of their addictions are objectified by the very addictions over which they supposedly have control. Part of the objectification of Kayla occurs through the repeated attempts of Kupono to "silence" her. In fact, at four different points in the choreography (0:44, 0:58, 1:32, 1:38), Kupono places one or both of his hands over Kayla's mouth, a silencing gesture that symbolically alludes to the ways in which an addiction erodes the addict's powers of choice and of self-definition. One of the most evocative of such moments occurs at one of the climactic moments of the song and the choreography. Immediately following the leg extension sequence, Kupono releases Kayla's extended leg and Kayla, appearing dazed, stands center stage in front of, and noticeably apart from, Kupono. Against the backdrop of the lyric "But you're onto me," Kupono, whose left hand rests possessively on Kayla's shoulder, sweeps his right hand in an exaggerated arc across and up Kayla's body, ultimately cupping his hand over her lower face. Kayla reacts by white-knuckle grabbing Kupono's hand and forearm and eventually ripping his hand from her mouth. The sequence of movements that follows reiterates this back-and-forth struggle between the addiction's compulsion to possess and the addict's desire to break free, to survive. Kupono places his hands on Kayla's upper thighs—first left, then right. With both hands, Kayla manages to push Kupono's hands down and away from her body. But Kupono quickly recovers and, over the next few seconds, his hands mark a proprietary pattern across Kayla's body. In rapid succession, his hands first meet at her lower abdomen. Although Kayla manages to swat away the right hand, it quickly sweeps up to grasp possessively at her upper torso. As Kayla swats at the hand that covers her breast, Kupono's other hand returns to cover her mouth. With both hands, Kayla manages to tear Kupono's hand from her mouth. Her head thrown back, her arms outstretched like a runner crossing the finish line, Kayla appears for a split second to be free of Kupono's grasp. But as she tries to advance beyond his possessive orbit, she is jerked to a halt by Kupono's hands, which have traveled, almost unnoticed by the spectator, to rest lightly on her hips. This sequence unfolds rapidly, lasting only about eight seconds of the routine, yet it very vividly illustrates the constant tug-of-war that the addict must endure between addiction and autonomy, and ultimately the choreography identifies that struggle as a losing battle for the addict. It is a stark and starkly honest representation of addiction—one that is all the more striking given its unconventionality. The choreography of this piece acknowledges addiction as a powerful, all-consuming force that at once overwhelms and possesses the addict, stripping her of the very psychological faculties that would enable the exercise of autonomy. Here, the addict is "always" brought back to her addiction by some invisible, but compelling, force that is both outside and beyond herself. She is trapped within the destructive cycle of her addiction, but she is not wholly (or, perhaps even partially) to blame for the havoc that that addiction wreaks. She is a dancer, following the lead of her partner. She is a puppet, acting on the directives of her puppeteer. She is an addict blindly following the demands of her addiction.

The middle portion of the routine, beginning at about 45 seconds in, consists of a series of movements that highlight the physical and emotional struggles in which an addict is perpetually engaged. This segment of the choreography begins at the conclusion of the tug-of-war hand sequence described above, with Kayla momentarily free from, then once again immediately possessed by, Kupono's grasp. In the next moments, Kupono lifts Kayla under both arms and throws her several feet across the performance space. Although the movement is executed gracefully, rather than violently, and the moment even bespeaks a kind of intimacy shared between the dancers, it also speaks quite clearly and directly to the hold and the power that the male partner (that is, the addiction) has over the female partner (that is, the addict). Indeed, lifts and throws turn on and presuppose the strength and skill of the male partner. Regardless of the degree of a lift's difficulty, its successful execution demands a heightened level of strength, skill, and physical dexterity on the part of the male dancer. His movements determine the height and the speed of the throw, as well as the directionality of the female's body both in the air and in the landing. All of these factors contribute significantly to whether the landing ultimately will be safe, steady, and successful. In other words, the lift, while relatively uncomplicated and lacking the theatricality of many more complex lifts featured on the program, nonetheless highlights the male's physical prowess and his command over his partner, over the choreography, and over the performance space. In this way, the lift-throw combination subtly emphasizes the addiction's sovereignty over the addict's body. That Kupono executes his movements so fluidly, so expertly, alludes to the mesmerizing power that illicit and controlled substances can exert on the body and mind—the way that the addiction seductively arrests the addict's power of choice, her discernment, until finally she is merely a body "soaring high" at the deft hands of her addiction.

Of course, the effective execution of the lift-throw combination also presupposes a great deal of skill, and even participation, on the part of the female partner. Her timing and technique are partly responsible for a successful and safe entrance into the lift-throw. The positionality of her body, and the distribution of its weight, while in the air contribute significantly to the quality, safety, and aesthetic appeal of the landing. In short, despite the common misconception that the female partner is a passive object that is lifted and thrown by her male partner, this dance reminds its viewers that the successful execution of a piece of choreography demands an equal commitment (of skill, of labor, and so on) by both dancers—a realization that poses serious challenges to the metaphor of waste. In particular, the (implicitly?) active role that Kayla assumes both here and elsewhere reminds spectators that the addict bears at least some responsibility for her addiction. But unlike the metaphor of waste, this choreography refuses to place the blame entirely at the doorstep of the addict, instead repeatedly acknowledging the power play—the dance—in which the addict and her addiction are perpetually engaged. This realization—like the dance that initiates it—is both haunting and hauntingly beautiful.

The power play enacted between Kayla and Kupono is reiterated over the next 20-plus seconds of the routine, as the couple fluidly executes a series of tumbles, kicks, and pseudo-lifts that culminates in the climax of the piece. Following the lift-throw, Kayla lands unsteadily on her left foot for a split second before collapsing, weak-kneed, to the ground, falling backward, and mock tumbling into a modified hero pose. Meanwhile, Kupono bounds across the stage in a series of cat-like movements, ultimately landing beside Kayla, first in a similar modified hero pose, then with both legs extended out in front of him. These movements are executed as Bareilles's voice sings, "I live here on my knees." The visual (and aural) allusion to hero pose here is, I suspect, ironic. A strengthening posture for the ankles and arches of the feet, the yoga posture stands in sharp contrast to those numerous moments earlier in the choreography when Kayla's feet falter or completely give way under her. It alludes to the physiological and even psychological impacts that addiction has on the material body: how addiction weakens the body's and the mind's defenses; how addiction wrests that body from the physical, relational, and environmental moorings that ground and center it; how addiction both literally and symbolically brings an addict to her knees. From their places on the stage floor, Kupono grasps Kayla around the waist and assists her in stepping over his body, a position from which Kayla first propels herself backwards and then executes a tumble-roll that concludes with Kayla springing to her feet. Meanwhile, Kupono also has risen to his feet, has crossed the several feet that separate him from Kayla, and has struck an odd tableau: his left knee bent, his left leg extended at a 90-ish-degree-angle from his body. Kayla kicks twice at Kupono's extended leg, while at the same time her upper torso convulses spasmodically and in no discernible rhythm or pattern. Next, Kupono places his hands on the front and back of Kayla's head and lifts Kayla vertically several feet off of the stage floor, her own feet kicking helplessly beneath her as she attempts and fails to gain some traction. As Kayla's feet once again make contact with the stage floor, she almost immediately launches into a kick sequence: first, with a back kick reminiscent of figure skater Denise Biellmann (a move that is executed while her hand is clasped by Kupono's), then with a fan kick that is executed over Kupono's stooped form (their handhold momentarily separated). In the final moments of this sequence, the pair executes a series of tumbles and jumps that are performed in unison.

Perhaps most notable in this section of the choreography are the various kicks that, when repeated so frequently within such a relatively short timeframe, become a visual leitmotif that warrants some serious consideration. In general, a kick is a physical gesture initiated by the foot and/or the lower leg that often is defensive in nature and that serves as a means of warding off a threatening force. To kick, in this respect, is "to show temper, annoyance, defiance, dislike, and so on; to rebel, be recalcitrant" ("kick, v.1"). Early in the sequence described above, as Kayla kicks twice at Kupono's extended leg, her gestures appear to be driven by temper, defiance, even dislike. Her torso convulses, suggesting that perhaps she is in the throes of a "bad high," and the kicks constitute a lashing out at the force (that is, her addiction) that she holds responsible for her current suffering. That Kayla is shown repeatedly to resist the compelling hold of her addiction directly challenges the deeply-entrenched belief that addicts are (or become) passive with respect to their addictions, willingly and willfully giving themselves completely over to their drug of choice. That these kicks are ineffectual, failing to unsettle, or even budge, Kupono visually underscores the stranglehold that an addiction has over an addict. The second set of kicks also is cast as ineffectual. After Kayla has been lifted vertically into the air, her feet flail underneath her, attempting (and failing) to gain traction on the stage floor below. (It is, I think, also noteworthy that Kupono's hands, which are placed on the front and back of Kayla's head, obscure her vision, either partially or completely, suggesting the compromised agency under which addicts daily labor.) Of course, this tableau once again highlights the addict's victimization at the hands of her addiction. Kupono plays the addiction as a force that controls without mercy, oppresses without conscience, and overpowers without resistance. Kayla, by contrast, is virtually helpless in his hands—no longer a puppet, but not quite a subject in her own right.

While the initial kicks in this sequence can be classified as defensive in nature, the two that conclude and punctuate the sequence are quite fluid and lyrical in execution, highlighting the virtuosity of the dancer (that is, Kayla). Here, Kayla's body moves effortlessly and nearly unencumbered through space. For a brief moment, she seems to give herself over completely to her training, to emotion, to the choreography, to the moment. The grace and the elegance of the final two movements allude to the "kick"—or "strong or sharp stimulant effect"—that controlled and illicit substances produce in the addict: the "thrill, excitement, pleasure," the "feeling of marked enjoyment," the high ("kick, n.1"). But the seeming carefree, "easy" nature of these movements also alludes to a related idiomatic expression—that is, "for kicks"—that would identify the actions (both the literal dance, as well as the addiction that it symbolically represents) as occurring "purely for pleasure or excitement, freq[uently] recklessly or irresponsibly" ("kick, n.1"). In other words, the gorgeous lines that Kayla's body traces in this section of the choreography need always be viewed in the context of the narrative that is unfolding on stage. These expertly-executed kicks remind viewers that Kayla is an incredibly talented dancer. But the narrative never allows viewers to forget that Kayla is an incredibly talented dancer *who is portraying an addict*. Are viewers, then, to attribute Kayla's grace and elegance to the years of disciplined training that have led her to *So You Think You Can Dance?* Are those aesthetically-pleasing movements intended to represent the "high" of an addiction? And, if so, then what are the emotional and ideological valences of those gestures? Do those kicks serve as an indictment of the addict, who gives herself too willingly, too completely to temptation? Do they allow viewers momentarily to glimpse, to perhaps understand partially, the all-consuming force that is an addiction—the seductive ways in which it overpowers an individual's will and suspends her "good judgment"?

There are, as well, other questions that are raised by this performance, questions that derive from common, idiomatic uses of the term "kick." Does this sequence represent the addict's attempts to kick her habit? Or is it an acknowledgement of the many ways—psychologically, physiologically, socially—that an addiction repeatedly kicks an addict in the teeth? Is Kayla experiencing the kick back, or recoil, of her addiction—the high that simultaneously is jolting and exhilarating? Or is she kicking the bucket before our very eyes? Are these gestures empowering: that is, is Kayla kicking addiction's ass? Or is she kicking off yet another bender? Kicking up her heels? Getting her kicks? Do the kicks signify that Kayla is alive and kicking? Or that she could just kick herself for succumbing, once again, to her addiction? The truly remarkable, even liberating, aspect of this performance is that the answers to such questions are neither forthcoming nor particularly easy to discern. Unlike the metaphor of waste, which asserts itself with the authority and the absolute certainty of a monolith, the metaphor that is traced by Mia Michaels's choreography seems always unsure of itself, tentative if not wholly ambiguous in meaning. It refuses to accept the authority of representation and, in doing so, it works to unsettle the authority of the metaphor of waste.

The climax of the choreography occurs about halfway through the 1:45 routine, when, immediately following the 20-second sequence described above, Kayla plants her feet firmly at center stage and extends her left arm into the air. This gesture is empowering, if somewhat ambiguous. Is it a declaration of the addict's liberation from her addiction? (Think Norma Rae.) Is it an affirmation of strength? (Think Rocky.) Is the addict appealing to the grace of God to deliver her from the clutches of addiction? Or does the gesture signal the addict's resignation to a force beyond her own will and agency—a God, or god, a choreographer, a dance, a moment? Here, determining what the gesture definitively "means" is less important than examining the implications of Kayla executing that possibly empowering gesture and Kupono halting it in mid-air. That Kupono grasps Kayla's extended forearm signifies the dominance and control that he presumes over Kayla. In this respect, his firm grasp of Kayla's forearm is not merely possessive, or even territorial, but it is controlling and all-consuming. This idea is reinforced by the soundtrack against which the choreography is set: "[Y]ou're neither friend nor foe/Though I can't seem to let you go. The one thing that I still know is that you're keeping me down." Here, the addiction is likened to the implied "you" (that is, gravity) addressed in the lyrics. Described as "neither friend nor foe," the addict is likened to an omnipresent but innocuous natural phenomenon by which bodies are attracted, or drawn, to one another. On one hand, gravity is a stabilizing force, anchoring us to the earth. It is about mutual attraction between bodies of mass—a point of which viewers are repeatedly reminded by Kupono's provocative physicality, his hypnotic gaze, and his seductive movements. Viewers also are reminded of gravity's stabilizing force by the many sequences in which Kupono is imaged "keeping [Kayla] down"—guiding her body through lifts and eventually back down to the stage floor; catching her body on freefalls and leading it to an upright position; directing, puppet-master-style, her body through a series of movements. On the other hand, gravity is oppressive. It presses on our bodies. It weighs on us. And ultimately it limits our freedom of movement. We can resist Earth's gravitational pull at best momentarily, and then only with the assistance of technology and ingenuity (for example, the invisible rigging that enables Elphaba to defy gravity at the climax of Act One in *Wicked*; the green screen technology that allows *Man of Steel* to "leap tall buildings in a single bound"; the still-miraculous feats of engineering that allow everyday people to "fly the friendly skies"). It is this love-hate relationship with the addiction/gravity/Kupono—a force, again, seen as "neither friend nor foe," but perhaps as a bit of both—that the choreography conveys so beautifully, and it is this thematic that poses the greatest challenge to the metaphor of waste. In some ways, this characterization of addiction is politically regressive as it attributes to the addict almost total responsibility for her addiction. After all, she "can't seem to let [him] go"—an admission that, in content and tone, at least implies not only agency on the part of the addict, but also an awareness that the choice that the addict repeatedly makes is less than desirable. However, the addict also and simultaneously is depicted in a life-and-death struggle with the addiction, which is culpable for "keeping [her] down." It is a small, but significant, challenge that works subtly, patiently, to erode the widely-held belief that addicts must always and only be blamed for their addictions and shamed for the consequences of those addictions.

This challenge is reinforced by Kayla's characterization at that moment in the choreography. For a split second at the instant her arm extends into the air, she is triumphant, as if finally, after so much toiling and hardship, she has liberated herself. But the triumph is fleeting as, in the next instant, Kupono grasps her arm firmly, decisively, possessively. Although little physical movement occurs during this nearly 10-second segment, it is nonetheless one of the most visually and ideologically powerful moments in the entire choreography. Most notably, this segment depicts the addict not as wallowing in denial and self-pleasure, but as actively struggling against the force that perpetually attempts to dominate and consume her. This struggle manifests itself most clearly in the physical contrasts that are drawn between Kayla and Kupono. His gestures are confident, precise. His grasp of her arm is unwavering. And his gaze is steady, his facial expression fixed somewhere between a triumphant smirk and a confident leer. By contrast, Kayla's gestures are weak, even sometimes tentative—especially as she fumbles at Kupono's wrist and attempts to wrest herself from his powerful grip. Her facial expression registers absolute and utter devastation. She sobs openly, even violently. She hangs her head, her tousled blonde hair partially obscuring her face. And she battles, ultimately in vain, to free herself from the commanding grip of Kupono. For Kayla, this is a life-or-death struggle, a point that is visually underscored by the exaggerated fanning of her fingers as they reach skyward and by the sharply-defined musculature on her extended arm. She desperately needs to be free of this force that shadows and oppresses her. But no matter what she does, she is perpetually ensnared by him. It is a moment fraught with pathos and ultimately this moment disallows the spectator from easily blaming the addict for her addiction. In fact, I would argue that this moment specifically, and the performance as a whole more generally, actively resists any consideration of "blame." Instead, the choreography decisively brings its dancers and its spectators back to the material body, acknowledging, as all live performances do, the fragility and the vulnerability of that body, something that regularly is lost in debates over who is to blame for an addiction. This performance reminds us of the internal struggles that constitute the addict's everyday life. It allows its spectators to "feel" some of those struggles in their own bodies, albeit imperfectly and only ever partially. And it finally privileges greater understanding over shaming, blaming, and scapegoating.

The final moments of the choreography are liberally peppered with gestures that depict the addiction as nurturing and the addict as vulnerable. (Is this the visual equivalent of Bareilles's lyric, "You loved me 'cause I'm fragile/ When I thought that I was strong./But you touch me for a little while and all my fragile strength is gone"?) The movements are slow, measured, deliberate. At one point, Kayla side-step shuffles several feet across the stage, her back to the audience, as Kupono tenderly holds her head in his cupped hand. At another point, Kupono slides one arm behind Kayla, resting it at the small of her back, and leads her through a modified "Tango swoop." Kayla leans back, her torso almost horizontal, and slowly moves her body in a semicircle before returning to vertical to face Kupono. And the piece ends, quite anticlimactically, with Kayla turning out of a kind of embrace and tentatively stepping away from Kupono, who now stands with his right arm extended at a right angle from his body, the mirror image of his own posture from the opening moments of the piece. On one level, such gentle intimacy between the pair alludes to the fairly common attitude that many addicts adopt toward their addictions: namely, the drug becomes the object of intense focus and affection, much like a significant other. In this performance, Kupono is the seductive lover who comforts, nurtures, and accepts Kayla unconditionally, just as, for many addicts, the drug replaces most/all intimate interpersonal relationships until the addict finally is alone. At the same time, Kayla is depicted as profoundly broken and in need of a "fix." The psychological and physiological brokenness of the addict is remarked upon time and again in this final segment of the choreography through the tentative, awkward positionalities that Kayla assumes with her body. That these tableaus contrast so radically with the controlled gracefulness of Kayla's earlier performance only works to reinforce the sense of brokenness that haunts the final moments of the choreography.

Yet the choreography refuses to scapegoat the addict. Indeed, Kayla is never depicted as reveling in her addictions and, in resisting this common temptation, the choreography disallows the audience to shame the addict for a weak will, a broken moral compass. Neither does the choreography permit spectators to blame the addict for her "poor choices." Indeed, what is emphasized in these final moments of Mia Michaels's quite brilliant choreography are the experiences of living through, within, and alongside an addiction—experiences that are metaphorically manifested as a dance. In the end, the addict is not thrown away. She is not marginalized. In fact, she is of central import to the final tableau, both in terms of how the dance was staged for a live audience and in terms of how the moment was shot and edited for an at-home audience. She occupies the visual foreground and the ocular center of the visual frame. Furthermore, she alone is granted the liberty of movement—the dancer's form of agency. In each of these ways, the addict is absolved of her presumed transgressions. These transgressions are, if not forgiven, then understood precisely because spectators are permitted to voyeuristically consume the highly seductive drug and vicariously experience the "high" that he produces. Meanwhile, that same addiction is shown to oppress the addict, rendering her once graceful movements stilted. As Kayla struggles (and, ultimately, fails) to approximate an aesthetically-pleasing tableau, spectators begin to understand what it might feel like to labor under the metaphorical, the ideological, and the empirical weight of an addiction.

Through the power of Kupono's movements, and through the raw sexuality that perpetually infuses his characterization, this piece allows its spectators to understand the all-consuming force that an addiction exerts over its prey. Through Kayla's tattered costume, her disheveled hair, and, most significantly, her many pained facial expressions, this piece enables its spectators to bear witness to the indignities that an addiction repeatedly forces an addict to endure. And, in the end, we do not know quite what to make of the narrative and the performance unfolding on stage. What are the implications of regarding Kupono as sexy, seductive? Is Kayla a victim or a (self-)victimizer? Should we marvel at the pair's mastery of this difficult choreography? Or should we be somewhat disconcerted by the dissonance that develops between the technical virtuosity and the narrative pathos? That this performance refuses to supply us with easy answers or pre-packaged responses is one of the most provocative ways that it challenges the authority of the metaphor of waste. The narrative that is charted through the movements of Kayla's and Kupono's bodies demands critical engagement on the part of its spectators. Those of us who watch—do we passively observe? Voyeuristically consume? Actively bear witness?—are forced to labor under the burden of meaning-making, even as the choreography and the narrative to which it alludes evade our attempts to master them. And in the end, we are left both exhilarated and exhausted by a performance that refuses to uncritically perpetuate overdetermined narratives about what it means, and how it feels, to be an addict.

The production of metaphor constitutes an exercise of power, as does its elucidation in the form of a study such as *Wasted*. Metaphor is both the pathway to our shared past as well as the means by which we progress forward. It is the location at which we simultaneously acknowledge and (hopefully) abandon the ideological shackles that have bound us to experiences that harm, that endanger, and that sometimes kill. Metaphor is a site of sheer possibility at which the virtually endless production of meaning is limited only by the scope of one's own creativity and/or the bounds of one's resources (creative or otherwise). It is the location at which we imagine a different world—a world perhaps no less circumscribed by metaphor, but a world in which the metaphors by which we live are significantly less prescriptive and determinisitic. Metaphor allows us to imagine that which under other, "normal(ized)" circumstances would be unimaginable. It is the vehicle through which we give voice to those (Other) experiences that cannot be spoken, and/or that refuse to be so, but that nonetheless need, or demand, to be heard. It empowers us to imagine beyond the realm of current possibility and, in doing so, it can instill in us a sense of hope for changed, alternative, improved material conditions.

It is this aspect of metaphor that predominantly undergirds the performance of Mia Michaels's "Gravity" routine. The choreography invites spectators to confront some of the most pervasive and insidious assumptions made by the metaphor of waste. It challenges the problematic notion that addicts possess a broken moral compass that is ultimately and exclusively responsible for their immoral (and often illegal) behaviors. It undermines the fallacious belief that addicts are driven by an uncontrollable impulse to destruction—destruction of self, of others, of community, of nation. It refuses to shame. And it contests the equation that historically has been drawn between addiction and death, returning its spectators finally to what it feels like to live within and experience the world through the addict's material body. What is so remarkable about this dance is the way in which it so vividly, so powerfully, imagines a world that is utterly and thoroughly unencumbered by the metaphor of waste. It populates that world with two vulnerable, but talented, bodies that simultaneously acknowledge and actively resist the wasteful prescriptions that I have discussed within the context of this study. As these bodies press against the limits of this deeply-entrenched metaphor, this dance refuses to romanticize the counternarratives that the bodies of its dancers trace in space and time. Neither does the choreography imagine a utopian world in which the metaphor of waste ceases to exist. Instead, it tackles that metaphor head-on, exposing the problematic assumptions that it makes about the nature of addiction and the lived experiences of the addict while also and simultaneously untangling the complicated ideological web that it has spun over the American cultural imaginary since the nineteenth century.

The metaphor that this dance charts is exhaustive rather than wasteful. It expends energy, time, creativity and, like all instances of live performance, it "saves nothing; it only spends" (Phelan 148). To suggest that this performance "saves nothing" and "only spends" is not to suggest that the choreography is wasteful. In fact, I would suggest quite the opposite: namely, that Mia Michaels's "Gravity" routine does not squander its resources (whether human or ideological or metaphoric), but rather it expends them quite meaningfully. The choreography exhausts the dancers' bodies—wringing from them every ounce of energy, of creativity, of talent, and of meaning possible. These young, fragile bodies labor under the exacting demands of the choreography and the production schedule. They toil against the unforgiving backdrop of instant celebrity. They persist tirelessly in their endeavors, in spite of (or is it because of?) the fleeting memory of reality television audiences and the tenuousness of the performance event itself. At the same time, these bodies endlessly push against the pre-existing meanings around addiction. They unearth "the metaphoric trappings that deform the experience" of addiction (Sontag 102). They challenge spectators to read "against interpretation" and, in doing so, they potentially liberate the addict, if only for the duration of a dance or a song, from the dangers of the metaphor of waste. These bodies relish in their possibility, resisting the overdetermined monolith of the metaphor of waste and welcoming into the realm of representation a wealth of competing metaphors that at least momentarily "deprive [the monolith] of meaning" (Sontag 102). In this respect, Mia Michaels's "Gravity" dance identifies metaphor as a site at which greater understanding and growth are fostered. These alternative metaphors exhaust the metaphor of waste, ultimately depriving it—but only temporarily—of its ability to confer meaning on the lived experiences of addiction. Nothing is squandered. Everything is spent.

Such is the power of metaphor.

At the same time, metaphor constitutes a means of social control by which one entity shapes and delimits the opportunities and resources available to another entity. It can significantly limit not only how individuals perceive themselves, but also how they experience themselves in and among the world. What is so perilous in the (re-)production of metaphor is that it not only describes, but it also and simultaneously creates the material conditions under which individuals live, labor, and love. Metaphor at once institutionalizes its ideologies and produces the set of lived experiences that those ideologies portend. To liken an addict to garbage, refuse, or waste, for instance, is to describe a perceived identity and to produce the incredibly wasteful socio-cultural institutions, mechanisms, and conditions from which that wasted identity is born and against which that wasted identity is lived. In this respect, metaphor paralyzes the material bodies to whose lived experiences and identities it lays claim. It ensnares them within its tangled web of signification and mercilessly coerces them to believe in the Truth that an addict is a waste.

Such is the peril of metaphor.

In the end, metaphor is never ideologically innocuous, but neither is it inherently liberating or inherently oppressive. Metaphor can, indeed, empower, but it also retains the ability to enslave and, in fact, most metaphors at once oppress *and* liberate, albeit often to radically different degrees. A metaphor simultaneously can be limitless and limited, a rigidly bounded representational landscape in which anything (and perhaps nothing) is possible depending on who is performing the metaphor, who is watching that performance, and in what context (social, cultural, historical, representational) that performance is unfolding. Mia Michaels's "Gravity" dance reminds us quite powerfully of the pleasure and the pain of addiction—the desire to "drown in [its] love," but "not feel [its] reign." It is a declaration of empowerment, an insistence that addiction "set [us] free, leave [us] be." But it also is simultaneously an acknowledgement of the all-consuming nature of addition. (The addict "never wanted anything so much," after all.) The song and the choreography cast addiction as predatory: a force that is "on to me and all over me." At the same time, addiction is represented as a gentle lover, as one that holds the addict "without touch," and "keep[s her] without chains." This dance constitutes but a moment—one moment in time—and as such poses a relatively insignificant challenge to the metaphor of waste from the margins of the American television industry. However, in the lament that this dance voices over that "something" that always brings us back to the metaphor of waste, it is at once meaningful and fragile, beautiful and tragic, momentous and insignificant.

Such is the power *and* the peril of metaphor.

Bibliography

"Aaron and Andrea." *Intervention*. A&E. 20 July 2009. Television.

"ABC's 'Extreme' Exploitation." *Documents*. The Smoking Gun. n.d. Web. 26 June 2014.

About the Drug Policy Alliance. Drug Policy Alliance. n.d. Web. 21 Sept. 2014.

Adams, James Truslow. *The Epic of America*. 2nd ed. New York: Little, Brown and Company, 1931.

Adams, Rachel. *Sideshow U.S.A.: Freaks and the American Cultural Imaginary*. Chicago: University of Chicago Press, 2001.

Albrecht, Karl. "The (Only) 5 Fears We All Share." *Psychology Today* 22 Mar. 2012. Web. 17 Dec. 2014.

Alexander, Anna and Mark S. Roberts. Introduction. *high cu/ture: reflections on addiction and modernity*. Edited by Alexander and Roberts. Albany: State University of New York Press, 2003. 1–15.

_____., eds. *high cu/ture: reflections on addiction and modernity*. Albany: State University of New York Press, 2003.

"Alyson and Tommy." *Intervention*. A&E. 6 Mar. 2005. Television.

Anderson, Benedict. *Imagined Communities: Reflections on the Origin and Spread of Nationalism*. New ed. London: Verso, 2006.

The Anonymous People. Dir. Greg D. Williams. Kino Lorber Films, 2014. DVD.

"The Anonymous People, by Greg Williams." *Projects*. Kickstarter. n.d. Web. 18 Oct. 2014.

"Anti-Smoking Activist Terrie Hall Dies." *Winston-Salem Journal* 17 Sept. 2013. Web. 25 Aug. 2014.

Arceneaux, Michael. "Why We Can't Blame Bobby Brown for Whitney Houston's Death." *The Grio*. 15 Feb. 2012. Web. 3 Dec. 2014.

Archer, Dale. "Philip Seymour Hoffman: The Curse of Addiction." *Psychology Today* 5 Feb. 2014. Web. 18 Oct. 2014.

Atlien. "Meet the Person Who Sold Whitney Houston's Casket Photo." *Straight From the A*. 16 Mar. 2012. Web. 26 Dec. 2014.

Austin, J.L. *How To Do Things With Words*. 2nd ed. Oxford: Oxford University Press, 1975.

Autopsy: The Last Hours of Whitney Houston. Reelz. 14 June 2014. Television.

Balsamo, Anne. *Technologies of the Gendered Body: Reading Cyborg Women*. Durham, NC: Duke University Press, 1996.

Banco, Lindsey Michael. *Travel and Drugs in Twentieth-Century Literature*. New York: Routledge, 2009.

Baumohl, Jim. "Editorial: Addiction and the American Debate about Homelessness." *British Journal of Addiction* 87(1992): 7–10.

——. "Inebriate Institutions in North America, 1840–1920." *British Journal of Addiction* 85(1990): 1187–204.

Baumohl, Jim and Jerome H. Jaffe. "Treatment, History of, in the United States." *Encyclopedia of Drugs, Alcohol, and Addictive Behavior.* Encyclopedia.com. n.d. Web. 17 July 2014.

Becker, Karin E. "Photojournalism and the tabloid press." *The Tabloid Culture Reader.* Edited by Anita Biressi and Heather Nunn. Maidenhead: Open University Press, 2008. 81–97.

Belsey, Catherine. *Critical Practice.* London: Verso, 1980.

Belushi Pisano, Judith, and Tanner Colby. *Belushi: A Biography.* New York, NY: Rugged Land, 2005.

Bennett, Carole. "Low Self-Esteem; A Disposition That Can Lead to Addiction." *From Heartache to Hope.* Psychology Today. 24 June 2013. Web. 1 June 2014.

Berlant, Lauren. *The Queen of America Goes to Washington City: Essays on Sex and Citizenship.* Durham, NC: Duke University Press, 1997.

Bernstein, Jonathan. *Pretty In Pink: The Golden Age of Teenage Movies.* New York: St. Martin's Press, 1997.

"Better Yet When Dead." *Coco Fusco.* Thing. n.d. Web. 5 Jan. 2015.

Bingham, Dennis. *Whose Lives Are They Anyway?: The Biopic as Contemporary Film Genre.* Piscataway, NJ: Rutgers University Press, 2010.

Bleich, David. "The Materiality of Rhetoric, the Subject of Language Use." *The Realms of Rhetoric: The Prospects for Rhetoric Education.* Edited by Joseph Petraglia and Deepika Bahri. Albany: State University of New York Press, 2003. 39–60.

Bogdan, Robert. *Freak Show: Presenting Human Oddities for Amusement and Profit.* Chicago: University of Chicago Press, 1988.

Boon, Marcus. *The Road of Excess: A History of Writers on Drugs.* Cambridge: Harvard University Press, 2005.

Booth, Stanley. "Joyless Indulgence." Rev. of *Wired: The Short Life and Fast Times of John Belushi*, by Bob Woodward. *Times Literary Supplement* 8 Mar. 1985: 269.

Bound by Flesh. Dir. Leslie Zemeckis. Mistress, Inc., 2012. Film.

"Brandon's Biography." *Tips From Former Smokers.* Centers for Disease Control and Prevention. 1 July 2014. Web. 1 Sept. 2014.

Brandt, Allan. *The Cigarette Century: The Rise, Fall, and Deadly Persistence of the Product That Defined America.* Reprint ed. 2007. New York: Basic, 2009.

Brehm, Jack Williams. *A Theory of Psychological Reactance.* Waltham, MA: Academic Press, 1966.

Brehm, Jack Williams and Sharon S. Brehm. *Psychological Reactance: A Theory of Freedom and Control.* Waltham, MA: Academic Press, 1981.

Bright Lights, Big City. Dir. James Bridges. Perfs. Michael J. Fox, Kiefer Sutherland, and Phoebe Cates. United Artists, 1988. DVD.

Brodie, Janet Farrell and Marc Redfield, eds. *High Anxieties: Cultural Studies in Addiction.* Berkeley: University of California Press, 2002.

———. Introduction. *High Anxieties: Cultural Studies in Addiction.* Edited by Brodie and Redfield. Berkeley: University of California Press, 2002. 1–15.

Bronfen, Elisabeth. *Over Her Dead Body: Death, Femininity and the Aesthetic.* New York: Routledge, 1992.

Brookes, Les. *Gay Male Fiction Since Stonewall: Ideology, Conflict, and Aesthetics.* New York: Routledge, 2009.

Brottman, Mikita. "Mondo Horror: Carnivalizing the Taboo." *The Horror Film.* Edited by Stephen Prince. Piscataway, NJ: Rutgers University Press, 2004. 167–88.

Brown, Edward M. "English Interest in the Treatment of Alcoholism in the United States During the Early 1870's." *British Journal of Addiction* 81(1986): 545–51.

———. "'What shall we do with the inebriate?': Asylum Treatment and the Disease Concept of Alcoholism in the Late Nineteenth Century." *Journal of the History of Behavioral Sciences* 21.1(Jan. 1985): 48–59. *Psychiatry Footnotes.* Google. n.d. Web. 7 Dec. 2014.

Buchanan, Jason. "Faces of Death." *The New York Times.* n.d. Web. 15 Aug. 2014.

Burns, Stanley B. *Sleeping Beauty: Memorial Photography in America.* 2nd ed. Santa Fe, NM: Twelvetrees Press, 1990.

Camhi, Leslie. Rev. of *Drunks,* Dir. Peter Cohn. *The Village Voice* 18 Mar. 1997: 80.

"Campaign Overview." *Tips From Former Smokers.* Centers for Disease Control and Prevention. 19 June 2014. Web. 25 Aug. 2014.

Canby, Vincent. "Reviews/Film: 'Wired,' in which Belushi Hails a Cabbie From Heaven." *The New York Times* 25 Aug. 1989. Web. 14 Nov. 2013.

Carnival and Sideshow Bibliography. House of Deception. n.d. Web. 30 June 2014.

Carr, Duane. *A Question of Class: The Redneck Stereotype in Southern Fiction.* Bowling Green: Bowling Green SU Popular Press, 1996.

Casciato, Cory. *Defining the Dead: What is a Zombie?* The Inevitable Zombie Apocalypse. 31 Mar. 2009. Web. 27 Oct. 2013.

Case, Sue-Ellen. *Feminism and Theatre.* Reissue ed. New York: Palgrave Macmillan, 2008.

Catsoulis, Jeannette. "A Documentary on Battling Addiction's Powerful Pull: 'The Anonymous People' Looks at the Recovery Movement." Rev. of *The Anonymous People,* Dir. Greg D. Williams. *The New York Times* 14 Mar. 2014. Web. 18 Oct. 2014.

"A Cautionary Tale?: The Man Booker Prize and the Commonwealth Short Story Prize: What Prizes Are For." *Commonwealth Writers.* Commonwealth Foundation. 14 Oct. 2014. Web. 11 Nov. 2014.

"CDC: Tips from Former Smokers—Bill: Smoking and Diabetes Don't Mix." *YouTube.* YouTube. 7 June 2013. Web. 1 Sept. 2014.

"CDC: Tips from Former Smokers—Shawn's Ad." *YouTube.* YouTube. 24 June 2014. Web. 7 Dec. 2014.

"CDC: Tips from Former Smokers—Terrie's Ad." *YouTube.* YouTube. 15 Mar. 2012. Web. 1 Sept. 2014.

"CDC Tips From Former Smokers—Terrie's Ad: Don't Smoke." *YouTube.* YouTube. 24 June 2014. Web. 1 Sept. 2014.

"CDC Tips From Former Smokers—Terrie's Ad: Teenage Regrets." *YouTube.* YouTube. 31 Jan. 2014. Web. 1 Sept. 2014.

Clark, David. "The Disease Model of Addiction." *Philosophy of Addiction.* AddictionInfo. n.d. Web. 28 Oct. 2013.

Cocca, Amy. "Lessons in Struggles with Mental Illness, Addiction." *The Morning Call* 17 Aug. 2014. Web. 21 Aug. 2014.

Colby, Tanner. "Regrettable: The Trouble Things I Learned When I Re-Reported Bob Woodward's Book on John Belushi." *Slate.* Mar. 2013. Web. 26 December 2013.

"Coley." *Intervention.* A&E. 10 Aug. 2007. Television.

Courtright, David T. *Dark Paradise: A History of Opiate Addiction in America.* Cambridge: Harvard University Press, 2001.

——. *Forces of Habit: Drugs and the Making of the Modern World.* Cambridge: Harvard University Press, 2002.

Craton, Lillian. *The Victorian Freak Show: The Significance of Disability and Physical Differences in 19th-Century Fiction.* Amherst, NY: Cambria Press, 2009.

Crowley, John William and William White. *Drunkard's Refuge: The Lessons of the New York State Inebriate Asylum.* Amherst: University of Massachusetts Press, 2004.

Custen, George F. *Bio/Pics: How Hollywood Constructed Public History.* Piscataway, NJ: Rutgers University Press, 1992.

Cyphers, Luke and Ethan Trex. "The Song Remains the Same." *ESPN Magazine* 11 Sept. 2011. Web. 29 May 2015.

Demastes, William W. "Preface: American Dramatic Realism, Viable Frames of Thought." *Realism and the American Dramatic Tradition.* Edited by Demastes. Tuscaloosa: University of Alabama Press, 1996. ix–xvii.

Djos, Matt G. *Writing Under the Influence: Alcoholism and the Alcoholic Perception From Hemingway to Berryman.* New York: Palgrave Macmillan, 2010.

Dodes, Lance and Zachary Dodes. *The Sober Truth: Debunking the Bad Science Behind 12-Step Programs and the Rehab Industry.* Boston: Beacon Press, 2014.

"Does the 'Biopic' Constitute a Genre?" *Boxclever Films*. 4 Mar. 2012. Web. 4 Jan. 2014.

Dolan, Jill. *Presence & Desire: Essays on Gender, Sexuality, Performance*. Ann Arbor: University of Michigan Press, 1993.

Douglas, Tom. *Scapegoats: Transferring Blame*. London: Routledge, 1995.

Drimmer, Frederick. *Very Special People*. New York: Amjon, 1973.

"Drug Addicts 'Suffer in Silence.'" *USA Today* 27 July 2006: 11a.

"Drug Sentencing and Penalties." *Criminal Law Reform*. American Civil Liberties Union. n.d. Web. 12 Sept. 2014.

Drunks. Dir. Peter Cohn. Perfs. Richard Lewis, Faye Dunaway, Dianne Wiest, and Howard Rollins. Northern Arts Entertainment, 1997. DVD.

Dube, Shanta R., Vincent J. Filetti, Maxia Dong, et al. "Childhood Abuse, Neglect, and Household Dysfunction and the Risk of Illicit Drug Use: The Adverse Childhood Experiences Study." *Pediatrics* 111.3(Mar. 2003): 564–72.

"DVD/Streaming." *Drunks*. n.d. Web. 20 May 2015.

Easton, Nina J. and Jack Mathews. "Another Chapter in the Strange Odyssey of 'Wired.'" *The Los Angeles Times* 13 April 1989. Web. 22 Oct. 2014.

_____. Rev. of *Wired*, dir. Larry Peerce. *Reviews*. Roger Ebert. 25 Aug. 1989. Web. 11 Nov. 2013.

Ellis, Bret Easton. *Imperial Bedrooms*. New York: Vintage, 2010.

_____. *Less Than Zero*. New York: Vintage, 1985.

Emery, Fred. *Watergate: The Corruption of American Politics and the Fall of Richard Nixon*. New York: Times Books, 1994.

Everitt, Lauren. "Whitney Houston and the Art of Melisma." *BBC News Magazine* 15 Feb. 2012. Web. 20 Nov. 2014.

Faces of Death. Dir. Conan LeCilaire. Aquarius Releasing, 1978. Film.

Faces of Meth. Multnomah County Sheriff's Office. n.d. Web. 15 Aug. 2014.

"The faces of meth: before and after." *Faces of Meth*. Multnomah County Sheriff's Office. n.d. Web. 28 May 2015.

Ferguson, Galit. "The Family on Reality Television: Who's Shaming Whom?" *Television & New Media* 11.2(2010): 87–104.

Ferrero, Raymond G., III. *A&E "Intervention" Condones Addict Abuse By Donna Chavous of Intervention911 and Silences Audience Outrage*. MarchmanActBlog. 16 April 2012. Web. 16 June 2014.

Ferro, Shaunacy. "The Science of PSAs: Do Anti-Drug Ads Keep Kids Off Drugs?" *Popular Science* 15 April 2013. Web. 14 Sept. 2014.

Fiedler, Leslie. *Freaks: Myths and Images of the Secret Self*. Reprint ed. 1978. New York, Anchor, 1993.

Fletcher, Anne M. *Inside Rehab: The Surprising Truth About Addiction Treatment—And How To Get Help That Works*. New York: Viking, 2013.

Ford, Dennis. *The Search for Meaning: A Short History*. Berkeley: University of California Press, 2007.

Foster, Susan Leigh. "Choreographing History." *Choreographing History*. Edited by Foster. Bloomington: Indiana University Press, 1995. 3–21.

Foucault, Michel. *The History of Sexuality, Volume 1: An Introduction*. Trans. Robert Hurley. Reprint ed. 1978. New York: Vintage, 1990.

Foucault, Michel. *Madness and Civilization: A History of Insanity in the Age of Reason*. Trans. Richard Howad. Reprint ed. 1965. New York: Vintage, 1988.

Franklin, Bob. *Newszak and News Media*. London: Arnold, 1997.

"Freak show." *Urban Dictionary*. 6 Nov. 2012. Web. 17 July 2014.

Freeman, Hadley. "Andrew McCarthy: From 80s Heart-Throb to Travel Writer." *The Guardian*. 29 Oct. 2012. Web. 23 May 2014.

"Frequently Asked Questions About the *Tips* Campaign." *Tips From Former Smokers*. Centers for Disease Control and Prevention. 19 June 2014. Web. 25 Aug. 2014.

Frieden, Tom. "Terrie Hall: A Beautiful Woman Who Saved Thousands of Lives." *Huffington Post* 19 Sept. 2013. Web. 24 Aug. 2014.

Fusco, Coco. "The Other History of Intercultural Performance." *TDR: The Drama Review* 38.1(Spring 1994): 143–67.

Galloway, Stephen. "The Consequences of Train-Wreck TV." *The Hollywood Reporter* 23 Aug. 2011. Web. 17 July 2014.

Geduld, Harry M. "Saturday Night Dead." Rev. of *Wired*, dir. Larry Peerce. *The Humanist* Nov./Dec. 1989: 45–6.

Genes of 'Bearded Lady' Revealed. Live Science. 21 May 2009. Web. 20 June 2014.

Gilbert, Matthew. "Vile 'Intervention' Pulls a Fast One." *The Boston Globe* 5 Mar. 2005. Web. 2 Jan. 2013.

Gilmore, Thomas B. *Equivocal Spirits: Alcoholism and Drinking in Twentieth-Century Literature*. Chapel Hill: University of North Carolina Press, 1987.

Glaser, Gabrielle. "Twelve Steps to Danger: How Alcoholics Anonymous Can Be a Playground for Violence-Prone Members." *ProPublica* 24 June 2013. Web. 12 Sept. 2014.

Glucksman, Mary. "Production Update." *FilmMaker*. 3.3(1995): 14, 50–55.

Gordon, Harold W. "Early Environmental Stress and Biological Vulnerability to Drug Abuse." *Psychoneuroendocrinology* 27.1–2(Jan./Feb. 2002): 115–26.

Grande, Laura. "Strange and Bizarre: The History of Freak Shows." *Things Said and Done*. Word Press. 26 Sept. 2010. Web. 1 July 2014.

"Gravity." Choreog. Mia Michaels. Perfs. Kayla Radomski and Kupono Aweau. *So You Think You Can Dance?* FOX 36-Toledo. 8 July 2009. Television.

Grim, Ryan. *This Is Your Country On Drugs: The Secret History of Getting High in America*. Hoboken, NJ: John Wiley & Sons, 2009.

Grimm, Erik. "Brain Research Shows Print Ads Have 0.3 Seconds to Prove Their Relevance to Readers." *Media Research Blog*. The International News Media Association. 30 June 2014. Web. 20 Aug. 2014.

Harmetz, Aljean. "Sanitizing a Novel for the Screen." *The New York Times* 18 Nov. 1987. Web. 23 May 2014.

Hirschberg, Lynn. "The Controversy Over 'Wired.'" *Rolling Stone* 27 Sept. 1984: 34–42, 102.

"History." *About.* Kirkbride Buildings. 2014. Web. 6 June 2014.

Hoffman, John and Susan Froemke. Introduction. *Addiction: Why Can't They Just Stop?* Edited by Hoffman and Froemke. New York: Rodale Inc., 2007. 14–18.

Holden, Stephen. "Why They Drank, How They Cope." Rev. of *Drunks*, Dir. Peter Cohn. *The New York Times* 14 Mar. 1997. Web. 18 Sept. 2014.

———. "A Woman Who Knows the Music Industry, and a Few Who Don't (Yet)." Rev. of *Sparkle*, dir. Salim Akil. *The New York Times* 16 Aug. 2012. Web. 11 Nov. 2014.

Holman, C. Hugh and William Harmon. *A Handbook to Literature.* 6th ed. New York: Macmillan, 1992.

"Houston, We Have a Problem … Again! Whitney Leaves Hollyweird Nightclub Lookin' Cray." *Bossip.* 10 Feb. 2012. Web. 17 Dec. 2014.

Howe, Desson. Rev. of *Wired*, dir. Larry Peerce. *The Washington Post* 25 Aug. 1989. Web. 11 Nov. 2013.

Huggan, Graham. *Nature's Saviours: Celebrity Conservationists in the Television Age.* London: Routledge, 2013.

Humphreys, Laud. *Tearoom Trade: Impersonal Sex in Public Places.* New York: Aldine de Gruyter, 1970.

Hurlburt, Roger. Rev. of *Wired*, dir. Larry Peerce. *Sun Sentinel* 28 Aug. 1989. Web. 11 Nov. 2013.

Iser, Wolfgang. *The Implied Reader: Patterns of Communication in Prose Fiction from Bunyan to Beckett.* Baltimore: The Johns Hopkins University Press, 1974.

"Jessica." *Intervention.* A&E. 13 June 2013. Television.

Johnston, Kristen. *Guts: The Endless Follies and Tiny Triumphs of a Giant Disaster.* New York: Gallery Books, 2012.

Juman, Richard. "The Case to Fund Addiction Treatment Right Now." *Content.* The Fix. n.d. Web. 30 Oct. 2013.

"Justice System Paradox: Crime Rate Down, Jail Census Up." *Alcoholism & Drug Abuse Weekly* 10.4(1998): 4–5.

Juzwiak, Rich. "The Strangest Love of All: *Being Bobby Brown* Turns 7." *Gawker* 30 June 2012. Web. 6 Jan. 2015.

———. "There's Nothing Strange About an Addiction to *My Strange Addiction*." *TV Guide* 30 July 2011. Web. 17 July 2014.

Kaufman, Amy. "Rehab Television Shows: Intervention or Exploitation?" *Los Angeles Times* 2 Jan. 2011. Web. 23 June 2013.

Kauffmann, Stanley. "Hates, Loves, Addictions." Rev. of *Drunks*, Dir. Peter Cohn. *The New Republic* 14 April 1997: 28, 30.

Keane, Helen. "Smoking, Addiction, and the Making of Time." *High Anxieties: Cultural Studies in Addiction*. Edited by Brodie and Redfield. Berkeley: University of California Press, 2002. 119–33.

Kendall, Marie Claire. "Should Hollywood Do More for Troubled Stars Like Philip Seymour Hoffman, Robin Williams?" *Breitbart* 13 Aug. 2014. Web. 21 Aug. 2014.

"kick, n.1." *Oxford English Dictionary Online*. Oxford University Press. Dec. 2014. Web. 24 Feb. 2015.

"kick, v.1." *Oxford English Dictionary Online*. Oxford University Press. Dec. 2014. Web. 24 Feb. 2015.

Kimmel, Daniel M. Rev. of *Drunks*, Dir. Peter Cohn. *Variety* 11 Sept. 1995: 20.

Kirkbride, Thomas Story. *On the Construction, Organization and General Arrangements of Hospitals for the Insane*. Philadelphia, 1854. *Google Book Search*. Web. 6 June 2014.

Kit, Boris. "Emile Hirsch to Play John Belushi in Biopic." *The Hollywood Reporter*. 28 Oct. 2013. Web. 25 Oct. 2014.

Knowles, Murray and Rosamund Moon. *Introducing Metaphor*. London: Routledge, 2006.

Koch, Wendy. "Diseased Ex-Smokers Testify in Graphic Anti-Smoking Ads." *USA Today* 28 March 2013. Web. 20 Aug. 2014.

Kosovski, Jason R. and Douglas C. Smith. "Everybody Hurts: Addiction, Drama, and the Family in the Reality Television Show *Intervention*." *Substance Use & Misuse* 46(2011): 852–8.

Krebs, Christopher P., Kevin J. Strom, Willem H. Koetse, and Pamela K. Lattimore. "The Impact of Residential and Nonresidential Drug Treatment on Recidivism Among Drug-Involved Probationers: A Survival Analysis." *Crime & Delinquency* 55.3(July 2009): 442–71.

Kristeva, Julia. *Powers of Horror: An Essay on Abjection*. Trans. Leon S. Roudiez. New York: Columbia University Press, 1982.

"Kristine." *Intervention*. A&E. 15 Feb. 2010. Television.

Lacey, Stephen. "Celebrity Tragedies Shine a Bright Light on Estate Planning." *Florida Today* 18 Aug. 2014. Web. 21 Aug. 2014.

Lakoff, George and Mark Johnson. *Metaphors We Live By*. Chicago: University of Chicago Press, 1980.

Lang, Annie and Narine S. Yegiyan. "Understanding the Interactive Effects of Emotional Appeal and Claim Strength in Health Messages." *Journal of Broadcasting & Electronic Media* 52.3(Sept. 2008): 432–47.

Laudet, Alexandre B. "The Impact of Alcoholics Anonymous on Other Substance Abuse Related Twelve Step Programs." *Recent Developments in Alcoholism* 18(2008): 71–89. *NIHPA Autor Manuscripts*. National Institutes of Health. n.d. Web. 29 Sept. 2014.

Leah. "Do Anti-Drinking Ads Backfire?" *Drinking Diaries.* 7 March 2010. Web. 1 Sept. 2014.

Lender, Mark Edward and James Kirby Martin. *Drinking in America: A History.* Revised and expanded ed. New York: The Free Press, 1987.

Lennon, Gary. *Blackout.* New York: Samuel French, Inc., 2011.

Less Than Zero. Dir. Marek Kanievska. Perfs. Andrew McCarthy, Jami Gertz, and Robert Downey, Jr. Twentieth Century Fox, 1987. DVD.

"Lethal New Mix of Heroin Has Killed EIGHTY Users Across the East Coast This Year." *Daily Mail Online* 16 Feb. 2014. Web. 21 Aug. 2014.

Letslk. "The Reality Show Being Bobby Brown Was More About Whitney Houston Than Him." *Black Like Moi.* Your Black World Network. 21 Mar. 2012. Web. 6 Jan. 2015.

Levine, Harry G. and Craig Reinarman. "The Trouble With Drink *And* Drugs: Why Prohibition and Criminalization Matter." *Addiction* 105(2010): 805–7.

Lilienfeld, Scott O. and Hal Arkowitz. "Does Alcoholics Anonymous Work?" *Scientific American* Mar./April 2011. Web. 29 Sept. 2014.

Linnemann, Travis and Tyler Wall. "'This is your face on meth': The Punitive Spectacle of 'White Trash' in the Rural War on Drugs." *Theoretical Criminology* 17.3(2013): 315–34.

López, Ian Haney. *Dog Whistle Politics: How Coded Racial Appeals Have Reinvented Racism and Wrecked the Middle Class.* Oxford: Oxford University Press, 2014.

Loue, Sana. "The Criminalization of the Addictions: Toward a Unified Approach." *The Journal of Legal Medicine* 24(2003): 281–330.

Lucas D'Oyley, Demetria. "On Blaming Bobby Brown." *The Root.* 23 Feb. 2012. Web. 6 Jan. 2015.

Lynch, Joe. "How A&E Got Rich Off of Recovery." *The Fix.* n.d. Web. 20 June 2013.

Macko, Mary Kathryn. "Why Is The National Anthem So Hard to Sing?" *American History.* Smithsonian National Museum of American History. 14 May 2014. Web. 29 May 2015.

Macy, Rebecca J., Connie Renz, and Emily Pellino. "Partner Violence and Substance Abuse Are Intertwined: Women's Perceptions of Violence-Substance Connections." *Violence Against Women* 19.7(July 2013): 881–902.

"Make Ads 'Stick' in Readers' Minds By Holding Their Attention Longer." *Marking Insights.* 5MetaCom. n.d. Web. 20 Aug. 2014.

Mann, Brian. "The Drug Laws That Changed How We Punish." *National Public Radio.* 14 Feb. 2013. Web. 10 Sept. 2014.

Many Faces 1 Voice. Faces & Voices of Recovery. 2013. Web. 18 Oct. 2014.

"Marci." *Intervention.* A&E. 31 Aug. 2009. Television.

Marvin, Carolyn and David W. Ingle. *Blood Sacrifice and the Nation: Totem Rituals and the American Flag.* New York, NY: Cambridge University Press, 1999.

Mathews, Jack. "Unveiled 'Wired' Shorts Out With Cannes Festival Audience." *Sun Sentinel* 20 May 1989. Web. 11 Nov. 2013.

Mattison, Ben. *The Social Construction of the American Daguerreotype Portrait.* American Daguerreotypes. n.d. Web. 15 Dec. 2014.

McInerney, Jay. *Bright Lights, Big City.* New York: Vintage, 1984.

Meizel, Katherine L. *Idolized: Music, Media, and Identity in American Idol.* Bloomington: Indiana University Press, 2011.

Miller, Mary Jane. "Report: SSI Cuts Harm Addicts, Limit Treatment Options." *Alcoholism & Drug Abuse Weekly* 10.15(1998): 1–2.

Moore, David and Suzanne Fraser. "Producing the 'Problem' of Addiction in Drug Treatment." *Qualitative Health Research* 23.7(July 2013): 916–23.

Muhammad, Dedrick. "The Reagan Era: Turning Back Racial Equality Gains." *The Huffington Post* 11 Mar. 2013. Web. 3 Jan. 2015.

Mullman, Jeremy. "Why Binge Drinking PSAs May Leave Some Reaching for Another Drink." *Advertising Age* 3 Mar. 2010. Web. 28 May 2015.

Murphy, Jennifer. "The Continuing Expansion of Drug Courts: Is That All There Is?" *Deviant Behavior* 33.7(2012): 582–8.

Murphy, Tim. "For Those Who Grieve Dead Celebrities, It's Like Losing a Family Member." *New York* 18 Aug. 2014. Web. 21 Aug. 2014.

Now I Lay Me Down to Sleep. 2015. Web. 29 May 2015.

"Obama Plans Clemency for 'Hundreds, Perhaps Thousands' of People Sentenced for Drug Law Violations." *News.* Drug Policy Alliance. 21 April 2014. Web. 21 Sept. 2014.

O'Connor, Anahad. "Using Ex-Smokers to Spur Others to Quit." *The New York Times* 28 March 2013. Web. 25 Aug. 2014.

"Origins." *Pages.* Alcoholics Anonymous. 2014. Web. 18 Oct. 2014.

Orr, Jessica. "To Be Effective, Anti-Drug Ads Should Focus on Thrill-Seeking Teens." *News.* University of Florida. 27 May 2004. Web. 9 Sept. 2014.

"Our Inebriates, Classified and Clarified." *The Atlantic Monthly* April 1969: 477–83.

Palmer, J.W. "Our Inebriates Harbored and Helped." *The Atlantic Monthly* July 1969: 109–19.

Parton, James. "Inebriate Asylums, and a Visit to One." *The Atlantic Monthly* Oct. 1868: 385–404.

"The Path to Creating 'The Anonymous People.'" *Renew Everyday.* 27 July 2012. Web. 18 Oct. 2014.

Patton, Cindy. *Inventing AIDS.* New York: Routledge, 1990.

Payne, Christopher. *Asylum: Inside the Closed World of State Mental Hospitals.* Cambridge, MA: The MIT Press, 2009.

Pechmann, Cornelia and Michael D. Slater. "Social Marketing Messages That May Motivate Irresponsible Consumption Behavior." *Inside Consumption: Consumer Motives, Goals, and Desires.* Edited by S. Ratneshwar and David Glen Mick. London: Routledge, 2005. 185–206.

Pegram, Thomas R. *Battling Demon Rum: The Struggle for a Dry America, 1800–1933*. Chicago: Ivan Dee, 1998.

"Persian Gulf War." *Topics*. History. n.d. Web. 9 Dec. 2014.

Peters, Jeremy W. "When Reality TV Gets Too Real." *The New York Times*. 8 Oct. 2007. Web. 31 Dec. 2012.

Phelan, Peggy. *Unmarked: The Politics of Performance*. London: Routledge, 1993.

Piazza, Jo. "National Enquirer Publisher Calls Whitney Houston Casket Photo 'Beautiful.'" *Fox News*. 23 Feb. 2012. Web. 26 Dec. 2014.

Powers, Ann. Rev. of *I Look to You*, by Whitney Houston. *The Los Angeles Times*. 26 Aug. 2009. Web. 23 Dec. 2014.

Quintanilla, Carl. "The Faces of Meth." *Nightly News*. Today. 11 Aug. 2005. Web. 15 Aug. 2014.

Race and the Drug War. Drug Policy Alliance. n.d. Web. 12 Sept. 2014.

Rainey, Naomi. "Hasselhoff: 'Reality shows have ruined TV.'" *British TV*. Digital Spy. 8 Feb. 2011. Web. 17 July 2014.

"Ray J Charged Cops After Whitney Death Jokes." *TMZ* 19 Sept. 2013. Web. 28 Oct. 2013.

Rengifo, Andres F. and Don Stemen. "The Impact of Drug Treatment on Recidivism: Do Mandatory Programs Make a Difference? Evidence from Kansas's Senate Bill 123." *Crime & Delinquency* 59.6(Sept. 2013): 930–50.

Rev. of *Wired*, dir. Larry Peerce. *Rolling Stone* 7 Sept. 1989. Web. 11 Nov. 2013.

Rev. of *Wired: The Short Life and Fast Times of John Belushi*, by Bob Woodward. *Kirkus Review*. n.d. Web. 7 Jan. 2014.

Reynolds, David S. and Debra J. Rosenthal, eds. *The Serpent in the Cup: Temperance in American Literature*. Amherst: University of Massachusetts Press, 1997.

Reynolds, James and Zoe Zontou, eds. *Addiction and Performance*. Newcastle upon Tyne: Cambridge Scholars Publishing, 2014.

"Richard." *Intervention*. A&E. 10 May 2010. Television.

Ron. "Whitney Houston—A Wasted LIfe." *Retired in Delaware*. Blogspot. 11 Feb. 2012. Web. 20 May 2015.

"Ro$e Love$ Mile$." *The Golden Girls: The Complete Seventh and Final Season*. Buena Vista Home Entertainment/Touchstone, 2007. DVD.

Russo, Lea. "Review Briefs." Rev. of *Drunks*, Dir. Peter Cohn. *Boxoffice* Dec. 1996: 56.

Scarry, Elaine. *The Body in Pain: The Making and Unmaking of the World*. New York: Oxford University Press, 1985.

Schechner, Richard. *Performance Studies: An Introduction*. 3rd ed. New York: Routledge, 2013.

Schroeder, Patricia R. *The Feminist Possibilities of Dramatic Realism*. Madison: Fairleigh Dickinson University Press, 1996.

_____. "Locked Behind the Proscenium: Feminist Strategies in *Getting Out* and *My Sister in This House*." *Feminist Theatre and Theory*. Edited by Helene Keyssar. New York: St. Martin's, 1996. 155–67.

Schudson, Michael. *Watergate in American Memory: How We Remember, Forget, and Reconstruct the Past*. New York: Basic Books, 1992.

"The Science of Drug Abuse and Addiction." *Publications: Media Guide*. National Institute on Drug Abuse. Dec. 2012. Web. 23 May 2014.

"Scientists Unveil a Bold New Definition of Addiction." *Content*. The Fix. n.d. Web. 2 Nov. 2013.

Scott, Olivia and Laurence Knott. "Buerger's Disease." *Doctor*. Patient.co.uk. 9 Sept. 2013. Web. 1 Sept. 2014.

Short, April M. "Meth Madness: How American Media's Drug Hysteria Vilifies the Poor." *Salon* 22 Feb. 2014. Web. 20 Aug. 2014.

Siegel, Jason T. and Judee K. Burgoon. "Expectancy Theory Approaches to Prevention: Violating Adolescent Expectations to Increase the Effectiveness of Public Service Announcements." *Mass Media and Drug Prevention: Classic and Contemporary Theories and Research*. Edited by William D. Crano, Michael Burgoon, and Stuart Oskamp. Mahwah, NJ: Taylor & Francis, 2002. 163–86.

Smith, Darvin. "AA Meeting Structure." *Lecture Notes/Class Handouts*. Dr. Darvin Smith. n.d. Web. 18 Oct. 2014.

Snider, Norman. "A Sordid Look at Stardom." Rev. of *Wired: The Short Life and Fast Times of John Belushi*, by Bob Woodward. *Maclean's*. July 1984: 54.

Sontag, Susan. *Illness as Metaphor* and *AIDS and Its Metaphors*. New York: Anchor, 1989.

_____. *Regarding the Pain of Others*. New York: Picador, 2003.

Sparkle. Dir. Salim Akil. Perfs. Jordin Sparks, Whitney Houston, Mike Epps, and Derek Luke. TriStar Pictures, 2012. Film.

Spillane, Joseph F. *Cocaine: From Medical Marvel to Modern Menace in the United States, 1884–1920*. Baltimore: Johns Hopkins University Press, 2002.

"squander, v." *OED Online*. Oxford University Press. Dec. 2013. Web. 29 May 2015.

"Stan Takes a Wife." *The Golden Girls: The Complete Fourth Season*. Buena Vista Home Entertainment, 2006. DVD.

Stowell, Sheila. "Rehabilitating Realism." *Journal of Dramatic Theory and Criticism* 6.2(Spring 1992): 81–8.

_____. *A Stage of Their Own: Feminist Playwrights of the Suffrage Era*. Ann Arbor: University of Michigan Press, 1994.

"Street Names and Slang Associated with Substance Addiction." *Addiction and Recovery*. NetPlaces. n.d. Web. 22 Oct. 2013.

Styan, J.L. *Modern Drama in Theory and Practice, Volume 1: Realism and Naturalism*. Cambridge: Cambridge University Press, 1981.

Sutherland, Max. "Print Ads: Two Second Hookers." *Articles*. I Have An Idea. 30 July 2002. Web. 20 Aug. 2014.

Szalavitz, Maia. "After 75 Years of Alcoholics Anonymous, It's Time to Admit We Have a Problem." *Pacific Standard* 10 Feb. 2014. Web. 29 Sept. 2014.

Tambling, Jeremy. *Allegory*. New York: Routledge, 2010.

Thompson, C.J. S. *The History and Lore of Freaks*. Reprint ed. 1930. London: Senate, 1996.

Thomson, Rosemarie Garland. *Freakery: Cultural Spectacles of the Extraordinary Body*. New York: New York University Press, 1996.

"throttle, v." *OED Online*. Oxford University Press. Sept. 2014. Web. 8 Dec. 2014.

"Tom." *Intervention*. A&E. 21 July 2008. Television.

"Too many laws, too many prisoners." *The Economist* 22 July 2010. Web. 12 Sept. 2014.

Topp, Leslie, James E. Moran, and Jonathan Andrews, eds. *Madness, Architecture and the Built Environment: Psychiatric Spaces in Historical Context*. Reprint ed. 2007. London: Routledge, 2011.

Tracy, Sarah W. and Caroline Jean Acker, eds. *Altering American Consciousness: The History of Alcohol and Drug Use in the United States, 1800–2000*. Amherst: University of Massachusetts Press, 2004.

"Trent." *Intervention*. A&E. 20 April 2007. Television.

Turner, J. Edward. *The History of the First Inebriate Asylum in the World By Its Founder*. New York, 1888. *Google Book Search*. Web. 3 June 2014.

Turque, Bill and Peter McKillop. "Why Justice Can't Be Done." *Newsweek* 29 May 1989: 36.

Valk, Ülo. "Cautionary Tale." *The Greenwood Encyclopedia of Folktales and Fairy Tales: A-F*. 3 vols. Edited by Donald Haase. Westport, CT: Greenwood Press, 2008. 170.

van Olphen, Juliana, Michelle J. Eliason, Nicholas Freudenberg, and Marilyn Barnes. "Nowhere to Go: How Stigma Limits the Options of Female Drug Users After Release From Jail." *Substance Abuse Treatment, Prevention & Policy* 4(2009): 1–10.

Verner, Amy. "Freak Shows and Human Zoos: The Selling of the 'Savage.'" *The Globe and Mail*. 20 Jan. 2012. Web. 10 July 2014.

"Vocal Range and Profile: Whitney Houston (Pre-Drugs)." *Critic of Music: The Latest Happenings in Music*. Blogger. 3 Nov. 2012. Web. 2 Dec. 2015.

Warner, Nicholas O. *Spirits of America: Intoxication of Nineteenth-Century American Literature*. Norman, OK: University of Oklahoma Press, 1997.

"waste, n." *OED Online*. Oxford University Press. Sept. 2013. Web. 22 Oct. 2013.

"wasted, adj." *Oxford English Dictionary*. Bowling Green State University Libraries. n.d. Web. 14 Oct. 2013.

Weiner, Barbara and William White. "The *Journal of Inebriety* (1876–1914): History, Topical Analysis, and Photographic Images." *Addiction* 102(2007): 15–23.

White, Hayden. *Tropics of Discourse: Essays in Cultural Criticism*. Baltimore: Johns Hopkins University Press, 1986.

"Whitney Houston." *Biography*. A&E Television Networks, LLC. n.d. Web. 6 Jan. 2015.

"Whitney Houston: Cop Claims Sgt. Ogled Her Dead Body." *TMZ* 18 Sept. 2013. Web. 28 Oct. 2013.

"Whitney Houston: Corroboration Over Pervy Comment About Whitney's Dead Body." *TMZ* 18 Sept. 2013. Web. 28 Oct. 2013.

"Whitney Houston: 'A Great Talent Squandered.'" *BBC News* 12 Feb. 2012. Web. 29 May 2015.

"Whitney Houston Jokes." *Funny Jokes*. BBM Live. 2013. Web. 24 Oct. 2013.

"Whitney: The Last Photo!" *National Enquirer* 5 Mar. 2012: 1.

"Whitney Houston—Star Spangled Banner." *YouTube*. YouTube. 13 Feb. 2012. Web. 29 May 2015.

"Why Meth Users Have Sores and Scabs on Their Faces." *Living Sober*. Northbound Treatment Services. 22 April 2013. Web. 20 Aug. 2014.

"Why Patient Advocacy Movement Is Muted for Addiction." *Alcoholism & Drug Abuse Weekly* 6 Feb. 2012: 3–4.

Wiedeman, Reeves. "The Sporting Scene: Singing the Anthem." *The New Yorker* 14 May 2012. Web. 29 May 2015.

Wilmington, Michael. "Belushi's 'Wired' Ride." Rev. of *Wired*, dir. Larry Peerce. *The Los Angeles Times* 25 Aug. 1989. Web. 11 Nov. 2013.

Wired. Dir. Larry Peerce. Perfs. Michael Chiklis, Ray Sharkey, J.T. Walsh. Taurus Entertainment, 1989. Videocassette.

Wired (1989). Rotten Tomatoes. n.d. Web. 11 Nov. 2013.

"wired, adj." *OED Online*. Oxford University Press. Dec. 2013. Web. 9 Jan. 2014.

Woodward, Bob. *Wired: The Short Life and Fast Times of John Belushi*. Reprint ed. 1984. New York: Simon & Schuster, 2012.

Woodward, Samuel B. *Essays on Asylums for Inebriates*. Worcester, 1838.

Wray, Matt. *Not Quite White: White Trash and the Boundaries of Whiteness*. Durham, NC: Duke University Press, 2006.

Yanni, Carla. *The Architecture of Madness: Insane Asylums in the United States*. Minneapolis: University of Minnesota Press, 2007.

Zieger, Susan. *Inventing the Addict: Drugs, Race, and Sexuality in Nineteenth-Century British and American Literature*. Amherst: University of Massachusetts Press, 2008.

Zoglin, Richard. "Finally, the Belushi Story." *Time*. 24 June 2001. Web. 11 Nov. 2013.

Index